OCT 3 1 2001

# Teachers' and Students' Cognitive Styles in Early Childhood Education

# Teachers' and Students' Cognitive Styles in Early Childhood Education

*Olivia Natividad Saracho*

**BERGIN & GARVEY**
*Westport, Connecticut • London*

**Library of Congress Cataloging-in-Publication Data**

Saracho, Olivia N.
   Teachers' and students' cognitive styles in early childhood
education / Olivia Natividad Saracho.
      p.  cm.
   Includes bibliographical references and index.
   ISBN 0–89789–486–3 (alk. paper)
   1. Cognitive styles in children.  2. Cognitive learning.  3. Early
childhood education.  I. Title.
BF723.C5S28   1997
155.4'13—dc21       96–52166

British Library Cataloguing in Publication Data is available.

Library of Congress Catalog Card Number: 96–52166
ISBN: 0–89789–486–3

First published in 1997

Bergin & Garvey, 88 Post Road West, Westport, CT 06881
An imprint of Greenwood Publishing Group, Inc.

Printed in the United States of America

The paper used in this book complies with the
Permanent Paper Standard issued by the National
Information Standards Organization (Z39.48–1984).

10  9  8  7  6  5  4  3  2

In memory of my father,
Pablo J. Villarreal, who loved life
to its fullest. He stimulated and
challenged my thinking.

# Contents

## IV. Future Directions

# Preface

This book is addressed to researchers, psychologists, child development specialists, early childhood educators, and especially to teachers. Its purpose is to help them understand the nature of children's cognitive style and to use that understanding to improve the learning activities provided to children; to help improve the teaching of children and, ultimately, their learning in school. The contents of this book are designed to help teachers deal with the individual differences that are found among the children in their classes, especially in regard to the ways that children perceive the world and make sense of it.

Cognitive style is a psychological construct that has been of interest to psychologists and educators for some time. To some extent cognitive style is related to children's general cognitive development; thus, research on cognitive style has been of interest to researchers, psychologists, early childhood educators, child development specialists, and teachers. Some educators feel that the academic performance of children could be improved if the schools provided a better match of learning activities to their predominant cognitive styles.

There are several different dimensions to an individual's cognitive style. One of these dimensions is field dependence independence (FDI), which characterizes field dependent (FD) and field independent (FI) individuals. This dimension is related to the way an individual perceives and understands an item as it is related to its context or is understood independent of its context. Another dimension is reflectivity-impulsivity. This dimension is related to the degree to which an individual thinks about his/her responses or responds quickly with relatively little thought. A third dimension is locus of control. This dimension is related to the degree to which an individual feels able to control his/her actions internally or feels that her/his actions are controlled by outside forces. There are other dimensions of cognitive style as well.

Research demonstrates that the various cognitive styles can affect children's intellectual functioning and their academic achievement. Teachers need to be aware of the cognitive style research that has been conducted recently and learn to use the results of this research to plan effective educational programs for children. This book has been designed to present such research, especially in the dimension of FDI. It gives an overview of cognitive styles research in terms of historical perspectives, theoretical underpinnings, and measurement approaches. It also reviews important findings emerging from contemporary research on young children's cognitive styles and their influence on teaching and learning. In addition, it provides implications for future research and classroom practice. The volume includes twelve chapters organized into four parts: (1) Background Information, (2) Students' Learning, (3) Teachers' Instruction, and (4) Future Directions.

Part I provides background information to describe cognitive style, its effects on the teaching-learning situation, and how to formally and informally assess cognitive style. Chapter 1, "Cognitive Style: Its Importance in Teaching and Learning," identifies several dimensions of cognitive styles, which have been identified through empirical research efforts. The various cognitive styles differ from one another in numerous characteristics. Over the past several years a large number of studies have examined these characteristics, which have been found to be stable and consistent over extended periods of time. This chapter summarizes the different dimensions of cognitive style and their educational implications, including its influence in the teachers' performance and the students' cognitive functioning.

FDI is considered a regular mode of processing information, but it contains more than simple elements. It develops slowly, conforming to the person's experiences. It differentiates characteristics between the FDI bipolar continuum that is high-level heuristic in arranging and regulating behavior in a broad variation of occasions (Witkin, 1976). Chapter 2, "Field Dependence Independence: An Important Dimension of Cognitive Style," describes the FDI dimension, the one most widely studied, in relation to factors such as age, sex, and cultural differences. To better understand the FDI dimension, the origin and characteristics as well as cultural, age, and sex differences of FDI are discussed.

Chapter 3, "Assessment Instruments," provides descriptions and procedures of formal and informal techniques to evaluate young children's cognitive style to individualize instruction in educational programs.

Part II deals with the students' learning. It describes FD and FI students in a classroom situation, their learning behaviors, and how FDI influences the early childhood curriculum, including social situations.

Chapter 4, "Portraits of Field Dependent Independent Children," provides a more detailed statement of the characteristics of FD and FI children. These children were administered several cognitive style tests and were videotaped during ten three-minute play periods. Extreme cases were chosen as examples of children who gave FD or FI performances during their play. At the end of all the case histories, the children's play behavior in relation to cognitive style is discussed.

In Chapter 5, "Students' Learning Behaviors," the cognitive behavior of young children in relation to cognitive style is discussed. The focus is on the stable features of organization of cognitive behavior. This chapter relates the role of cognitive style to student's learning.

Chapter 6, "The Role of Field Dependence Independence in the Early Childhood Curriculum," considers research trends in the area of cognitive styles in relation to the early childhood curriculum. Cognitive style appears to affect how pupils learn, how teachers instruct, and how students and teachers interact in classroom contexts. The FDI cognitive style dimension is explored in relation to its role in the early childhood curriculum, especially with instructional approaches, teaching materials, and classroom organizations.

Chapter 7, "Field Dependent Independent Characteristics in Young Children's Social Behaviors," reviews studies which have independently investigated young children's cognitive style and social behaviors with emphasis on their play. The limited studies examining the relationship between cognitive style and social behaviors in young children are presented. Common characteristics in young children's cognitive style and play behaviors are compared. These characteristics have been validated in several studies. This chapter suggests that cognitive style manifests itself in different ways at different times in young children's lives, and presents several possible ways of explaining this phenomenon.

Part III deals with the teachers' instruction. It describes FD and FI teachers in a classroom situation, their instructional behaviors, and the consequences of matching teachers and students.

Over the past decade, researchers have shown increasing interest in cognitive style as a way to understand the teachers' influence on student learning. FD teachers have been shown to rely on small group instructional techniques and extensive use of classroom discussions in which the opportunity for directing and structuring the activity is controlled by the children themselves. In addition, FD teachers use questions that are more factual, usually requiring brief, technical responses. FI teachers prefer to structure their classrooms quite differently, showing stronger preference for the use of large group instructional techniques such as whole group instruction, lectures, and direct teaching. These teachers are also more likely to ask more questions at a higher conceptual level. Chapter 8, "Portraits of Field Dependent Independent Teachers," provides a more detailed statement of the characteristics of FD and FI teachers. These teachers were administered several cognitive style tests and were videotaped during ten three-minute instructional periods. Extreme cases were chosen as samples of teachers who gave FD or FI performances during their classroom instruction. At the end of all the case histories, the teachers' instructional behavior in relation to cognitive style is discussed. In Chapter 9, "Teachers' Instructional Behaviors," support is provided for the study and use of various cognitive style constructs in understanding how they influence teaching, and the implications this influence holds for teacher-student interactions in the classroom, as well as aspects of student learning.

Several studies have been conducted on the interactive effects of teachers-students' cognitive styles, considering the individual differences in both teachers and students. The relationship between cognitive style and classroom behaviors has been attributed to the match and mismatch of teachers' and student's cognitive styles and to the cognitive style of individual students and teachers. Chapter 10, "Matching Teachers and Students," describes the significance of matching the students' and teachers' cognitive styles in the classroom and teacher-student compatibility. It also discusses studies related to the match and mismatch of students and teachers. It compares classroom behaviors of teachers and students who match and mismatch in cognitive styles. It describes the way students who are matched or mismatched to their teachers' cognitive styles behave, as well as how their teachers behave toward them in the classroom. Although differences in the students' and teachers' behaviors were found based on whether they matched or mismatched in cognitive style and sex, the major differences were found based on the teachers' cognitive styles.

Part IV provides researchers and educators with future directions, including how early childhood teachers can be better prepared to meet the students' individual differences and how cognitive style can improve educational practice.

In many classrooms, the need to respond to the range of individual differences is met by setting different expectations for children's academic learning. More often, however, all children are expected to learn the same things in the same way, with some children expected to learn more than others or allowed to take more time to learn what is expected of all children. The FDI dimension of cognitive style influences how teachers teach, students learn, and teachers and students interact. Professional preparation curricula must include information about experiences with learning and teaching styles to help teacher candidates identify and accommodate various learning styles. Therefore, knowledge of cognitive style must be included in programs that prepare teachers. Teacher candidates should learn, in their educational programs, to handle both FD and FI cognitive styles for teaching, learning, and ultimately, nourishing cognitive flexibility in themselves and in their students. Chapter 11, "Preparation of Early Childhood Teachers," suggests content, strategies, and experiences that can prepare early childhood teachers to respond to the students' individual differences based on their cognitive style. Chapter 12, "Potential Roles of Cognitive Style in Educational Practice," addresses the issues of how to respond to individual differences in educational settings. It suggests that knowledge of cognitive style can be used to match learning tasks to individual children to develop cognitive flexibility, thus creating curriculum flexibility. It concludes that cognitive style seems to be a valid construct at this time and that educators should use knowledge of students' and teachers' cognitive styles to improve the quality of young children's education. It is important to continue to increase awareness of individual differences in the children and teachers in striving to improve educational opportunities for all children.

Each chapter identifies important issues that relate to the content of each chapter, to introduce the reader to current concerns. Most of these issue highlights are referenced to current periodicals and professional journals and are written to encourage readers' contemplation and further investigation. For this reason the references section is compiled at the end of the volume.

This volume would not have been written without the love, encouragement, and support of my parents, Pablo J. and Francisca S. Villarreal; my brother, Saúl M. Villarreal; my sister, Lydia Gonzalez; and my best friend and mentor, Bernard Spodek, Professor of Early Childhood Education at the University of Illinois at Urbana–Champaign. I would also like to thank the following individuals for the help they have provided me in developing this book: Elida de la Rosa, Sharon Teuben-Rowe, Dumrong Adunyarittigun, Cynthia Gerstl, Edward Salners, and Mary Ellen O'Ferrall. They helped identify some of the resources that I used. I especially wish to thank Ms. Lynn Taylor, Assistant Vice President, Editorial, and Leanne Jisonna, Editorial, at Greenwood Press, for the encouragement and support they provided throughout the development of this book.

# Part I

# Background Information

Chapter 1

# Cognitive Style: Its Importance in Teaching and Learning

## INTRODUCTION

Numerous studies of teachers and students have been conducted to better understand the education process. Many of the studies have focused on teachers' and students' personal characteristics. It has been assumed that individual personality factors translate directly or indirectly into good teaching and learning performance. Studies that have focused on teacher and student behavior have assumed that effective teaching and successful learning can be determined by what teachers and students do (Solas, 1992). An alternative approach to understanding the nature of the teaching and learning process is to go beyond what teachers and students appear to be and to inquire about their ways of thinking. One way is to understand teachers' and students' cognitive styles and their relationship to teaching and learning. Their cognitive styles influence their responses to different situations. As such, they impact on the teachers' performance and on the students' cognitive functioning. This chapter will describe the different dimensions of cognitive style, and their educational implications.

## COGNITIVE STYLE

Cognitive style identifies the ways individuals react to different situations. It is one way to characterize individual differences. While the level and pattern of abilities derive from the individual's genetic endowment, cognitive style influences how abilities develop. Cognitive style describes consistencies in using cognitive processes. It does not describe the content or cognitive level of an individual's performance. Cognitive styles include stable attitudes, preferences, or habitual strategies that distinguish the individual styles of perceiving, remembering, thinking, and solving problems.

Individuals actively process and transform incoming information, structuring new knowledge and integrating it within the memory structure. This process contributes to the individual's intellectual development, extending his/her repertoire of cognitive skills that have been accumulating throughout life.

The term "cognitive style" might be more appropriately referred to as "personal style" (Witkin, 1949). The cognitive style characteristics describe the individual's mode of understanding, thinking, remembering, judging, and solving problems. An individual's style determines the cognitive strategies applied in a variety of situations. Messick (1984) differentiates between the application of styles and strategies. "Styles imply a general orientation to task situations, while strategies are attuned to particular types of tasks and situations" (p. 62). In performing cognitive style tasks, young children select from a range of strategies that are transformed into stylistic responses.

These responses are wide stylistic characteristics that become obvious in an individual's experience (Anastasi, 1988) and behavior, such as perceptual styles, personality, intelligence, and social behavior. These modes of functioning are distinctive as well as highly consistent and stable (Saracho & Spodek, 1981, 1986; Witkin et al., 1962/1974; Witkin et al., 1954/1972).

## Dimensions of Cognitive Style

Empirical research has identified several dimensions of cognitive style. Although the dimensions of cognitive style differ from one another in several ways, they have some similarities. Messick (1976) provided a summary of nineteen different "cognitive-style" dimensions (e.g., field dependence/independence, scanning, breadth of categorization, conceptualizing styles, cognitive complexity versus simplicity, reflection versus impulsivity, leveling versus sharpening, constricted versus flexible control, and tolerance for unrealistic experiences). Each dimension of cognitive style is viewed as a bipolar contrasting mode of functioning and indicates a different set of interacting attributes referred to as "dynamic gestalt" (Vernon, 1972). Table 1.1 summarizes these dimensions of cognitive styles.

Using the definitions of the different dimensions of cognitive styles, Witkin et al. (1977) stipulated several basic characteristics of all cognitive styles.

1. Cognitive styles involve the form rather than the content of cognitive activity. Individual differences allude to *how* people perceive, think, solve problems, learn, and relate to others. Cognitive style is defined in process terms. This property is a natural consequence of the origin of cognitive style dimensions that took place in laboratory studies, where process was the central concern. The experimental research on the processes underlying FD and FI behavior is far-reaching (Witkin et al., 1954/1972). These processes suggest educational implications, such as ways of teaching students to use preferred problem-solving strategies.

2. Cognitive styles are widespread dimensions that cut across the boundaries

**Table 1.1**
**Nine Cognitive Styles**

1. *Field independence versus field dependence*: an analytical, in contrast to a global, way of perceiving (which) entails a tendency to experience items as discrete from their backgrounds and reflects ability to overcome the influence of an embedding context.

2. *Scanning*: a dimension of individual differences in the extensiveness and intensity of attention deployment, leading to individual variations in the vividness of experience and the span of awareness.

3. *Breadth of categorizing*: consistent preferences for broad inclusiveness, as opposed to narrow exclusiveness, in establishing the acceptable range for specified categories.

4. *Conceptualizing styles*: individual differences in the tendency to categorize perceived similarities and differences among stimuli in terms of many differentiated concepts, which is a dimension called conceptual differentiation, as well as consistencies in the utilization of particular conceptualizing approaches as bases for forming concepts (such as the routine use in concept formation of thematic or functional relations among stimuli as opposed to the analysis of descriptive attributes or the inference of class membership).

5. *Cognitive complexity versus simplicity*: individual differences in the tendency to construe the world, and particularly the world of social behavior, in a multidimensional and discriminating way.

6. *Reflectiveness versus impulsivity*: individual consistencies in the speed with which hypotheses are selected and information processed, with impulsive subjects tending to offer the first answer that occurs to them, even though it is frequently incorrect, and reflective subjects tending to ponder various possibilities before deciding.

7. *Leveling versus sharpening*: reliable individual variations in assimilation in memory. Subjects at the leveling extreme tend to blur similar memories and to merge perceived objects or events with similar but not identical events recalled from previous experience. Sharpeners, at the other extreme, are less prone to confuse similar objects and, by contrast, may even judge the present to be less similar to the past than is actually the case.

8. *Constricted versus flexible control*: individual differences in susceptibility to distraction and cognitive interference.

9. *Tolerance for incongruous or unrealistic experiences*: a dimension of differential willingness to accept perceptions at variance with conventional experience.

*Sources*: Samuel Messick, The criterion problem in the evaluation of instruction: Assessing possible, not just intended, outcomes. In M.C. Wittrock and David E. Wiley (eds.), *The evaluation of instruction: Issues and problems* (chapter 6) (New York: Holt, Rinehart and Winston, 1970). Adapted and reprinted by permission of Holt, Rinehart and Winston, Inc.; N. Kogan, Educational implications of cognitive styles. In G. S. Lesser (ed.), *Psychology and educational practice* (p. 246) (Glenview, IL: Scott, Foresman and Company, 1971). Reprinted by permission of G. S. Lesser.

of the human mind and integrate them into a holistic entity. Reflecting their pervasiveness, cognitive styles are broader than cognition and include personality characteristics. For example, socially oriented people are especially attentive to what others say and do, and use the information they receive from others to determine their own beliefs and feelings. In determining cognitive style, non-cognitive attributes also can be assessed. Cognitive styles also can estimate nonverbal or perceptual methods. Perception can be measured using objective, controlled techniques to identify an individual's cognitive style. Nonverbal perceptual techniques that are used to assess a person's cognitive style relieve the disadvantage that students out of the mainstream culture commonly endure on standard verbal assessment procedures (Witkin et al. 1966).

3. Cognitive styles are consistent and stable over time, although some may easily be altered. However, most people maintain the same cognitive style over time. Such stability makes stylistic dimensions very useful in long-range guidance and counseling.

4. In relation to value judgments, cognitive styles are bipolar. This characteristic is especially important in differentiating cognitive styles from intelligence and other ability measures where having more of an ability is better than having less of it. In contrast, cognitive styles have different values in each pole. For example, the FDI dimension describes the cluster of competence in cognitive articulation and impersonal orientation at one end of the pole, while it describes the cluster of social orientation and social skills plus less competence in articulation at the other end. The characteristics at the end of each pole are appropriate for different tasks. For example, a study (Quinlan & Blatt, 1972) showed that psychiatric student nurses who were judged to be good by their mentors were compared on tests of FDI to similarly viewed student surgical nurses. The psychiatric student nurses were found to be relatively FD while the surgical student nurses were found to be relatively FI. Since effective work in psychiatric nursing relies heavily on an interest in people and on social sensitivity rather than analytical skills, this is a good fit for relatively FD individuals. In comparison, surgical nurses do not need social interests and sensitivities, because they rarely work with conscious patients. The nurses' success usually depends on how quickly they can find the correct forceps from a complex array of instruments on a surgical tray. Therefore, this job is more appropriate for relatively FI persons.

According to Witkin et al. (1962/1974), the more neutral character of cognitive style growing out of its nonvalued bipolarity is less threatening and provides more information about individuals than scores on ability tests such as the IQ.

An example of a dimension of cognitive style may help clarify its nature. The literature shows that the field dependence independence (FDI) has been most widely investigated. Chapter 2 describes this dimension in detail.

## EDUCATIONAL IMPLICATIONS

Cognitive style includes more than intellectual ability. The work by Witkin et al. (1954/1972, 1962/1974) on psychological differentiation was a pioneering effort in defining structural constraints of personality in cognitive processes. Individual consistencies in cognitive behavior are derived from a wide range of behaviors and strategies employed to cope with specific situations, tasks, stimulus-constraints, and purposes for which they are especially relevant and suited. Since cognitive style relates to a person's psychological and educational attributes and is part of each individual's personality, it becomes an important factor in schooling because it influences the performance of students and teachers.

## Teacher Performance

Educators and researchers are concerned about teacher classroom performance and are always looking for ways to improve it. Teachers need to have an intellectual basis for their performance, to act skillfully and to plan and evaluate their performance (Saracho, 1988e).

## Students' Cognitive Functioning

Children's cognitive functioning refers to how they respond to and make sense of their world. Assessing this functioning makes more sense than relying on a simple score on a standardized intelligence test. The types of errors children make while taking an intelligence test may provide more information about their cognitive performance than does a test score (Sigel, 1963). The children's experiences and assessments of their intellectual growth should be used as a frame of reference to obtain accurate knowledge about the nature of children's cognitive performance (Hunt, 1961).

## Classroom Interactions

The classroom is a social system where interaction between students and teachers occurs. Learning outcomes are the results of these interactions. Researchers have identified different learners' responses to various forms of instruction related to differences in cognitive style. Just as students with different cognitive styles favor certain learning strategies, so do teachers with different cognitive styles favor certain teaching techniques. Therefore, it is not enough to consider just the cognitive style of the classroom students. Teachers' and students' cognitive styles must be considered together in making decisions about instructional strategies and planning learning alternatives.

Since cognitive styles affect both teacher instruction and student learning, it is important to understand the educational implications of teachers' and students' cognitive styles separately, as well as the results of classroom interactions. When teachers and students with the same or different cognitive styles are placed together in classrooms, one can predict varied consequences related to whether teachers and students are matched or mismatched.

For decades schools have been concerned with individual differences in the classroom. Too often the solution offered is to provide alternative pacing of instruction. Programmed learning, individually guided education, and mastery learning are but a few of the many solutions offered. These alternatives, however, do not necessarily consider the students' or teachers' predominant modes of cognitive functioning. Perhaps, with a better understanding of the concept of cognitive style and with the development of techniques to extend the repertoires of teachers and students, new ways of meeting individual differences can be developed.

## SUMMARY

Cognitive styles reflect the individual's psychological differentiation, and behavioral or intellectual responses to situations. This holistic view of cognitive styles is integrated in a wide range of psychological phenomena meaningfully affecting the individuals' cognitive processes (Saracho, 1987b).

Several dimensions of cognitive styles were summarized to illustrate an individual's stylistic differences. Cognitive styles have been perceived as habitual modes of processing information, but they are more than simple habits. They develop slowly based on the individual's experiences. Therefore, it is essential to discriminate between cognitive styles that are high-level heuristic in organizing and controlling behavior in a wide variety of circumstances (Witkin, 1976).

The stability and pervasiveness of cognitive style across diverse spheres of behavior indicate deeper roots in the individual's personality structure that include more than the notion of characteristic modes of cognition. Cognitive styles consist of generalized habits of information processing developing in congenial ways around underlying personality trends. Cognitive styles are, thus, intimately interwoven with an individual's total personality. They are one component of the matrix that determines the nature of adaptive characteristics and defense mechanisms. From this perspective, a core personality structure is manifested in the different levels and domains of the individual's psychological performance (e.g., intellectual, affective, motivational, defensive) and its manifestation in cognition is cognitive style.

Cognitive styles consider individual differences among people, which is a psychological construct. The existing cognitive style theory is incomplete. Cognitive style theory needs to be structured in a broader theoretical framework to be able to understand the psychological differences in cognitive style. Further conceptualization and empirical work are needed to support its wide range of psychological differentiation, causes, and consequences.

Chapter 2

# Field Dependence Independence: An Important Dimension of Cognitive Style

Over the past five decades researchers, educators, and psychologists have investigated various aspects of cognitive style, a psychological construct. They have concentrated on functional components of cognitive processes, especially how they affect the individuals' mental, personality, and social behaviors. These modes of functioning become evident in an individual's perceptual and intellectual experiences in a highly consistent and pervasive manner. The term "cognitive style" implies a consistent way in which individuals process information.

Cognitive style reflects a person's way of responding and performing in diverse situations. Field dependence independence (FDI) characterizes one dimension of perceiving, remembering, and thinking as an individual apprehends, stores, transforms, and processes information.

While several dimensions of cognitive style have been examined, the FDI dimension is one which has generated the most research for cognitive restructuring and social behaviors. Field dependent (FD) and field independent (FI) individuals have different behavioral characteristics that identify their cognitive styles and categorize them as a more FD (global or undifferentiated) or a more FI (analytic or differentiated) person. FD and FI cognitive styles represent distinctly different methods of processing information. FI people use internal referents to guide them in processing information, while FD people use external referents. FI people differ in the techniques they use in dealing with complex and confusing events and in reacting to a variety of circumstances in a cognitive way. To better understand the FDI dimension, the origin and characteristics as well as the cultural, age, and sex differences of FDI will be discussed.

## ORIGIN OF FDI COGNITIVE STYLES

FDI had its origins in the laboratory, and its concepts and methods of assessment reflect that beginning. The early work in FDI was concerned with how subjects locate the upright position in space (for example, Witkin, 1949, 1950, 1952; Witkin & Asch, 1948). Originally, FDI was assessed in space orientation conditions. An individual was placed in a tilting chair and then the room itself might be tilted.[1] Bodily cues conflicted with visual cues. The modes of resolution ranged from greater reliance on internal mechanisms to greater reliance on the visual field (Wapner & Demick, 1991). People perceive which way is up based on the information they receive from the visual environment. They also use perceptions from within their bodies to continuously adapt themselves to the downward pull of gravity in maintaining upright posture and balance. Generally, perceptions from the visual field and the body would complement each other and an accurate location of the true upright position could be obtained. Research was designed to provide conflicting cues from gravity and from the visual field. Witkin and his associates' early experiments used a simpler, more manipulable visual framework, but they still had to simultaneously separate the visual and bodily standards (Witkin et al., 1977). In the Rod-and-Frame Test, for example, a titled square frame in an otherwise dark room induces similar conflict. The cues that are used to arrange a rod in the vertical position provide a measure of FDI. Witkin and Goodenough (1981) report relationships between laboratory tests (showing FI cognitive style) and high scores on paper-and-pencil tests of restructuring abilities, but they admit that additional empirical support for the whole causal model is needed.

The test situation consisting of the "separation of an item (body or rod) from an organized field (room or frame)" prompted Witkin and Goodenough (1981, p. 15) to use Gottschaldt's (1926) hidden figures task as the basis for the Embedded Figures Test. Chapter 3 describes these and other FDI assessment techniques.

FDI identified the degree of difficulty in separating an item from an organized field or overcoming an embedding context. Greater or less disembedding or analytic ability shows itself across an individual's perceptual and intellectual abilities (Witkin & Goodenough, 1981). Perceptual and intellectual functioning correspond to elements of articulation, with individual differences ranging from an articulated field approach to a global field approach.

Restructuring skills and interpersonal competencies cluster in opposite poles of the FDI single dimension. A person is assessed and placed on a continuum between these poles. At one end of the pole is the analytic cluster with restructuring skills, while at the other end is the global cluster with interpersonal skills. These individual differences continue across both perceptual and intellectual performance. The responses to a broad range of circumstances are referred to as "style," and the approach surrounding both the perceptual and intellectual undertakings is referred to as the "cognitive" style.

The original FDI concept proposes that FD individuals, who are limited in their ability to disembed figures, also have an interpersonal orientation. In contrast, FI individuals are more competent in disembedding ability but have an impersonal orientation (Witkin & Goodenough, 1981). Kogan and Block (1991) refute this, suggesting that while FD persons may be interpersonally oriented, their social orientation does not translate into actual interpersonal skills. Saracho's (1991a) study supports this view: (1) FI children were more popular than FD children, (2) FD children often rejected other FD children as their playmates, and (3) FI children preferred other FI children (Saracho, 1991a). Treating FDI as a bipolar dimension suggests that it is a value-free construct.

The theoretical framework that has progressively emerged in the FDI literature represents successive attempts to conceptualize, first, the early observed self-consistent individual differences in the mode of orientation, and, later, the ever-broadening patterns of self-consistencies. Through the continuous interplay between theory and research, the conceptualization of FDI has eventually been broadened to include personality structure and its development (Witkin & Goodenough, 1981).

From Witkin's starting point as a laboratory investigator of perception, his search for an understanding of individual differences in FDI led him into many disciplines including education, psychology, biology, and anthropology and many conceptual areas including socialization, educational concerns, and cross-cultural concerns. Obviously, many new research directions have been stimulated during the process. The *Social Sciences Citation Index* shows that Witkin is among the most cited authors. These citations and the rapidly growing literature on FDI are objective assessments of his influence in the social sciences. While Witkin saw individual differences as an important issue, he viewed them in value-neutral terms as well as in cognitive, affective, and motivational domains.

## CHARACTERISTICS OF FIELD DEPENDENCE INDEPENDENCE

In the most current theoretical formulation, Witkin and Goodenough (1981) delineated a bipolar value-neutral dimension where FD and FI individuals had specific psychological strengths. Saracho and Spodek (1981) provide a contrasting comparison of FD and FI individuals on Table 2.1. They compare and contrast these behaviors using the extremes of both cognitive styles. The performance strategies in FDI are remarkably prevalent and compatible. Sufficient research reveals that the persons' differences in these characteristics are constant over time.

Since its introduction (Witkin et al., 1954/1972), the FDI theory has been an ever-changing framework, continuously integrating discoveries and new insights about the nature of its dimensions (Goodenough, 1986). It will continue to change in the future under the impetus of newly emerging evidence (Witkin &

**Table 2.1**

**Comparison of Field Independent and Field Dependent Characteristics**

| Field Independent Persons | Field Dependent Persons |
|---|---|
| 1. tend to be analytical; | 1. tend to be global; |
| 2. can solve problems whose materials require structuring; | 2. take longer to solve the same kinds of problems; |
| 3. can abstract an item from the surrounding field; | 3. are guided by the organization of the field as a whole; |
| 4. employ specialized defenses such as intellectualization and isolation; | 4. use global defenses, such as repression and denial; |
| 5. are independent of authority; | 5. are influenced by authority figures or by peers; |
| 6. are dependent on their own values and standards; | 6. use external sources of information for self-definition; |
| 7. are impersonal and socially detached; | 7. have a strong interest in people, respond to people's emotional expressions, and like to have people around them; |
| 8. favor occupations in which working with others is not essential, such as astronomy or physics; | 8. prefer occupations which require involvement with others, such as elementary school teaching, selling, or rehabilitation counseling; |
| 9. favor impersonal abstract subjects, such as mathematics and the physical sciences. | 9. are oriented to subject areas which relate most directly to people, such as the social sciences. |

Goodenough, 1981). As seen now, the FI person is analytic, confident, and self-reliant; while the FD person is holistic, uncertain, and dependent upon others. This definition, used by researchers in many fields (e.g., social psychology), is actually a late 1970s view. In Witkin's final work, FDI embraces three major constructs: (1) reliance on internal versus external referents; (2) cognitive restructuring skills; and (3) interpersonal competencies (Witkin & Goodenough, 1981). The three-construct definition relates special abilities with each end of the continuum (Goodenough, 1986). For example, FI describes the ability to disembed or restructure visual stimuli, referred to as "cognitive restructuring," while FD relates to competency in interpersonal relations. Persons with autonomous, self-reliant modes of processing (FI style) develop cognitive restructuring abilities, while persons depending on others for information and approval (FD style) develop abilities to socialize.

Another development in the study of FDI is a notion of cognitive flexibility, the degree to which persons with both FD and FI styles show a degree of flexibility in their activities (Saracho & Spodek, 1981, 1986; Witkin & Goodenough, 1981). Flexible individuals have both analytic and interpersonal competencies but fixed individuals are stronger in one set of competencies than in another.

Field dependence and field independence are value-neutral qualities of an individual. FI children can solve problems (often spatial in character) that demand structuring or reorganization of any information, while FD children exhibit a social sensitivity that equips them with good interpersonal relations with others (Kogan, 1987). It is important to be aware that no one style is considered better than the other.

Most persons have, to some extent, the characteristics of both cognitive styles. The individual's performance techniques in cognitive styles are extremely pervasive and congruent. There is sufficient evidence to show that an individual's cognitive style characteristics are considerably stable over time.

Since its introduction in 1949 (Witkin et al., 1962/1974), the theory of FDI has been for Witkin "an ever-changing framework, continuously incorporating new discoveries and new insights about the nature of the dimensions" (Goodenough, 1986, p. 6). "It will appear quite different in the future under the impetus of newly emerging evidence" (Witkin & Goodenough, 1981, p. x).

### Early Childhood Education

Research over the last decades on FDI in relation to early childhood education has continued throughout this decade. In agreement with Witkin et al. (1977), early childhood researchers (e.g., Coates, 1972, 1975; Kogan, 1987; Saracho, 1991a) have considered FDI to be a cognitive style that is bipolar and stable, affecting the way a person thinks, feels, and behaves. FDI influences the way persons perceive and process information and the way they interact with their environments. The overlap in the cognitive, personality, and social domains relates FDI to early childhood education (Messick, 1984), an overlap that is acknowledged as a cognitive, affective, and sociological phenomenon. FDI appeals to early childhood researchers because of its bipolarity: "each pole has adaptive value under specified circumstances" (Witkin et al., 1977, p. 16). The characteristics at each end of the pole (i.e., each type of learner) combined with learning situations suggest that any student can succeed under appropriate conditions. Thus, as a practical matter, teachers might match learning situations to children's cognitive styles. It is also the most popular dimension among educators, psychologists, researchers, and individuals in other disciplines. The FDI construct also has been related to cross-cultural contexts (Berry, 1976; Huang & Chao, 1995; Witkin & Berry, 1975) as well as such factors as age and sex. The following sections will discuss additional components of FDI in relation to cultural differences, age, and sex.

## CULTURAL DIFFERENCES

Encouraged by an effort to increase perspectives on the FDI concern, Witkin conducted cross-cultural studies in his later years (Witkin & Berry, 1975). First, he compared cultures to examine particular hypotheses regarding socialization factors in the development of field independence. This research raised his interest in cross-cultural method, and he searched for the elements in different cultural settings conforming to FD and FI ways of functioning.

Most cross-cultural research of subsistence-level cultures strengthens the inference that hunters are more FI than farmers. For example, the Eskimo hunters of the Arctic Wastelands of North America and the Aboriginal hunters of the desert Wastelands of Australia are viewed as the most FI people of the world (Witkin et al., 1977). Witkin and Berry (1975) reported that hunting and gathering people are more FI than farming people because hunting and gathering people need to spot animals or objects from the background. In contrast, farming people need to socialize with others.

According to Witkin, the cognitive style that portrays a cultural group is strongly adjusted to the ecocultural context. In this expectation, the cognitive disembedding skills related to a FI cognitive style is more suitable for the hunter, who usually draws information from the environment to locate game and to return home from the hunt. In comparison, the more immobile life of the farmer demands less disembedding skills. However, the greater and more intricate organized social clusters where the farmer lives demand social-interpersonal skills.

Sociocultural factors influence every facet of human development, including child-rearing practices, family styles, sociolinguistic patterns, and socialization and behavior patterns (Saracho & Hancock, 1983). In cultures where the family is strongly valued, socialization practices stress cooperation among the family group (Mirandé 1985; Saracho & Hancock, 1983). Witkin (1976) suspected that genetic factors, child-rearing practices, and socialization experiences govern the persons' FDI. According to Ramírez (1982, 1989), persons coming from a culture that is different from that of the school are less competitive, less sensitive to spatial incursions by others, less comfortable in trial and error situations, and less interested in the details of concepts, materials, or tasks that are nonsocial. However, flexibility does occur. Apparently, cultural differences influence cognitive styles. The following sections describe the influence that cognitive styles have on cultural groups such as Mexican Americans, African Americans, Native Americans, and Asian Americans.

### Mexican Americans

Some researchers (e.g., Kagan & Buriel, 1977; Saracho, 1983b) have demonstrated a significant relationship between differences in FDI and the Mexican American culture. Other researchers (e.g., Berry, 1976; Ramírez, 1982, 1989; Witkin, 1976) attribute this to the Mexican American parents' focus on social integrative values to encourage their children to become socially oriented, an evolutionary process where a series of affiliations steadily adjusts the relationships of the child to the family and society. For example, the social patterns of most Mexican Americans include the acceptance of authority at home, church, and state; maintenance of personal loyalty to friends, and sensitivity to praise and criticism (Mirandé, 1985; Saracho & Hancock, 1983). Berry (1976), Ramírez (1982, 1989), and Witkin (1976) believed that a typical prosocial orientation of Mexican American children supports their field dependence. Since family attachment is strong, a greater emphasis is placed on cooperation than on competition.

Socialization practices that emphasize strong family ties and respect for and obedience for elders are practices that are believed to define a relatively FD cognitive style (Saracho, 1991a). In much of the literature on cognitive style, Mexican American children are depicted as more FD. It would seem to psychologists and educators that *all* Mexican Americans are homogeneous in their cognitive styles. Saracho (1983b, 1983c, 1983e, 1989e), however, contests this assumption. Saracho (1991a) described a range of cognitive styles that depicts any group of Mexican American children as containing more FD types. She reports a diversity of cognitive styles among Mexican American children and a range of social skills. Young children were also sensitive to each other's cognitive styles.

Research on parents' beliefs toward socialization practices fails to demonstrate the parents' influence in their children's FDI (Holtzman, Díaz-Guerrero, & Swartz, 1975; Sanders, Scholz, & Kagan, 1976). According to Saracho (1983b, 1983c, 1983e, 1989e), 5-year-old Mexican American children can be FI at an early age. Mexican American children's degree of inference increased based on their field independence as they get older. Thus, in the case of Mexican Americans, their FDI has been oversimplified, misunderstood, and misinterpreted (Saracho, 1983c, 1989e). Extensive research must be conducted before generalizing that all Mexican American students are FD.

### African Americans

Studies (e.g., Perney, 1976; Ramírez & Price-Williams, 1974; Shade, 1981, 1982) show a pattern suggesting that African Americans have a FD cognitive style. African Americans have a unique perceptual pattern. Performance patterns are basically similar among all socioeconomic classes within an ethnic group (Stodolsky & Lesser, 1967). Such similarities are credited to shared African roots, the American "Black" experience, and current African American concerns and political movements. The American "Black" living in a bicultural environment obtains behavior patterns from both African American ethnic behavior and mainstream Euro-American culture. Hale (1983) believes that the emotion-charged, people-oriented quality of African American expression reflects the African heritage.

African Americans may be relatively homogeneous because of "the recognition that 'color' affects the environmental responses of all African Americans, regardless of social class" (Shade, 1984, p. 1). African Americans do not develop visual information as assumed. The perceptual style of African Americans varies from other cultural groups in many ways. The favored learning modality for African Americans is kinesthetic and tactile instead of visual (Shade, 1984). Thus, they learn more effectively when they are able to create movement and encounter hands-on experiences. The African American culture sets a high value on oral and nonverbal communication. People learn by listening and demonstrate understanding by speaking. African American persons are more effective when they present their work orally. Their verbal communication style employs dramatic talking with rhythm, word order, and nonverbal mannerisms (Gilbert & Gay, 1985).

African Americans are often raised in extended families that provide many opportunities for social interactions (Hale, 1983). Children raised this way recognize people and understand and interpret facial expressions and nonverbal reactions (Shade & Edwards, 1987). African American children have been found to be more people oriented. They learn to focus on animate instead of inanimate objects (Damico, 1985). As a result, African Americans relate more to people and events and are less attached to objects. Most African Americans have characteristics of FD cognitive styles such as cooperation, interdependence, tactile learning, hands-on experiences, nonverbal reactions, facial expressions, and their relationships to people and events (Saracho & Gerstl, 1992).

African American cognitive style integrates the need to have an overall, global, or holistic picture of a learning task (Howard, 1987) and to use intuitive instead of deductive or inductive reasoning (Shade, 1981). Obviously, the learning style of African Americans may be relatively FD (Shade, 1981) and relational (Hale, 1983).

### Native Americans

The Native American cognitive style varies from tribe to tribe. Native American experiences in America, both on and off the reservation, including their relative segregation from mainstream society and their language differences, influence cognitive style. The Native American culture contains a generalistic orientation, where tribal members are interested in both people and things (Shade, 1984). Many have assumed that the Native Americans' traditional socialization and child-rearing patterns make them more FD, but these assumptions have not been supported (Swisher & Deyhle, 1987).

The major mode of learning for Native Americans is visual (Brewer, 1977; Rhodes, 1988; Swisher & Deyhle, 1987, 1989; Tafoya, 1989), which influences their high FI scores in tests of cognitive style. Native American students learn by observing others (Brewer, 1977; Tafoya, 1989). The focus on visual learning may help Native American students to generate excellent skills in visual perception and discrimination. They develop classification and categorization skills early in life. Rural or reservation students can discriminate between different classes of animals, the abundant brands used on the animals, and kinds of cloud formations (Brewer, 1977). Traditional Native American populations use a thought mechanism that differs from that of mainstream populations (Rhodes, 1988; Swisher & Deyhle, 1989).

Many Native American students in the primary grades are said to use global (FD) strategies in reading (More, 1987b). Teachers believe that Native American children use concrete rather than abstract materials (More, 1984); however, these are only teachers' impressions. The concrete materials used in the learning tasks may have been more culturally relevant. Thus, concrete/abstract variations of Native American students may be associated with culture irrelevance/relevance instead of cognitive style differences. Both concrete strategies and group interactions are attributes of FD cognitive style.

A review of studies on the Native American students' performance on visual, auditory, and kinesthetic perceptual tasks shows that Native American children are more effective at processing visual information, which is a characteristic of FI cognitive style (Kaulbach, 1984). Cullanine (1985) found that non–Native American elementary students are slightly more FI than Native American students from two relatively isolated Indian villages. However, Dinges and Hollenbeck (1978) found traditional Native Americans to be more FI than Anglo-Americans. Canadian Eskimos and northern Indians who represent hunting/gathering societies are more FI. Their living styles and child-rearing practices require the ability to impose an organizational structure on a field (e.g., unmapped territory) (MacArthur, 1968). Weitz (1971) categorized two Native American cultural groups (Algonkian and Athapaskan): urban-transitional and traditional, male-female, and older-younger. She found that the overall group was very FI and the more traditional people were more FD than the urban-transitional Native American people. In addition, field independence increased with age and females were more FI than males. More (1984, 1987b) supported that field independence increased with age for school-age Native American children. Hence, Native American children become more FI as they develop (More, 1987a).

The Native American students' mode of learning has both FD and FI characteristics. According to Saracho and Gerstl (1992), FD Native American students: (1) need new material introduced globally; (2) cooperate and elude competition; (3) take part in small-group work and student-initiated ventures; (4) maintain social interaction; (5) hesitate to assume a leadership role; and (6) are oriented toward peers. In comparison, FI Native American students (1) view details as meaningful and (2) manipulate and experiment.

Obviously, Native American students have both FD and FI characteristics. Differences in FDI cognitive styles have far-reaching educational implications.

## Asian Americans

Asian Americans are considered to be more FI because they do better at tasks requiring restructuring ability than social sensitivity. Differences exist within this group. Cognitive styles of Filipino American preschoolers may be more FD than other Asian American children. Chan, Takanishi, and Kitano (1975) explored the learning characteristics of preschool Asian American children to establish similarities and differences in their cognitive styles. Chinese, Japanese, Korean, and Hawaiian children's FI scores were comparable across groups to their Anglo-American counterparts. Young children from these ethnic groups may enter school with a well-formulated FI perceptual style (Chan, Takanishi, & Kitano, 1975). Hong Kong Chinese Americans are more FI than other Asian American groups (Dawson, Young, & Choi, 1974). Huang and Chao (1995) compared Chinese and American students. They found that these subjects were FI regardless of their country of origin or gender. These students may have been analytical to start with and, given this, they were successful in the school environment that emphasizes analytical thinking. Chinese American children are likely to enter school with a highly reflective response style, taking a relatively long time to respond to questions (Kitano, 1983). Asian American children enter school with a good understanding of visual discrimination skills and quantitative concepts (Kitano, 1983). Asian Americans have distinct learning styles, depicted by a visual-perceptual response or preferred visual images or graphic representations that foster learning, analytic skill, or the ability to identify figures embedded in a complex background field, and spatial reasoning ability (Griggs & Dunn, 1989).

South Pacific males are substantially more FI than females, but Hawaiian Americans are more FI than the other South Pacific Islanders (Hansen, 1984). Research comparable to that of Ramírez and Castañeda (1974) on Mexican American students has not been conducted with Asian American students' cognitive styles and their cultural values, but differences do exist. According to Tong (1978), FDI cognitive style is interesting and valid for Asian Americans, although it needs the power to justify other historical and cultural complexities of the Asian American experience.

### Conclusion

Culture includes a pattern of beliefs and values that delineates a way of life and impact on how people act, judge, decide, and solve problems. In each culture, reality is uniquely conceptualized through implicit and explicit assumptions and derivative generalizations which together construct a coherent system (Saracho & Gerstl, 1992).

Social, cultural, and environmental surroundings of ethnic groups differ in regard to their cultural/cognitive styles. While it was once stylish to reject the cultural assets and diversity in ethnic groups, social researchers now show equal respect and appreciation for the similarities and differences among ethnic groups (Saracho & Gerstl, 1992). Individual differences can be considered in assessing the interaction of cognitive style and ethnic groups (Saracho, 1989b).

Studies on FDI among cultural groups both support and dispute the assumptions held about FDI children and their sociability. These inconsistencies must be considered in determining the FDI of persons from other cultures.

## AGE DIFFERENCES

Research shows that as persons get older, they become more FI (Saracho, 1983b, 1983c, 1983e, 1989e; Witkin et al., 1954/1972), with a slight difference in field independence among 8- and 13-year-old children and adults (Witkin, 1949). McCleod (1987) studied three groups of male and female students ages thirteen to twenty-one years. He found 16- to 18-year-old students were more FI. Developmental trends showed a decrease in field dependence into late adolescence, then an increase in field dependence beginning in early adulthood (19- to 21-year-old group). Crosson (1984) found that older creative women were more FD. Such outcomes are similar to other researchers' conclusions: Adults in their middle years are more FI than both younger and older people. Although Saracho (1983e) found some 5-year-old children to be FI, young children are predominantly more FD and their potential to separate an object from the context develops with age. Busch, Watson, Brinkley, Howard, and Nelson (1993) found that 3- to 5-year-old children achieved higher scores as they got older. Using 7- to 11-year-old children, Gelderloos, Lockie, and Chuttoorgoon (1987) found that the spontaneous development of FDI through maturation may be accelerated through the experience that an educational system can provide students with a more stable internal frame of reference. Children become more FI as they grow, reach a peak in young adulthood, and then become more FD (e.g., Vaught, Pittman, & Roodin, 1975; Bigelow, 1971; Cecchini & Pizzamiglio, 1975; Massari, 1975). FI characteristics increase from childhood to young adulthood periods and decrease from young adulthood to old age (Witkin, Goodenough, & Karp, 1967; Witkin et al., 1954/1972), though several studies challenge these results. Consequently, age differences may be confusing the sex differences (Saracho, 1983c, 1989e).

## SEX DIFFERENCES

Sex differences vary among studies: (1) some show no sex differences, (2) others show males more FI, and (3) yet others show females more FI. Peplin and Larsen (1989) report no sex differences in college students on two FDI tests. Van Blerkom (1987) found no sex differences with undergraduate students. Ennis and Lazarus (1990) found no sex differences in 7-year-old children.

*FI Males versus FI Females.* Sex differences in FDI suggest that males are slightly but consistently more FI than females (e.g., Witkin et al., 1976). Men are more FI than women (Balistreri & Busch-Rossnagel, 1989; Witkin et al., 1954/1972). Seven-year-old boys achieved higher FI scores than 7-year-old girls (Forns-Santacana, Amador-Campos, & Roig-López, 1993).

Apparently, the degree of field independence surfaces consistently greater for males than for females, although several studies differ in their findings (e.g., Cecchini & Pizzamiglio, 1975; Ruble & Nakamura, 1972; Pawelkiewics & McIntire, 1975; Massari, 1975). Studies suggest that women have been influenced by the orientation and appropriateness of the tasks based on their sex roles (Balistreri & Busch-Rossnagel, 1989). Many researchers have challenged these results. They have found that females were more FI than males (Bush & Coward, 1974; Hyde, Geiringer, & Yen, 1975; McGilligan & Barclay, 1974; Perney, 1976; Witkin, 1950). Sherman (1967) asserts that sex differences are artifacts in space perception and do not necessarily suggest that males are more ''analytical'' than females.

Much of the research suggests individual variability within the sexes, particularly with elementary school, early childhood, and younger children. Four-year-old preschool children, for example, were studied, and girls were found to be more FI than boys (Chynn, Garrod, Demick, & DeVos, 1991). The existence of gender differences has been less clear with young children. Kloner and Britain (1984) report that 4- to 5-year-old girls were more FI than boys. Busch, Watson, Brinkley, Howard, and Nelson (1993) found that girls ages three to five had higher FI scores than the boys. Kogan's (1976, 1983) review of the literature suggests girls may be initially more FI than boys and that the differences reverse after ages five and six. He hypothesized that FDI surfaces somewhat earlier in females than in males. Busch, Watson, Brinkley, Howard, and Nelson (1993) found that girls were developing more rapidly in their field independence trait, which is consistent with Kogan's suggestion that field independence may not develop as a coherent construct in boys until age five or six. However, when kindergarten to fourth-grade children were studied, common factor solutions for boys and girls were found (Hardy, Eliot, & Burlingame, 1987), although early differences may have been disguised by the heterogeneity of age. Busch et al. (1993) caution researchers in assessing the performance of boys. This assessment represents an immature stage of field independence, or it is an index of an entirely different construct. They believe that boys under six must be assessed with caution.

### Conclusion

Differences in cognitive styles that have been found may be influenced by age and the people's socialization. Children develop through a steady evolution within a social context. Expectations and values construct the individual's FDI. Thus, the increased socialization of the child may account for the sex differences among young children.

### SUMMARY

FDI assesses the person's psychological differentiation, displaying a person's response and performance in a circumstance. This holistic theory of FDI is merged in a broad range of psychological phenomena meaningfully influencing the person's cognitive mode (Saracho, 1987b). FDI characterizes a person's way of perceiving, remembering, and thinking as the person apprehends, stores, transforms, and processes information. The term "cognitive style" usually denotes an individual's congruent techniques of responding and performing in diverse situations, where behaviors are actually observed. Such behaviors identify individuals' cognitive styles and categorize them as more FD (global or undifferentiated) or more FI (analytic or differentiated).

FDI is considered a regular mode of processing information, but it contains more than simple elements. It develops slowly, conforming to the person's experiences. It differentiates characteristics between the FDI bipolar continuum that is high-level heuristic in arranging and regulating behavior in a broad variation of occasions (Witkin, 1976).

FDI is intrinsically embedded in the person's complete personality within the affective, temperamental, and motivational realms. It is an element of the person's surroundings that concludes the nature of conforming attributes and protective methods. From this perspective, a core personality formation is evident in the different stages and realms of a person's psychological functioning (e.g., intellectual, affective, motivational, defensive) and its disclosure in cognition is FDI.

FDI determines one dimension of individual differences among people. FDI theory will continue to flourish if it is structured in a progressive theoretical framework to fully understand the individual's psychological variation. Further conceptualization and empirical work can promote its extensive realm of psychological differentiation, motives, and effects. Research and theory should continue within a cohesive psychological framework.

## NOTE

1. These are described in Chapter 3.

# Chapter 3

# Assessment Instruments

Over the past several years, researchers and practitioners in education have become interested in assessing individuals' cognitive style, especially the field dependence independence (FDI) dimension. FDI is a bipolar continuum with field dependent (FD) individuals on one extreme and field independent (FI) individuals on the other extreme. The preceding chapter provided a complete description of the FDI dimension. This chapter describes formal and informal techniques to assess cognitive style, to individualize instruction in educational settings.

## STANDARDIZED ASSESSMENT INSTRUMENTS

Several instruments are used to assess the FDI dimension. *The Embedded Figures Test* (EFT) (Witkin et al., 1971), *Rod-and-Frame Test* (RFT) (Oltman, 1968), *Body-Adjustment Test* (BAT), and *Block Design* subtest of the *Wechsler Intelligence Scale for Children* (WISC) (Goodenough & Karp, 1961) are standardized tests of cognitive style that are most commonly used. These tests are very different from each other in form; they also measure different traits. However, a moderate degree of overlap is found among these measures.

The need to identify FDI in young children has forced some researchers to adjust some of these tests for young children. The tests that have been adapted for young children include the *Rod-and-Frame Test, Tilting-Room-Tilting-Chair Test, Embedded Figures Test, Articulation of the Body-Concept Scale*, and *Goodenough-Harris Drawing Test*.

Scores on these tests reflect a person's perceptual ability and thinking styles. A high score on these tests means the person is FI, while a low score means the person is FD. There is a consistency in these scores among the various age groups (8 to 21) for all tests of cognitive style. Researchers rely on these tests to determine the individual's cognitive style.

These tests are described in this section to show how researchers have assessed cognitive style. Some of these tests require controlled laboratory procedures. Since they are much too elaborate for teachers to use in the classroom, teachers can use paper-pencil tests and classroom assessments. All tests require an individual to separate an item from the field or context of which it is part—and which therefore exerts a strong influence upon it—to break up a field or configuration. The tests described below were selected on the basis of their frequent use, simplicity, and effectiveness. These tests are described according to how they are being used: *Standardized Paper and Pencil Tests* and *Standardized Laboratory Tests*.

## Standardized Paper and Pencil Tests

1. The *Embedded Figures Tests* (EFT)[1] are standardized tests that require individuals to separate an item from the field in which it is embedded. Originally Gottschaldt (1926) developed these figures when he examined the role of past experiences in perception. To increase difficulty in the figures, colored patterns were superimposed on Gottschaldt's black-and-white outline complex figures. A simple figure is "hidden" in an integrated pattern of a larger figure. The person's task is to locate a specific simple figure within a larger complex figure. For example, outlines can create the boundaries of several prominent subpatterns in the complex patterns. The EFT has several versions that are appropriate for different age groups:

1. The adult EFT is individually administered and the *Group Embedded Figures Test* (GEFT) is administered in a group. Both versions are appropriate for adults.
2. The *Children's Embedded Figures Test* (CEFT) is appropriate for children as young as age five.
3. The *Preschool Embedded Figures Test* (PEFT) is appropriate for children ages three to five.

The adult EFT, which is individually administered to adults, and the GEFT are standardized measures that are composed of a series of 24 complex figures, where a simple figure is hidden in each complex figure. An individual has a five-minute time limit to locate the simple figure in the complex figure. The adult looks for a specific simple figure within a large complex figure. The simple figure is embedded in a complex pattern of a larger figure such as its outlines may be integrated along the boundaries of several prominent subpatterns in the complex figure (see Figure 3.1). Jackson (1956) reduced the EFT to a series of twelve complex figures with a three-minute instead of a five-minute time limit.

The EFT was modified into a simpler form to be used with young children (ages five to nine years) by Goodenough and Eagle (1963). Complex figures

**Figure 3.1**
**Sample Items from the Embedded Figures Test**

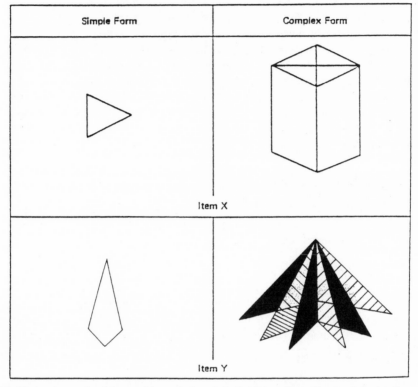

| Simple Form | Complex Form |
|---|---|
| | |
| Item X | |
| | |
| Item Y | |

were illustrations of familiar but caricatured objects. Such complex figures were constructed out of plywood and color in a jigsaw puzzle format. Young children would look for a simple form that was blended into one of the pieces of the jigsaw puzzle. A knob was attached to the piece with the simple form and several others to make this test self-corrected. When the attached knob on a piece of the jigsaw puzzle was pulled, only the correct simple form piece could be detached. This design allowed easier disembedding than in the regular EFT. The time limit was deleted and children were given another opportunity to succeed to reduce pressure and frustration. Children who pulled the wrong knob for their first choice were permitted to pull another knob and experience success. This procedure eliminated feelings such as failure that are experienced during the administration of the EFT. Finally, the children would sit at some distance from the complex figure, stand up, search for the simple figure, and pull a knob.

**Figure 3.2**
**Sample Items from the Children's Embedded Figures Test**

This form of administration extends action to a concrete situation and adds variety, as compared to the sitting and studying form of the EFT. Goodenough and Eagle's (1963) version of the EFT for 5- to 9-year-old children was considered reliable and valid, but its bulkiness and the expense of its construction made the test impractical for wider use.

The *Children's Embedded Figures Test* (CEFT) is another form of the EFT that was modified by Karp and Konstadt (1963, 1971) for children who are five years of age or older. This form of the EFT has most of the features of the Goodenough and Eagle (1963) version. It has several similar simple forms and complex figures and eliminates some of the practical disadvantages of the Goodenough and Eagle (1963) version. The CEFT, like the EFT, has a series of 25 complex figures where a simple figure is embedded and is administered individually. The cut-out models of the simple forms that are presented to the child have the shape of a tent (triangle) and a house, which makes it easy for the child to remember and search for the simple form in the complex figure (see Figure 3.2).

The CEFT is presented in the form of a game. The examiner tells the child that "this is like the game in the Sunday papers where a hidden animal, for example, must be found in a forest" (Witkin et al., 1971, p. 18).

The CEFT was later modified to be used with younger children. Coates (1972) developed the *Preschool Embedded Figures Test* (PEFT) for 3- to 5-year-old children. The PEFT and CEFT have many similarities. The PEFT, like the EFT and CEFT, has a series of 24 complex figures where a simple figure is embedded and administered individually. The cut-out model of the simple form that is shown to the child has the shape of a tent (triangle), which makes it easier for the young child to remember and search for the simple form in the complex figures. Coates (1972) took the CEFT, removed the color from the complex figures, and reduced the number of distracting simple forms in the complex figures. Each complex figure is outlined in black on a white background (see Figure 3.3). Nine of the original figures are included in the PEFT. For each complex figure, the children search for a simple equilateral triangle embedded in the figure and trace it with their fingers. To simplify the language, the simple figure is referred to as a tent.

2. *Articulation of the Body-Concept (ABC) Scale*[2] is a measure that identifies

**Figure 3.3**
**Sample Item from the Preschool Embedded Figures Test**

characteristics exhibiting a person's level of articulation. The individual uses a pencil to draw a person on white paper. Then on another piece of paper, the individual draws a person of the opposite sex. The language is simplified with young children. Both drawings are assigned a single rating using three basic criteria: ''(1) the form level of the drawings, (2) the degree to which the identity and sex are differentiated in the drawing and (3) the level of detailing in the drawing'' (Saracho, 1983a, p. 232). Detailed definitions of these categories are described in Table 3.1. These categories were used to formulate a five-point rating scale based on the definition of these characteristics. An individual's position on the five-point scale specifies his/her degree of FDI. At least two persons independently evaluate the different levels of articulation. The criteria have been used to specify characteristics on a five-point scale.

**Table 3.1**
**Characteristics of Drawings Reflecting Level of Sophistication**

A. Form level
   1. Primitive features
      a. Circles or ovals for body and limbs
      b. Triangular or rectangular body with limbs stuck on
      c. Other forms lacking attempt at human shape (e.g., absence of waist, shoulders, etc.)
      d. Limbs in form of sticks or ovals, shapeless, ending in prong-like or claw-like fingers; no shaping of hands; prong-like or claw-like toes
      e. Contact point of limbs to trunk involving overlapping or transparent joining; limbs stuck or detached (as opposed to integrated body parts)
      f. Grossly unequally sized arms, legs, ears, fingers, etc., combined with primitive form, uncontrolled lines
      g. Indiscriminately attached or misplaced body parts (e.g., arms attached at center of trunk)
   2. Sophisticated features
      a. Definite, shaped body outline; head, neck, shoulders well integrated into body outline and leading into trunk and appendages
      b. Attempt at human-like shape, proportioning
      c. Adequate profiling (e.g., trunk and legs facing in same direction, etc.)
B. Identity and sex differentiation
   1. Primitive features
      a. Objectively interchangeable male and female figures
      b. Difference between figures only in hair and/or hat treatment
      c. Minimal inadequate trunk differentiation (i.e., triangle trunk for female, oval for male, but otherwise identical; or belt for male and buttons for female as only difference)
   2. Sophisticated features—marked and adequate role assignment, expressed in clothing and/or shape (also expressed in hair, features, appropriate accessories, uniforms, etc.)
C. Level of detailing
   1. Primitive features
      a. Body parts omitted (e.g., absence of neck, nose, ears, or eyebrows; fingers attached directly to arms with hands omitted)
      b. No clothing indicated
      c. Facial features expressed by dots or ovals
      d. Inadequate or inconsistent clothing (e.g., buttons but no neckline, cuffs or hemline; hat, but no other clothing; toes shown in otherwise clothed figure; tie, but no neckline, etc.)
   2. Sophisticated features
      a. Consistent, well-rationalized detailing; clothing; facial expression; shoes
      b. Figure cast in role with good attempt at presentation of action
      c. Figure cast in role with presentation of accessories consistent with this role (e.g., cowboy with smoking gun, etc.)

*Source*: Witkin et al. (1962/1974), pp. 119–120.

3. The *Goodenough-Harris Drawing Test* (GHDT) (Harris, 1963) is a standardized measure that is used to assess conceptual thinking. This measure is similar to the ABC Scale in that individuals draw a set of male and female figures and the degree of detail on both drawings determines the individual's degree of FDI. More detail in the drawings indicates more field independence, while less detail denotes more field dependence. Criteria in this measure are observable characteristics in the drawings. Details of the drawings are specified on a checklist and a point is earned for each detail that is drawn on the picture such as eyes, ears, nose, mouth, and other details. The drawings are evaluated separate from each other by specifying details on two checklists: one with 71 items for the female drawing and another with 73 items for the male drawing. The checklist makes the scoring on the GHDT more precise; it is easier to assess the drawings and is less time-consuming (Saracho, 1986b). At least two persons independently check off on the checklist each observable detail found on each drawing, add the checks to obtain a score for each drawing, and record on the appropriate space on the checklist the total score for each drawing. The highest score for the female drawing is 71 and 73 for the male drawing. To determine an individual's FDI, both scores are added and divided by two. A high score indicates a person is FI, while a low score indicates the person is FD (Saracho, 1984c, 1985a, 1986b).

The similarity between the GHDT and ABC Scale (e.g., description, procedures) suggests that the scoring procedures for the ABC Scale can be replaced with the scoring procedures for the GHDT. The set of male and female drawings for the ABC Scale is rated on a five-point scale, which many think is a narrow range of scores. This narrow range of scores creates difficulty in obtaining a sensitive score for the FDI construct. According to Saracho (1984c, 1985a, 1986b, 1990a), the standardized measures that are used to assess FDI are time-consuming, because they are usually individually administered, which makes it expensive to use with large numbers of individuals. Since the ABC Scale requires persons to draw a set of male and female drawings, it reduces the examiner's time. The GHDT resembles the ABC Scale, has a wider range of scores, is inexpensive, and is easy to administer. The GHDT assesses conceptual thinking, but its similarity to the ABC Scale makes it practical to use in wide-scale assessment of the individual's FDI and provides better discrimination of cognitive style. The GHDT can appropriately be used to identify cognitive style, especially that of young children. Drawings make the assessment one of power rather than speed (Saracho, 1986b). Children draw the set of female and male drawings at their own pace, comprehend the task, do not experience the pressure of a time limit, and are free to express themselves without frustration.

This endorsement has been supported. Saracho (1984c, 1985a, 1986b) validated the use of the GHDT as a measure of cognitive style. She examined the relationship of scores on the ABC Scale, CEFT, and PEFT to those on the GHDT for children ages three to eight. She used a variety of reliability and validity procedures and found the GHDT to be an appropriate FDI measure for

**Figure 3.4**
**Drawings by a Five-Year-Old Girl (Scores for GHDT = 27, ABC Scale = 2, and PEFT = 9) (Reproduced with permission)**

both preschool and primary school children (Saracho, 1984c, 1985a, 1986b). She used three persons to independently assess the drawings for the ABC Scale and the GHDT; however, she suggests that if raters are trained to achieve 98 percent criterion, at least two rates must be used. Figure 3.4 provides a comparison of these measures with a 5-year-old child.

### Standardized Laboratory Tests

1. *Rod-and-Frame Test* (RFT)[3] is an apparatus with a luminous square frame and a luminous rod that moves separate from the frame. Both the frame and the rod are pivoted at the center to make the frame tilt to the left or the right. An individual is tested in a dark room and can only see the luminous frame and rod in tilted positions. The luminous frame is tilted, and then the examiner tells the individual to correct the rod from the tilted frame into a straight position. Individuals must "extract" the luminous rod from the luminous frame and ad-

**Figure 3.5**
**Rod-and-Frame Test**

*Source*: Witkin et al. (1977). Copyright 1997 by the American Educational Research Association.
   Reprinted by permission of the publisher.

just the rod. They use their body position as a reference to adjust the luminous rod into a straight (vertical) position. When the individual reports that the luminous rod is in a straight (vertical) position, the examiner determines the individual's degree of FDI, which is the degree of the tilt of the rod from the straight (vertical) position. A small tilt indicates independence of the field and reliance on the body; whereas a large tilt indicates the degree of dependence (see Figure 3.5). The individual is tested while sitting erect, to be able to refer to the body to install the rod in a straight position. The test consists of three series, each containing eight trials:

*Series 1*: The person is tilted to one side (at 28 degrees left or at 28 degrees right) while the frame is tilted to the same side (at 28 degrees left or at 28 degrees right). The person must adjust the rod to the upright (straight) position from an initial tilt of 28 degrees (at times to the same side as the frame, at times to the opposite side of the frame).

*Series 2*: The person is tilted to one side while the frame is tilted to the opposite side (both at 28 degrees).

*Series 3*: The person is erect while the frame is tilted to the left or right (at 28 degrees).

To help children understand the procedures, they are presented with instructions in a form of a "game." The examiner provides them with the rules before they enter the experimental room. The examiner demonstrates the procedures and gives the child the opportunity for practice trials. In addition, the examiner explains the concept "vertical" in concrete words and precise reference criteria. For example, to explain vertical position, the examiner tells the child that the luminous rod should be in the same position as the telephone pole. In Witkin et al.'s (1962/1974) operational formulation of FDI, the RFT is given equal weight with the EFT in a composite index on the basis of the important relationship that was found between the two measures. Dreyer, Dreyer, and Nebelkopf (1971) validated the CEFT, PEFT, and portable RFT and found that this strong relationship can be extended down to kindergarten children ranging in age from five to six years. For children 4½ years of age, the relationship between the PEFT and RFT breaks down.

The portable RFT was modified to use with young children. Oltman (1968) adapted a portable rod and frame apparatus to facilitate the ease of administration of the RFT with young children. However, 4-year-old children wiggled and removed their heads from the chin rest in the portable rod and frame apparatus, which restricted young children from focusing on the task. Coates (cited in Kogan, 1976) modified the RFT by placing a rod and frame on a wall without requiring any of the children's visual obstructions or physical restraints. For the second trial of the task, a large standard (2 × 18 inches) was placed approximately five inches to the left of the RFT and the child was told to make the stick in the middle stand up straight just like the one on the side.

2. *Tilting-Room-Tilting-Chair Test* (TRTCT)[4] assesses a person's visual and bodily standards in perception of the upright position, while the object of perception is the body rather than an external object, such as the rod in the RFT. The person judges his/her position of the body itself in space. The apparatus is a box-like room (70 × 71 × 69 inches) that is suspended on a ball-bearing pivot so that the individual can tilt the apparatus to any degree (e.g., to the left or to the right). Inside the box-like room is a chair that is also tilted to the left or the right separate from the room. A person sits in a chair that can be tilted clockwise or counterclockwise. The chair is projected into a small room that can be tilted clockwise or counterclockwise, independent of the room. After the person sits, the chair and room are moved to a tilted setting. Then the person adjusts the chair to an upright position (vertical). The standard test consists of two parts: (1) *The Room-Adjustment Test* (RAT) and (2) *The Body-Adjustment Test* (BAT).

*The Room-Adjustment Test* (RAT) is composed of eight trials where in four trials (Series 1a) the room and chair are initially tilted to opposite sides and in four trials (Series 1b) to the same side. At the beginning, the room is always

**Figure 3.6**
**Body-Adjustment Test**

*Source*: Witkin et al. (1977). Copyright 1997 by the American Educational Research Association.
Reprinted by permission of the publisher.

tilted 56 degrees while the chair is tilted 22 degrees. For each trial, the chair remains in its initial position of the tilt, while the person directs the examiner how to move the room to a position he/she perceives as upright (straight).

Children are presented with demonstrations in advance of the test procedures and are shown how the apparatus works. They sit in the chair of the apparatus. The examiner shows them the movement of only the room, only the chair, and both together. The examiner tells them in simple terms the "rules of the game" and plays the game with them.

The *Body-Adjustment Test* (BAT) is structurally similar to the RFT. An item (body or rod) is surrounded by a visual field (frame or room) where persons are assessed in relation to the degree to which they perceive the item as determined by the surrounding framework (see Figure 3.6). Some persons perceive their bodies as upright when they are aligned with the room and tilted at the same angle. Those who find themselves in this position report that they are perfectly straight. In comparison, other persons, regardless of the position of the surrounding room, bring their bodies more or less to the upright position. They perceive the body as an entity discrete from the surrounding field; while persons at the other extreme have a profound effect on their perception of the position of the body. Thus, persons are assessed between the two extremes: one field dependence and the other field independence.

The BAT is composed of six trials, where in three trials (Series 2a) the room and chair are initially tilted to the same side and the other three trials to the opposite sides. The room is first tilted at 35 degrees and the chair at 22 degrees. For each trial, the room remains tilted while the person instructs the examiner how to move the chair to a position she/he perceives to be upright (straight).

The raw score for both the RAT and BAT in each of the series is the degrees from the true upright (straight) position for the different trials of the series.

3. *Rotating-Room Test* (RRT) (Witkin et al., 1962/1974) is an apparatus that resembles the TRTCT. It is a fully enclosed, light-proof room (5 feet high × 5 feet wide × 4½ feet long) and is mounted on a chassis that is driven above a circular track 22 feet in diameter. Persons can move the unit smoothly, because the track is heavily waxed and the unit rides on pneumatic tractor tires. The room can be tilted from side to side on the chassis, above a horizontal axis to form an arrangement to the circle described by the center of the rotating room. The room is black on the inside, has prominent white borders, and has two pictures hung on the front wall to clearly represent its normal and horizontal axis. In addition, a chair is tilted to one side or the other above the same axis.

The RRT has postural factors that are altered by rotating the person about a circular track in order that the vector of the force felt by the person's body is the effect of the downward pull of gravity and an outward-acting centrifugal force. Persons adjust their bodies or the room where they are seated to positions that they perceive as upright (vertical). Initially, at each trial, both are objectively in an upright position. As in the TRTCT, the person's attention to postural sensations produced by the force on the body assists him/her to tilt body and room toward alignment with this force. When the person goes along with the visual field, he/she perceives body and room as straight in their initial positions.

## Comparison of Cognitive Style Measures

The cognitive style measures have been standardized. Several researchers have found these measures to be valid and reliable through a variety of procedures that were used with young children ages three to eight. They believe that these reliable and valid procedures provide a strong justification to reduce the length of the tests for most purposes.

These measures are described in Table 3.2 and are summarized in Table 3.3.

The FDI assessment instruments summarized established that persons differ in their modes of perception. Witkin (1949) shows that individuals' perceptions symbolize deep-rooted elements of their psychological structures. Persons exhibit characteristic modes of perceiving and dealing with situations related to usual facets of their psychological structures. A psychological justification supports the agreement among all of the FDI assessments. More than one measure

**Table 3.2**
**Description of Cognitive Style Measures**

*Rod-and-Frame Test (RFT)*: an apparatus with a luminous square rod and frame that needs to be adjusted to the center of the frame.

*Tilting-Room-Tilting-Chair (TRTCT)*: a box-like room suspended on ball-bearing pivots. Both the room and chair tilt independently to any degree to the left or right to be adjusted to an upright position.

*Articulation of the Body-Concept (ABC) Scale*: a five-point rating scale that assesses a set of male and female drawings based on the details on the pictures.

*Embedded Figures Tests (EFT)*: a series of complex figures that have a simple figure embedded in each complex figure. The *Children's Embedded Figures Test* has been modified to be used with children over five years of age while the *Preschool Embedded Figures Test* has been modified to be used with children ages three to five.

*Goodenough-Harris Drawing Test (GHDT)*: a checklist of 71 items for female pictures and 73 items for male pictures is used to assess the amount of detail in each picture to determine the cognitive style of young children whose ages range from three to eight.

Adapted from Saracho (1988).

should be used to confirm an individual's FDI. Studies on the FDI dimension mostly use cognitive restructuring tests that probably concentrate on the individual's cognitive restructuring instead of his/her own personality. For instance, studies show the EFT is related more to the WISC for Children's Block Design than to the RFT, although the EFT is more reliable. The WISC is an intellectual measure; therefore, this relationship suggests an intellectual factor in the individual's cognitive style.

## INTELLECTUAL FACTORS

Witkin et al. (1962/1974) described performance assessments to determine the individual's FDI as personality assessments instead of ability assessments. Personality assessments can be influenced by general reasoning ability. Since reasoning ability is required to process information in these tests, ability is difficult to isolate from personality factors in problem-solving tests. Solutions to problems generally involve ''parts'' that can be separated from the context in which they are embedded and restructured into new relationships. Individuals with a basic ability to ''break up'' a configuration can solve perceptual and problem-solving situations. The individual's analytical or global way of experiencing reflects his/her problem-solving and perceptual activities. An analytical field approach refers to the style of functioning characterized in both the individual's perceptual and intellectual behavior, including the ability to overcome an embedding context and to experience items as discrete from the field in which they are found. A global field approach leads to the perception of the dominant organization of the field, and items are ''fused'' with their background (Witkin et al., 1954/1972, 1962/1974). The capacity to actively and analytically cope

**Table 3.3**
**Summarized Description of Standardized Cognitive Style Tests**

| Test | Method | Subject's Task | Scoring Procedure |
|---|---|---|---|
| *Rod-and Frame Test* | Laboratory | Adjust rod to the center | The degree to which the person tilts the rod from the center on an average of eight trials for each series. |
| *Tilting-Room-Tilting-Chair Test* | Laboratory | Adjust the room to the center | The degree to which the person tilts the room from the center on an average of four trials for each series. |
| | | Adjust the chair to the center | The degree to which the person tilts the chair from the center on an average of eight trials for each series. |
| *Rotating-Room Test* | Laboratory | Adjust the room to a straight position | The degree to which the person rotates the room to a straight (vertical) position on an average of four trials for each series. |
| | | Adjust the chair to a straight position | The degree to which the person rotates the chair to a straight (vertical) position on an average of four trials for each series. |

**Table 3.3 (continued)**

| | | |
|---|---|---|
| *Embedded Figures Test* | Pencil and paper test | Find a simple figure in a series of 25 colored complex figures | The total number of simple figures the person finds in the complex figures. |
| *Children's Embedded Figures Test* | Pencil and paper test | Find a simple figure in a series of 24 colored complex figures | The total number of simple figures the child finds in the complex figures. |
| *Preschool Embedded Figures Test* | Pencil and paper test | Find a simple equilateral triangle in a series of 24 uncolored complex figures | The total number of simple figures the child finds in the complex figures. |
| *Articulation of the Body-Concept (ABC) Scale* | Pencil and paper test | Draw a set of male and female drawings | The amount of detail included in both drawings, which is assessed by a minimum of two trained raters who independently assign a single rating to both drawings on a five-point scale. |
| *Harris-Goodenough-Drawing Test* | Pencil and paper test | Draw a set of male and female drawings | The amount of detail included in both drawings, which is assessed by a minimum of two trained raters who independently |

Adapted from Saracho (1990).

with the field, evident in perceptual tasks, is extended over to perceptual activity and is represented in general reasoning ability. In the relationship between general reasoning ability and the FDI, (1) the RFT appraises the personality better than tests such as the EFT, and (2) tests such as the EFT overlap with general and spatial ability but the RFT does not overlap (Saracho, 1988d; Witkin & Goodenough, 1977).

When individuals can separate their bodies from their environments, they are able to set apart a figure from the background in a structure. Witkin et al. (1962/1974) carried a series of perceptual studies where subjects separated their bodies (as in the tilting-room-tilting-chair and rotating-room tests) from surrounding contexts. Individuals who can restrict the context in one of these conditions may also do so in other conditions. The different tests reveal individual differences in conditions that identify extractions of an "item" from the field in which it is found. Witkin, Goodenough, and Karp (1967) report a high level of inter-task consistency among the RFT, EFT, RAT, and BAT for 8- to 21-year-old persons. These tests measure spatial relationships that determine the individuals' FDI (Witkin et al., 1954/1972), but some researchers doubt the accurateness of the Block Design subtest of the Wechsler Intelligence Scale for Children (WISC) (Goodenough & Karp, 1961). Several researchers suggest the Articulation of the Body-Concept (ABC) Scale (Witkin et al., 1962/1974) and Goodenough-Harris Drawing Test (Saracho, 1984c, 1985a, 1986b) as good assessments to determine FDI (Linn & Kyllonen, 1981). Such a dispute over the original assessments increases the importance of using a minimum of two measures to determine the individual's FDI.

## Intelligence Measures

Several studies (e.g., Coates, 1975; Goodenough & Karp, 1961; Linn & Kyllonen, 1981; Saracho, 1983d, 1984c, 1985a, 1986b; Schimek, 1968; Sherman, 1967) show that cognitive styles reflect several intellectual facets. Results from these studies indicate that FI persons function more efficiently than FD persons on standardized intelligence tests. Both intelligence and cognitive style tests require persons to overcome embedded contexts.

Many researchers are troubled with the assessment of individuals' cognitive styles because of the influence of intelligence on the cognitive style tests. Halverson and Waldrop (1976) report that preschoolers' social behaviors relate to their verbal intelligence and FDI. Similar studies (Coates, 1975; Goodenough & Karp, 1961) support the relationship between cognitive style and intelligence. Coates's (1975) study of 4½-year-old children reveals that the Preschool Embedded Figures Test had an intellectual factor that also is found in the Wechsler Intelligence Scale for Preschool and Primary Children (WIPPSI) Block Design and Geometric Design. Goodenough and Karp (1961) confirm this outcome. The intellectual factor has a perceptual analytic element.

Other researchers also report the relationship between cognitive style and intelligence. Saracho (1984c, 1985a, 1986b) supports this relationship using the Children's Embedded Figures Test and the Goodenough-Harris Drawing Test with 6- and 8-year-old children and the Preschool Embedded Figures Test and the Goodenough-Harris Drawing Test with 3-, 4-, and 5-year-old children. Witkin et al. (1962/1974) report relationships among cognitive styles tests and the Stanford-Binet and Weschler Intelligence Scale for Children. All of these researchers found some intellectual aspects of cognitive style. However, Witkin et al. (1962/1974) criticize the effects of intellectual factors in the cognitive style measures, crediting the similarities in the subtests to the relationship between intelligence and cognitive style test scores and not to tests.

Resemblance in individuals can be predicted because those individuals who do well in intelligence tests are those who can overcome embedded contexts. Dubois and Cohen (1970) disagree with Witkin et al. (1962/1974). They found that the relationship between cognitive style, embedded contexts, spatial-perceptual skills, and nonverbal organization was small. Dubois and Cohen (1970) confirmed that FDI is one factor of intelligence; this conclusion cannot be generalized on the basis of one study. Additional research studies may support the relationship between intelligence measures and FDI measures. For example, studies that used the EFT as a measure of cognitive style usually had a higher relationship with the Weschler Intelligence Scale for Children's Block Design than with the RFT, although the RFT is more reliable as a measure. Witkin et al. (1962/1974) found a relationship between FDI and the total IQ scores on the Stanford-Binet and the WISC with 10- and 12-year-old children. Other studies that used all relevant measures manifested an element depicting an analytical field approach on the Picture Completion, Block Design, Object Assembly (e.g., Goodenough & Karp, 1961; Cohen, 1957), Body-Adjustment Test, Rod-and-Frame Test, and Embedded Figures Tests (Kogan, 1971).

## CLASSROOM ASSESSMENTS

The ABC Scale, GHDT, and the different forms of the EFT are easy to use, especially by classroom teachers. Several other practical instruments have been developed for classroom teachers to use. These classroom assessments are described below.

1. *Field-Sensitive and Field-Independent Child Behavior Observation Instruments* (Ramírez & Castañeda, 1974) are five-point rating scales that provide teachers with information on the child's cognitive style in different observable situations rather than a test. The frequencies of the child's observable behaviors are rated on a five-point scale: (1) not true, (2) seldom true, (3) sometimes true, (4) often true, or (5) almost always true. These ratings describe overall impressions of the child's cognitive style. For instance, a child may be predominantly FD, but in some situations he/she may respond in a FI way. These rating scales suggest (1) the extent to which a person is bicognitive and (2) ways to promote such a style.

The teacher rates the child on a five-point scale for each behavior on the observation instrument. Ratings suggest the frequency with which specific behaviors are manifested and indicate the child's primary cognitive style. The behaviors are observed and recorded during several situations over a period of time. The child's performance in a specific setting is observed and rated on this scale. The information obtained from the situation-specific ratings assists the teacher to map out a child's individual program (Ramírez & Castañeda, 1974). Table 3.4 provides sample items from this instrument.

2. *Learning Style Inventory* (LSI) (Dunn, Dunn, & Price, 1978) is a survey of the students' responses to a series of questions about their environmental, emotional, sociological, and physical choices and the way(s) they think they function in specific situations. A computer system analyzes the students' responses to show the important components in the students' learning styles. A manual guides teachers on how to effectively diagnose the students and select their learning alternatives. Learning alternatives are suggested when some components indicate a need for more than one source or strategy. Such information makes teachers conscious of individual differences for resources that students need and the size of the instructional area to provide for those students who prefer to work independently, with peers, with the teacher, or other person(s). In addition, this information helps teachers to design and implement an ideal learning environment for individuals and groups of students who have similar learning patterns (Dunn, Dunn, & Price, 1978). Although this inventory does not determine FDI, it has some of the characteristics of the FDI construct.

## PLAY AND THE ASSESSMENT OF COGNITIVE STYLE

The relationship between cognitive style and play has been identified in a series of studies.[5] Therefore, play can be used to asses the students' cognitive style. The following sections discuss ways to assess cognitive style through play.

### Theoretical Considerations

Play parallels a person's bodily and social processes (Erikson, 1950). Each playful effort is patterned by the necessities inherent in the interacting forces of the whole personality. Therefore, Witkin et al. (1954/1972) examined play for personality factors related to perception. Play, with the protection of its "make believe" world, allows players to experiment with concrete expressions of their many conflicting needs, conscious and unconscious. The player is ringmaster and selects the impulses that will inadvertently be accepted, obstructed, and granted admission. Such selective acts display some of the reinforced attitudes and values that are part of the players' repertoire reflecting their experiences, needs, and historical antecedents. The language in which they express their play ideas also influences their selection of strategies to cope with their concerns. Play gives the players a special freedom. In the play world, the players are

**Table 3.4**
**Sample Items from the Observation Instrument Developed by Ramírez and Castañeda (1974)**

*Observable Behaviors*

| **Field-Sensitive** | **Field-Independent** |
|---|---|
| *Relationship to Peers* | |
| Likes to work with others to achieve a common goal. | Prefers to work independently. |
| *Relationship to Teacher* | |
| Openly expresses positive feelings for teacher. | Rarely seeks physical contact with teacher. |
| *Instructional Relationship to Teacher* | |
| Seeks guidance and demonstration from teacher. | Likes to try new tasks without teacher's help. |
| *Characteristics of Curriculum* | |
| Performance objectives and global aspects of curriculum are carefully explained. | Details of concepts are emphasized: parts have meaning of their own. |

unfettered by reality's demands and can test the unreal, impossible, socially tabooed, and repressionally bound.

*Developmental Assessment.* Play can be used to assess children in a natural context to the degree that play supports their exhibition of maximum competence. Children are motivated to play, but they are also confronted with the desire to impose rules on their play. Therefore, a tension develops between doing what brings pleasure and subordinating those same actions to rules that restrict that pleasure. The pursuit of desire offers a strong motivational element to act while the omnipresence of rules presents impulse control. Children's play actions reflect this "desire:rule tension." The ability to have one's actions led by meaningful rules, first appearing in symbolic play, is generalized to other facets of children's lives (Pellegrini, in press).

Obviously, the play situation by its very nature invites children to experiment with concrete formulations and syntheses based on their impulses and ideas. Children's behavior during conflicts is inherent in the choices imposed; their ways of enduring, the confidence with which they cope with themselves and the field, and their quality of awareness of self and objective realities are all factors that can be seen to mold the form of play, but they also are all factors that must enter other life operations (Witkin et al., 1954/1972).

Researchers suggest several play measures to identify children's cognitive styles. These include *The Miniature-Toy Play Situation, Play Rating Scale,* and *Anecdotal Records on Children's Play.* The following play assessments are based on the children's cognitive styles:

## The Miniature-Toy Play Situation

The *Miniature-Toy Play Situation* (MTPS) (Witkin et al., 1954/1972) is an assessment that elicits relevant personalty information regarding the child's perceptual performance. The miniature-toy play situation was tested with 8-, 10-, and 13-year-old children. Each child is presented with a wide assortment of structured and unstructured play materials to make up a play or story and to set the stage for it. Detailed accounts are made of the children's play and their accompanying behaviors. Each protocol is assessed for personality characteristics of the players that might be related to their performance in FDI tests. One broad and useful aspect of the total play production is the organizational pattern (OP) that is imposed by the players upon the thematic and configurational aspects of their play. Each play record is rated on a seven-point scale based on the quality of the children's organizational patterns. In addition, ratings are specified and restricted to elements of play, namely, the ways of enduring in play in relation to feelings, sexual concerns, and use of animal objects.

*Test Materials and Equipment.* The play situation is a brightly lit three-sided cubicle which stands in an otherwise darkened room. A low table running the width of the cubicle (4 feet 8 inches wide and 2 feet 1 inch deep) is used as the "stage" for children to play. From the rear wall of this stage and immediately facing the player is a strongly illuminated, one-way-vision mirror (3 feet 3 inches × 2 feet 4½ inches). Behind the mirror is a small, darkened room where one or more observers record the child's play. The brightly lit area situates the child and her/his play in full clear view of the observers, who also are not able to be seen by the child. To the right of the stage, forming the right-hand wall of the cubicle, are three low, recessed shelves containing the play materials that are arranged in the same standard pattern for all children. Finally, in the left-hand wall of the cubicle is a small window, beyond which the experimenter is seated. Thus, seated, somewhat out of range, the experimenter is able to observe the child and, when necessary, to communicate or maintain contact with him/her.

The play materials used include (a) objects commonly encountered in the daily living of 8- to 13-year-old children, with a greater representation of those likely to be important at these ages; (b) objects seldom encountered in concrete reality, but generally experienced as symbolic expressions of several facets of early impulse problems; and (c) unstructured materials. Therefore, the collection consists of (1) many dolls, some defined and others undefined as to their ages, sex, roles, relationships, and functions; (2) furniture and accessory household objects; (3) motorized vehicles and heavy work equipment such as a steam shovel, a heavy truck, and airplanes; (4) domesticated animals; (5) objects of warfare; (6) a variety of wild and water animals; and (7) blocks (including different colors, shapes, and sizes), clay, water, and sheets of paper. The objects are all approximately to scale, but with enough scale differences to interfere with the smooth performance of a few of the more obsessional children. An attempt is also made to provide color and size variation within the same class of objects, because in some situations color may influence the child's choices. Some broken objects are also included.

*Test Procedures.* The child enters the play cubicle and is told to "make up a story or play and to set the stage for it." She/he is also instructed that at the end he/she is going to be asked to describe the production, and that a photograph will be taken of the final stage set.

The experimenter remains seated outside the cubicle at the window in the left wall unless the child asks for help or requests additional materials. The experimenter does not keep active contact with the child unless the child initiates the contact. The purpose is to keep the contact between the child and experimenter an easy and informal one, and also keep the situation as free as possible from adult pressures. Children who show prolonged reluctance to play are first verbally encouraged; then, if necessary, they are advised to "just explore the toys" until an idea comes to them.

Only within broad limits is any attempt made to restrict the play. No limitations are placed on efforts to extend the play into areas other than the stage. Time limits are not attempted except in extreme instances. If the play is severely constricted or finished in less than ten minutes, the child is invited, but not forced, to play again. On the other hand, if play lasts over an hour and there are scheduling difficulties, the child is invited to bring the play to a speedy close. Thus, the procedures attempt to offer maximum opportunity for play satiation.

Children who do not provide a spontaneous account of their production are asked to describe or explain it at the end. If no explanation is provided, questions are asked informally, but no effort is made to apply more than this mild pressure against the recurrent encountered lack of a clear conception, or, at least, of a verbalized conception of the central play ideas.

*Recording Procedures.* Two or three simultaneous play samples are recorded. The experimenter's record, made as unobtrusively as possible out of the child's usual line of vision, is interrupted at any point children are not at ease. The other play samples are recorded from behind the one-way-vision mirror. Children should be unaware of the presence of these observers, and the experimenter should make sure record operations are unobtrusive.

After records are inter-compared for a complete account of the play manipulations, of verbal accompaniment, if any, and of cues about the child's accompanying flux of affects, this composite running account, sketches of the placement of objects on the stage of successive phases in the play, a photograph of the final stage setting, and the child's interpretation of his/her play encompass the play record.

*Analysis.* In evaluating play, both the configural (form) and thematic (content) aspects of play are used, because these seem to express personality differences. The *thematic* material of the play may be explicitly stated by the player, or at least easily inferred on the basis of the conventional meaning of the materials used. Some children may create a verbal translation of their play as it unfolds. Most children may direct their play from a level of thinking at which conceptualization is not sharp enough to permit more than fragmentary verbal material. Hence, at the end of the play, many may not be able to provide a descriptive account of their play. Meanings of the play, therefore, have to be read from apparent material of play, inferred from contexts, or interpreted tentatively from commonly occurring symbolic equivalents of play usages. Moreover, most of even the explicitly manifest themes can suggest the existence of disguised or symbolically expressed ideas that presumably stemmed from unconscious or at least only minimally conscious impulses.

In evaluating each play, the ideas or attitudes are expressed in *form* qualities. Some of these form qualities are intrinsic in organizational features of the whole play or its parts and some in its spatial properties. In relation to patterns of organization, play productions exhibit variation in tempo of development in quality of continuity. A play can shift smoothly throughout to a close, be left unclosed, suffer frequent disruptions, move from one theme to another, repeat a larger theme or elements of it, create only a simple idea, or enrich the theme with supplementary or side themes. The motor-expressive and spatial forms of the play that accumulated meanings from preverbal days can offer valuable information about the player. Hence, the way children control and position the concrete materials, the tightness or looseness of the groupings and structures they create, the associations of these groups and structures to the total play area available, the form of their arrangement (e.g., circular, linear, squared, amorphous clustering) are considered. Attention is also given to other structural attributes that are customary symbolic carriers of deep-lying concerns and attitudes, such as special attention to doors, windows, walls, roofs, and concrete definitions of the inner-outer, high-low, open-closed, dependent-independent, stable-unstable, symmetrical-asymmetrical attributes of the groupings and structures.

The material from the play records indicates the child's perceptual performance from the analysis of the form instead of the thematic aspects of the play. The form features assess the effect of anxiety provoked during play as well as the nature and effectiveness of the child's strategies of coping with this anxiety. A rating scale can facilitate the analysis of the child's play in relation to cognitive style. It can identify children's patterns of performance during play.

*Rating Scale for Organizational Pattern* (OP) (Witkin et al., 1954/1972). A seven-point rating scale can be used to assess the child's pattern of performance in enacting the play. A high rating[6] is given only if the child plays with some freedom, manages concrete play materials, sustains some conscious grip of how he/she plays (as evidenced by ability to verbalize about it), and keeps a logical mastery over the play ideas. Succeeding step intervals show progressive loss in level of mastery and logical execution of the course and content of the play. Lack of mastery is indicated in several ways, but it is depicted predominantly as ''(1) loss of continuity of the play ideas or forms, (2) the eruption of irrelevant and irrational material into the play operations with incomplete rational assimilation of these intruding elements, or (3) some form of play inhibition.'' (Witkin et al., 1954/1972, pp. 384–385).

The criteria in defining successive step intervals of the Organizational Pattern (OP) Rating Scale were arrived at pragmatically from the play records of 10-year-old boys, and the implicit values stemmed from general knowledge of the children's psychological functioning. These values were, however, affiliated to semiobjective standards. The ratings of the OP seven-point scale are as follows:

1. Spatial organization and development of the play ideas are competent throughout and free from intrusion of irrelevant, bizarre, or eruptive concepts. The theme is appropriately completed. The player manages concrete materials and understands the central idea of her/his play well enough to verbalize it at least briefly.

2. The play idea is well developed except for occasional disturbance in either spatial or conceptual organization. The play has only passing or mildly irrational elements, but reveals minor blocking as mild constriction, avoidance or contact with most materials, or inability to verbalize about the play.

3. Spatial and ideational organization is appropriate in most of the play, but there are minor irrational components that disrupt the beginning or may later be introduced into the play, although some rationale is provided before the play is concluded.

4. Marked irrationality or irrelevance of content or spatial forms invades the play, but a rationale is provided or integrated into the play before the play is completed.

5. The dominant segment of the play constructs a logically developed body of forms or concepts, or both, regardless of the interruption of markedly illogical components that are kept and not integrated into the body of the play.

6. The play attempts to express forms or ideas in some organized way, but meaningless and illogical material usually interferes with its coherence; or moderately inappropriate material causes instability or marked anxiety.

7. The play efforts cannot maintain any initiated idea or form organization because of constant intrusion of marked discontinuities or eruptive material.

The scale does not distinctly discriminate each point. However, the wide and actual distinctions in the records themselves make this scale a useful assessment tool.

While this approach to assessing cognitive style through play is used in experimental situations, it suggests ways that teachers can use play to evaluate cognitive style in a less elaborate manner. Teachers can observe children's play and record the ways in which they play, identifying characteristics of play that are related to different cognitive styles.

### Play Rating Scale

The *Play Rating Scale*[7] (PRS) (Saracho, 1984a), a sixteen-item rating scale, records young children's play in four different play areas (physical, block, manipulative, and dramatic).

1. *Physical play* describes the children's use of their bodies to perform large actions such as running, jumping, climbing, digging, or riding a tricycle. FI children prefer to participate in physical play (Saracho, 1990a, 1991a, 1991b, 1994).

2. *Block play* describes the children's play with small unit blocks to miniaturize their world, large hollow blocks to build large structures, and block accessories to add a dramatic content to their construction. Their block structures range from simple construction to elaborate structures. When young children improve their ability in playing with blocks, their science and mathematics skills are cultivated; therefore, it is assumed that FI children play in this area (Saracho, 1995a). Also, according to Saracho (1990a, 1991a, 1991b, 1994), FI children prefer block play.

3. *Manipulate play* describes how children operate relatively small pieces of equipment such as puzzles, cuisenaire rods, peg sets, or a series of wood cylinders. Manipulative materials can be used to compare, seriate, or manipulate equipment. Through manipulative play teachers can teach reading, science, and mathematics, which are subjects preferred by FI children (Saracho, 1995a). Saracho (1991a, 1991b, 1994) also found that FI children were the ones who engaged the most in the manipulative play.

4. *Dramatic play* describes how children pretend and act out roles that relate to their real life experiences such as home, beauty parlor, post office, restaurant, or grocery store. Since dramatic play relates to social studies, it is assumed that this type of play is preferred by FD children (Saracho, 1995a).

In each of these play areas, various behaviors are observed, recorded, and scored, including (1) frequency of play, (2) ability and creativity to communicate ideas, (3) social levels of participation in play, and (4) capacity to lead in play activities. These behaviors identify the children's FD and FI characteristics.

*Frequency of play* refers to how often children play in a specific area. Studies indicate that FD individuals are more socially oriented and since play is a form of social behavior, it is believed that FD children participate more in social play (Saracho, 1985a, 1995a, 1996a).

*Ability and creativity to communicate ideas* in each play area refers to the way children code and communicate meanings using words, pictures, gestures, objects, or a combination of these. Their communication system can be in forms of both linguistic and nonlinguistic media (e.g., graphic, music, gestural). If children assume and act out social roles with a high degree of intercommunication among the players, their play behaviors reflect FD characteristics (Saracho, 1996a). In addition, Saracho (1996b) observed that FD children more than FI children communicated ideas during their play. FI children communicated the least ideas in physical, block, manipulative, and dramatic play (Saracho, 1995b, 1995c).

*Social levels of participation in play* in each play area categorizes children's play into five hierarchies of social play. FD children exhibited higher levels of socialization (Saracho, 1996b), especially in dramatic play (Saracho, 1995b, 1995c). However, the FD and FI children's socialization varies with each level. This variation is described below.

a. *Solitary Play* is when the child plays alone. FD preschool children are more socially oriented in their play, whereas FI preschool children engage more in solitary play. Saracho (1987b, 1996b) found that FI children more than FD children play at this socialization level.

b. *Onlooker* is when the child looks at other children's play. Since the onlooker does not engage in play, FI children may be the ones who only look at children's play (Saracho, 1985a).

c. *Parallel Play* is when the child plays alone but parallel to one or more children. According to Saracho (1987b, 1995b, 1995c), FI children engage in parallel play.

d. *Associative Play* is when the child plays in a group activity. Saracho (1987b) found that FD children engage in associative play.

e. *Cooperative Play* is when the child plays in an organized group activity that includes elements of division of labor to accomplish a final goal. FD children engage in co-operative play (Saracho, 1987b, 1996b).

*Leader or follower* is when children assume several social roles and follow certain rules. Peer interactions and conflicts evolve mutual role relationships, such as becoming leaders or followers. Children are leaders when they initiate activities but are followers when they depend on others to initiate activities. It is assumed that FI children will exhibit more leadership abilities (Saracho, 1985a).

## Anecdotal Records on Children's Play

*Anecdotal Records on Children's Play* (Saracho, 1992) also can be used to assess their cognitive styles. At least two persons are trained to observe and record the children's play behaviors during free play or activity times for a period of time. Children are permitted to display any play behaviors during these times. Anecdotal records are kept for these children to be used as a way of gathering information about a play situation. Observers look at and listen to what is happening, then record it accurately. They record brief accounts of a play situation. Factual descriptions of incidents, behaviors, or events provide illustrations of the different play situations. The following guidelines are followed in recording anecdotes:

1. Background information is recorded (e.g., date, time, child's name, and setting) when the event occurs.

2. Descriptions of specific events and the child's reactions, actions, and comments are cautiously recorded.

3. The collection of anecdotal records identifies behaviors by portraying specific situations and featuring selected behaviors.

4. Systematic observations describe events that identify patterns in young children's behavior.

**Figure 3.7**
**An Example of an Anecdotal Record**

Child _Ida Iaron*_____ Age ___5 years 1 month___ Sex _Female___

Date _September 25, 1998_ Time _9:31-9:32_ a.m./p.m.

Setting _Dramatic Play__ Observer _Ira Gonzalez_

Observation No. _1_____

| Observations | Interpretations |
|---|---|
| Ida was playing in the (housekeeping area) {next to Darron and Don}. | (dramatic play area) {parallel play} |
| Don picked up a truck and the wheel fell off. Ida and Don discussed ways to use the truck without the wheel. Ida tried to fix the toy and was not successful. | |
| [She left it on the table and went to another activity]. | [initiated her own activity] |
| /Ida picked up a roll of paper towels and played with it pretending it was a musical instrument (flute). She drew some circles on the side and tooted through one side./ | /used her make-believe ability to improvise by using the roll of paper towel as a musical instrument/ |

*In changing the subjects' names for anonymity, names beginning with the letters D and I were substituted. These letters indicated the subjects' FDI. For example, Ida was a FI child and Darron a FD one.

After a period of time, the children's modes of play are identified from the anecdotal records. At least two raters interpret these recordings. First, each observer independently examines the anecdotal records and identifies the different forms of play (e.g., manipulative, dramatic) and the children's play behaviors (e.g., communicates ideas, initiates own play) exhibited in each play area. Then the observer writes comments on the right-hand side in relation to the characteristics of cognitive style. Figure 3.7 illustrates this procedure. Observations were interpreted in the following way:

**Examples**

1. Ida is playing in the dramatic play area.

2. Ida substituted a roll of paper towel for a flute. Thus, she used her make-believe ability to make improvisations.

3. Ida was playing next to Don and Darron, which suggests that her social level of participation may best be described as parallel play.

4. Ida left the truck on the table and went to another activity. Apparently, Ida initiated her own play activity when she created a musical instrument and played it.

Inter-rater reliability of these records indicates that these procedures are valid and reliable play assessments of cognitive style (Saracho, 1992, 1995a, 1996a). These types of cognitive style assessments are encouraged because they are administered within a natural context, which may provide more accurate assessments.

## PERSONALIZED EDUCATIONAL PROGRAMS

Information obtained from these assessments has implications for learning. This source of information can help teachers to anticipate which students can function in a traditional, an individualized, an open, or an alternative program. The information also suggests the best resources (e.g., programs, tapes, instructional packages, contracts, films, games, small group techniques) for the different individual students. For instance, slow learners remember information better with tactual, visual-tactual, or tactual kinesthetic experiences.

The FDI construct also affects students' learning. FD and FI persons with similar intelligence may vary in their ability to use different kinds of information. For instance, FD students react better to material with social content, while FI students react better to material with impersonal content (Witkin & Moore, 1974). FI students are able to learn material that needs structure and are able to organize this material with ease. In comparison, FD students learn better from material that is organized and structured, such as explicit instructions in problem-solving strategies, for clearly defined performance outcomes. FD students prefer group and discovery experiences, whereas FI students select independent work and impersonal instructional approaches (Saracho & Spodek, 1981, 1986, 1994).

Research establishes that the FDI construct contributes to the students' selection of learning strategies and the learning process.[8] The students' cognitive styles can be determined early in their school careers to design curriculum and instructional approaches according to the students' cognitive styles.

Individuals can learn to perform and respond better in ways that differ from their primary cognitive styles. The most productive strategy is to increase each student's repertoire beyond his/her primary cognitive style. The students' cognitive styles need to be assessed to determine whether they are FD or FI (Ramírez & Castañeda, 1974; Saracho & Spodek, 1981, 1986). First, learning experiences corresponding to the students' primary cognitive styles are designed and implemented to provide students with a feeling of comfort and security in the school environment in order that learning is accomplished and successful (Saracho & Spodek, 1981, 1986).

After the students feel secure, the teacher can present each one with activities that are less compatible with that learner's cognitive style. Some degree of ''cognitive-style dissonance'' may assist in directing the student in moderately different directions. Consequently, a FI student can participate in activities such as chairing a committee or working with a group to make gifts for a sick fellow student. Such activities compel social sensitivity, a FD characteristic. Conversely, a FD student can participate in FI activities that demand the use of analytic skills, such as working alone to solve a problem in relation to a building structure or a mathematics assignment (Saracho & Spodek, 1981, 1986).

## SUMMARY

Cognitive styles determine people's personalities, such as their social and cognitive performances, better than any intellectual test by itself could do. An assessment of the individual's cognitive style provides more information than mental performance or achievement levels. It reveals the individual's cognitive patterns, learning in the different subject matter areas, and the nature of the teacher-student interactions in the classroom (Saracho, 1990a). Such information can be used in planning learning activities for individual children.

## NOTES

1. See Witkin (1950) for a detailed description of the EFT tests.

2. Witkin et al. (1962/1974) describe this measure in detail and provide specific examples of its scoring procedures.

3. Witkin (1949) and Witkin et al. (1962/1974) provide a full description of this test; Witkin and Asch (1948) report a study of the factors governing perception in this type of situation.

4. Witkin (1949) and Witkin et al. (1962/1974) provide a full description of this test; Witkin (1949) reports a study of the factors governing perception in this type of situation.

5. See Chapter 7 for a detailed description of the relationship between children's cognitive styles and their social behaviors, which are integrated in their play.

6. It is assumed that the most tightly knit organization is found in children who in their perception are able to resist the visual field. Scores in the perceptual tests reflect the values of the rating scale. Thus, this procedure makes the ''direction'' of the perception and personality scores correspond.

7. A copy of the PRS with specific instructions is available upon request from Olivia N. Saracho, Department of Curriculum and Instruction, University of Maryland, College Park, MD 20740.

8. Chapter 6 describes the FD and FI students' learning behaviors.

# Part II

# Students' Learning

# Chapter 4

# Portraits of Field Dependent Independent Children

Cognitive style describes the individual's distinctive ways of functioning, including the individual's perceptual styles, personality, intelligence, and social behavior. The cognitive style of field dependence independence (FDI) characterizes the individual's way of thinking, remembering, and understanding. For example, field independent (FI) individuals utilize internal references to process information, while field dependent (FD) individuals use external referents that assist them to process information.

This suggests that individuals differ in the way they respond to situations based on their cognitive styles. Teachers would be better able to understand the children in their classes if they were to consider their particular cognitive styles. They can observe the children's behavior in the classroom to identify their cognitive styles. For example, the following portraits identify more clearly the characteristics of FD and FI children. These characteristics were identified in a natural context. That is, while children were playing.

In identifying the children's cognitive style characteristics, an attempt was made to compare and contrast children from the extremes of FD and FI cognitive style.

The children who were observed were Anglo-Americans, African Americans, and children from other ethnic groups. They also came from different socioeconomic levels. Three cognitive style tests were administered to 100 5-year-old children in early childhood programs. To observe children in a natural context, they were videotaped during their play. Each child was videotaped ten times for a three-minute observation during ten three-minute play periods.

The tests used were the Children's Embedded Figures Test (Karp & Konstadt, 1971), Articulation of the Body-Concept (ABC) Scale (Witkin et al., 1962/1974), and the Goodenough-Harris Drawing Test (Harris, 1963; Saracho, 1984c,

1985a, 1986b). Reliability, validity, and descriptions of these measures were provided in Chapter 3.

Based on the scores of these cognitive style tests, five extreme FD and five extreme FI children were selected to be portrayed. The three-minute videotaped sessions of these children were transcribed as the bases for these portraits. These observations provided examples of the play behaviors of children with different cognitive styles. Two transcriptions per child were randomly selected for inclusion in the portraits.[1] Children and teachers who were considered more FD were assigned a name beginning with the letter D, while those who were considered more FI were assigned a name beginning with the letter I. This process helped to identify the child's and teacher's cognitive style when their behavior was described.

## PORTRAITS

Five extreme cases were chosen as samples of children who gave FD or FI performances during their play. At the end of all the portraits, a general discussion of the children's behavior is discussed.

### Field Independent Children

**FI Child 1:** *Ida*[2]                          **Sex:** Female

#### Observation 1

[During breakfast, *Ida* stands and speaks with Ilse and Isaac and then walks to the center of the room where a box of unifix blocks is on the floor. Some cubes are arranged in a $2 \times 2 \times 4$ tower. *Ida* adds several blocks to expand the tower to a $2 \times 2 \times 6$ with one block on top. *She* then pretends to paint the tower with a paint brush that is in the box of blocks. *She* stops, looks around the classroom, and takes three more blocks from the box *she* pretends to paint.]

#### Discussion

*Ida* only interacts with FI peers who match *her* cognitive style and engages in FI-oriented activities (such as blocks, pretending in an abstract way to paint).

#### Observation 2

[*Ida* is playing in the housekeeping area next to Darron and Don. Don has a toy in his hand, while *Ida* has the wheel to the toy. *Ida* takes the toy away from Don. Ms. Dreyfuss walks past this area.]

*Ida*: The wheel fell off.

Ms. Dreyfuss: That's okay.

[*Ida* tries to fix the toy and is not successful. Therefore, *she* leaves it on the table and goes to stand next to Ms. Ibsen (the other teacher). Since Ms. Ibsen is speaking to someone, *Ida* walks away and goes to get a musical instrument made of paper towel rolls. *Ida* is playing a card game with Ilse. Neither child says anything. *Ida* shuffles the cards. Ilse takes the cards from the box. *Ida* looks around the classroom and then faces Ilse and picks a card.]

Ilse: [shaking her head]: No.

[Ilse picks another card.]

### Discussion

*Ida* engages in a social activity with two peers who do not match *her* cognitive style. This behavior is similar to the one reported in the FDI literature of mismatch dyads (Oltman, Goodenough, Witkin, Freedman, & Friedman, 1975) which shows that FI persons are more aggressive. *Ida* appears to be very assertive when *she* takes a toy away from *her* mismatch peer to attempt to solve the problem by fixing the toy.

*Ida* then walks away from *her* mismatch peer and attempts to attract the attention of the FI teacher who matches *her* cognitive style. As a FI person who is insensitive to others, the FI teacher is unaware of *Ida*'s search for attention.

*Ida* then goes to play cards, a FI activity, with a matched peer in a FI way (no social interactions occurred).

### FI Child 2: *Irene*                    Sex: Female

### Observation 1

[*Irene* is playing "Doctor" with Don. Ida is watching. *Irene* has a stethoscope in *her* ears. Don is lying on the floor. The floor is covered with a long piece of white paper.]

*Irene* [listens to Don's heart and yells]: Next!

[Since Irma does not move, *Irene* yells again to Irma.]

*Irene*: Next! Irma.

[She calls her over with *her* finger, then points to the paper. Don gets up. Irma comes over and pretends to be the patient. *Irene* examines Irma. *Irene* listens to her heart. Irma tries to get up. *Irene* gently pushes her back down.]

*Irene*: Lay down.

[Irma tries to say something, but *Irene* does not let her.]

*Irene*: Shhh, I can't hear.

[*She* "listens" to Irma's head.]

*Irene*: Irma, okay.

[Irma gets up. *Irene* gives the stethoscope to Isaac. Then Irma and *Irene* leave and go play checkers. Ira is watching Irma and *Irene* play checkers.]

### Discussion

The FDI literature indicates that FI individuals set up their own standards. *Irene*, like FI persons, tries to control the play of others. *She* plays doctor, assuming the most important role in the play episode, and tells others what to do. There is no social interchange between *Irene* and the other children. *She* plays with matched peers (Isaac, Irma, Ira). Ira watches by himself, a FI behavior; while Don follows *Irene*'s directions, a FD behavior.

### Observation 2

[*Irene* is sitting in the housekeeping area playing with Ira. *She* gets up and walks over to Ms. Dreyfuss.]

*Irene* [in a singing voice]: Ms. Dreyfuss, will you help me get my shoes on?

Ms. Dreyfuss [in a singing voice]: Why are you talking like that?

*Irene* [singing]: Because I can't get them on.

Ms. Dreyfuss [bending down to help *Irene*]: These shoes are all wet. You know what? Put on the shoes you wore here today.

[*Irene* takes the shoes and goes back to the housekeeping area to play with Ira. *She* puts on *her* shoes.]

Ira: Okay, I go first.

[Then they play checkers.]

### Discussion

*Irene* is playing with Ira, who matches *her* FI cognitive style. Both FI children are playing checkers, a FI activity. *She* asks the FD teacher rather than the FI teacher for help.

### FI Child 3: *Isaac*                    Sex: Male

### Observation 1

[*Isaac* discusses plans with Irving and Ilene to decide who will be Mr. Meoge when they play "Karate Kid." *Isaac* then demonstrates what karate looks like.]

*Isaac*: Watch Ilene.

[*He* kicks twice. Ms. Dreyfuss sees them.]

Ms. Dreyfuss: No karate. I don't like that. I'll have to ask you to change it now.

*Isaac* [protesting]: . . . but, we're not . . .

Irving [interrupting]: How about circus?

*Isaac* and Ilene [together]: We already played that!

[Ira joins the discussion.]

**Discussion:**

*Isaac* is playing with two peers and is later joined by another one; all these children match *his* FI cognitive style. The FD teachers do not permit them to play karate and *Isaac* protests, a FI behavior (sets up *his* own values).

**Observation 2**

[*Isaac* is cooking. *He* is working with Ira, Inga, Inez, Irma and Ms. Ibsen. They are making jello.]

Ms. Ibsen: [announces]: Everyone will get a chance.

*Isaac*: That's for you.

Ms. Ibsen [asks the group]: Why do you think that that's that color?

*Isaac* [calls out]: Cause that's in the water!

Ms. Ibsen: Good, *Isaac*, pour yours in. Ira, give me all of it, give me all of it. Inga, you're gonna do the boiling water.

[*Isaac* throws away the empty jello boxes.]

Ms. Ibsen: No, Irma, you have to wait till the water boils. Don't touch anything, I have to check on the boiling water. Sit on your hands. Sit on your hands.

[All children follow the directions.]

**Discussion**

*Isaac* engages in an activity with four peers and a teacher, who all match *his* FI cognitive style. The teacher encourages analytic thinking (FI ability) by asking them to determine why the water turned a certain color. *Isaac* provides the correct response.

**FI Child 4:** *Ilene*                    Sex: Female

**Observation 1**

[*Ilene* finds a paper from the Polaroid camera on the table, takes the paper to Ms. Dreyfuss.]

*Ilene*: She, she took a picture and this come out of the camera. Here [giving the paper to an adult in the room].

Adult: What is it?

*Ilene*: It's trash.

Ms. Dreyfuss: Trash? Ow.

[*Ilene* laughs, looks at the paper, and tries to read it. *She* then sits down next to Ms. Dreyfuss and looks at a book with her. Inez also looks at the book.]

Inga and *Ilene* [ask the teacher]: Can you get us one of those for our playground?

[Ms. Dreyfuss smiles. Ira and Darron then join the group. They look and speak to each other. The director of the school enters the room and speaks with the teacher. All children stop talking and listen to the director.]

### Discussion

*Ilene* solves the problem when *she* finds the trash on top of the table by taking it to Ms. Dreyfuss, her teacher. *Ilene* tells Ms. Dreyfuss where *she* found the paper from the camera. *Ilene* also looks at the paper and tries to read it and then looks at a book (analytic behaviors) with Inez, who matches *Ilene*'s cognitive style.

### Observation 2

[*Ilene* is playing with a "musical instrument" made of a roll of a paper towel. *She* blows into the roll, but it does not make the appropriate sound. *Ilene* looks at it, shrugs *her* shoulders and tries again. It still does not work. *Ilene* shrugs *her* shoulders again and walks over to Ms. Ibsen. *Ilene* stands and watches Ms. Ibsen help Inez, Dewey, and Irma make instruments.]

*Ilene*: Ms. Ibsen, this won't work.

Ms. Ibsen: Maybe because it's bent at the bottom.

[*Ilene* tries to fix the end. This time it works.]

Ms. Ibsen: There you go, there you go.

[*Ilene* walks over to the observer to show her that it works. *Ilene* then walks over to Irma.]

*Ilene*: Irma, blow harder.

[*She* demonstrates.]

Irma: [exclaims]: No!

[Irma fixes the instrument. Then *Ilene* and Irving are playing with "musical instru-
    ments."]

Ms. Ibsen: Find something else to play.

[*Ilene* begins to pretend *she* is playing a guitar.]

*Ilene*: What about the horn?

Ms. Ibsen: As long as it's quieter. It's nice to be quieter.

*Ilene*: What about a hawk?

Ms. Ibsen: A hall?

*Ilene*: Not a hall, halls are m-e-l-i-s." (*She* probably means medicine.)

Ms. Ibsen: A hawk?

[Then Inga joins in. *Ilene* and Irving begin to play the instruments again.]

Someone: She asked you not to do it in here.

*Ilene*: How about we all be a band? We gonna copy off of Irving.

Ms. Ibsen: What do you call the leader of a band?

Irving: The captain?

Ms. Ibsen: Close. It starts with a "C" sound.

Irving: Either the leader of band or an orchestra.

Inga: I get it. I know what it is. (Pause) know what it is.

Ms. Ibsen: What is it?

Inga: The conductor.

Ms. Ibsen: Good. So who's the conductor?

*Ilene* [exclaimed]: No! These are not your rubber bands.

[*Ilene* walks away and again pretends to play the guitar.]

**Discussion**

*Ilene* attempts to solve a problem when *she* wants to play a musical instrument. *She*
makes one out of a roll of paper towel. Then *she* fixes the end of it, because *she* could
not get it to make a sound. *Ilene* later pretends to be playing a guitar.

*Ilene* seeks more often the people who match *her* FI cognitive style. When *she* cannot
make a sound with *her* instrument, *she* seeks the help of *her* FI teacher. *Ilene* also engages
in activities with FI children (Irma, Irving, Inga).

**FI Child 5:** *Ira*                                    **Sex:** Male

**Observation 1**

[*Ira* is discussing plans of what to play with Isaac, Ilene, and Irving. They decide to play the Three Stooges].

Irving: I'm Moe.

  Hi, Moe, Hi, Moe.

*Ira*: I want to be the bald one.

Isaac: I'm the leader and they're Moe, Larry, and Curly.

*Ira*: Oh, who's the short guy?

[They talk about being a clown, Pee Wee Herman. *Ira* demonstrates. They play Simon Says for about ten seconds. They talk about someone changing their name. Isaac kicks and hits *Ira* in the stomach. Ms. Dreyfuss tells *Ira* and Isaac to find something to do. *Ira* walks over to Ms. Dreyfuss and looks around the room.]

*Ira*: I want the color forms.

**Discussion**

*Ira* is interacting with children (Isaac, Ilene, Irving) who match *his* FI cognitive style. *Ira* and Isaac fight with each child, and the teacher, who mismatches their cognitive style, has to separate them. Both FI children's failure to attempt to resolve their disagreement suggests that they set their own values and lack social skills. The FDI literature (Oltman et al., 1975) also shows that when two FI matched dyads are together, conflict arises over a situation requiring decisions.

**Observation 2**

[*Ira* is playing ''Memory'' with Don, Darron, and Ida].

Darron (to Ida): Don't cheat, don't cheat!

[Ida takes her turn but does not make a match. *Ira* takes *his* turn and makes a match. Darron shakes his head.]

Darron: Okay, it's Don's turn.

[Don goes and does not make a match. *Ira* goes again.]

Darron: No, that's not fair. First it's Ida's turn.

[Ida takes another turn and fails to match. Then *Ira* takes another turn, and is able to match.]

*Ira*: I don't know how I do that.

Darron: Now it's Don's turn.


[Ida touches a card.]


Darron: No, no, no. *Ira* got that.
　　　　No, no, no. *Ira* got that.

### Discussion

*Ira* is interacting with children (Isaac, Ilene, Irving) who match *his* FI cognitive style. When *Ira* engages with mismatch peers, *he* and Ida become assertive. This behavior is observed in FDI studies that were conducted with mismatch dyads (Oltman et al., 1975). The FI person is usually more aggressive.


## Field Dependent Children


**FD Child 1:** *Darron*                **Sex:** Male

### Observation 1

[*Darron* is "cooking" by *himself* in the housekeeping area. *He* then walks to another section of the room, watches some children, gets the "Legos" and returns to the housekeeping area. *He* pretends to build. Then *he* is joined by Isaac.]


*Darron*: I'm making a computer, Isaac.

Isaac: I know.


[Isaac hands a rectangular shaped block to *Darron*.]


*Darron*: It's remote control.

Isaac: No, it's not.

*Darron*: Yes, it's remote control, Isaac.


### Discussion

*Darron* is playing in a social area (housekeeping) where social interaction (a FD behavior) occurs to a greater extent. *He* engages with the computer in a concrete way (making a pretend computer rather than using one). *His* FD mismatch peer (Isaac) is using analytic materials (rectangle).

### Observation 2

[*Darron* is playing "Memory" with Ida, Don, and Ira. Irma is watching.]

Ira: Don, it's your go.

*Darron*: Nooo, don't go. She's bothering us.

Irma: I'm not doing anything.

Don: Yea, look [pointing to a camera].

*Darron*: No, not she, she [pointing to Irma].

Irma: I'm telling on you all.

Don: All right. You're not, you're not, you're not.

*Darron*: Come on! Now we're all gonna get in trouble.

Don: She always tells on somebody who says something.

*Darron*: She always tells.

Don: Yea, who needs her?

Ira: Oh!

Don: All right, we need her, we need her.

*Darron*: Let's play.

Ira: It's my turn.

*Darron*: No, it's Don's turn.

Ira: Go, Don.

[Ida picks a card for Don.]

Ira: No.

Ida: You can't do that. That's not fair. You can't pick for Don. It's not your turn. Put that back.

Don: Cause Ida can't pick you when it's not your turn.

[Irving walks over.]

*Darron* [to Don]: Pick a card.

[Don tries to pick.]

*Darron*: No, that's wrong.

Ira: I can't concentrate.

*Darron*: I didn't want that. You see what you made me do? You bother us.

[Irving walks away.]

*Darron*: Let's start all over.

[*Darron* begins to sing. Don sorts cards. *Darron* mixes them up.]

*Darron* [to Don]: Then you're not playing.

[Don gives the cards to *Darron*.]

*Darron*: I go.
[*He* picks what looks like a zebra.]

### Discussion

*Darron* and Don are having a conflict with Irma. In the FDI literature of mismatch dyads (Oltman et al., 1975) the FI persons are more often aggressive. Irma is very assertive when she bothers the other children and plans to tell on them.

    *Darron* uses a global defense (denial) when *he* blames another child for what *he* did, such as when *he* says that *he* didn't want to do that, but someone made *him* do it.

**FD Child 2:** *Don*              **Sex:** Male

### Observation 1

[*Don* is arguing with Darron.]

*Don*: I'm the good guy.

Darron: Oh, man, I don't want to be the bad guy.

*Don*: Okay. I'll be the bad guy.

Darron: No, I'm the bad guy.

[This argument continues for about two minutes while Ida, *Don*, and Darron walk around the room. They stop arguing and sit at the table. Then Ida and Darron begin to draw a picture. *Don* watches.]

### Discussion

Both *Don* and Darron want to be the good guys, because good guys are the ones who are liked by people. Thus, they respond to people's emotional expressions and want people to like them, FD behaviors.

### Observation 2

[*Don* is working at the table with Ms. Ibsen. *He* is making a guitar by taping an egg carton and a roll of paper towels together. *Don* walks across the room to ask Inga if she has any rubber bands.]

Inga: No, go ask Ms. Ibsen.

[*Don* does. Then *Don* walks around the classroom for a long time (2½ minutes) before deciding upon an activity. *He* tells Ms. Dreyfuss *he* wants to play with something in a plastic bag.]

Ms. Dreyfuss: Okay.

[*Don* removes five plastic bags from the hooks, reaches into the fifth bag and removes a heart-shaped object. Over the object *he* is sewing, there is a needle and thread. *Don* returns all bags to the hooks. Then *Don* sits down and works on *his* heart.]

### Discussion

*Don* is having difficulty solving a problem. *He* asks Inga for a different material instead of trying to use another kind of material that is available at *his* table or taping the egg carton and roll of paper in a different way. After searching for rubber bands, *he* decides to use a needle and thread. According to the FD characteristics, FD persons take longer to solve problems.

Inga suggests that *Don* seek help from the FI teacher, who matches Inga's cognitive style. However, *Don* seeks the assistance of the FD teacher, who matches *his* FD cognitive style.

**FD Child 3:** *Derrick*        **Sex:** Male

### Observation 1

[*Derrick* is sitting at a table. In front of *him*, *he* has a gingerbread man made out of paper.]

Ms. Iserman: *Derrick*, are you done?

*Derrick*: Yes.

Ms. Iserman: Put *your* name on the back.

*Derrick*: I already did.

[*Derrick* continues to sit at the table watching other children play. Ms. Iserman walks over and touches *Derrick's* gingerbread man.]

Ms. Iserman: If *you* want, *you* can glue on some hair or do whatever *you* want. Here's some glue.

[*Derrick* glues on eyes.]

### Discussion

*Derrick* finishes *his* project and waits for someone to tell *him* what to do. Finally, the FI teacher (Ms. Iserman) checks *his* gingerbread man and gives *him* the glue to add eyes, which *he* does. Thus, *Derrick* depends on authority for direction.

**Observation 2**

[*Derrick* is leaning over a table looking at a bug in a jar. Damien and Doris are with *him*.]

Doris: What's that green stuff?

*Derrick*: That's his doo-doo, he has to go to the bathroom.

[They all laugh.]

Damien: Yea, he has to go to the bathroom.

[They laugh again.]

Doris: What kind of a bug is it?

*Derrick*: It's an anteater.

Damien: No, it's a beetle.

*Derrick*: It's a beetle, anteater. It's a girl. Girls doo-doo. Boys poo-poo.

[They laugh again.]

*Derrick*: Yea, that's what that green stuff is.

[They continue to watch the bug.]

Ms. Dehaven [to the group]: Do you know where we found it?

*Derrick* and Damien: Where?

**Discussion**

*Derrick* decides to participate in an activity with *his* FD matching peers (Doris, Damien) and *his* FD teacher, who matches *his* FD cognitive style. There is a great deal of interaction among these FD persons.

**FD Child 4:** *Dewey*                    **Sex:** Male

**Observation 1**

[*Dewey* asks Ms. Iserman to get a certain game down from the shelf. She gives *him* the game *he* asks for, but tells *him* that the game does not have any pieces. *He* returns the game to Ms. Iserman and asks for another one.]

Ms. Iserman: This one?

*Dewey*: No, the other one.

[She hands *him* a snap together with a 3-D puzzle. *He* tries to put the pieces together but is not successful. *He* is sitting on the rug alone.]

**Discussion**

*Dewey* asks *his* FI teacher for a game. She gives *him* a puzzle, a FI game. This game may be appropriate for that teacher but not for *Dewey*, who is not able to put the puzzle together. This may be the result of a mismatch in cognitive style between the FD child and FI material or because of a mismatch in ability.

**Observation 2**

*Dewey* is sitting in the block corner with a bucket of blocks in front of *him*. A truck is in the bucket.]

*Dewey* [asks Delores]: Do you want to play?

[Delores shakes her head to indicate ''no,'' says something to *Dewey*, and walks away.]

Delores: I won't say so.

[Dean walks over to the block corner and takes a truck out of the bucket. *Dewey* tries to grab the truck from Dean.]

*Dewey* [yells across the room]: Ms. Iserman, Ms. Iserman, I want to play alone without Dean!

Ms. Iserman: Well, then, tell Dean to play somewhere else.

*Dewey* [to Dean]: Go play somewhere else. *Dewey* wants to play by himself.

Dean: I don't want to.

Ms. Iserman: Well, sometimes you want to play by yourself. You can take the truck and go somewhere else and play.

[Dean leaves the truck and walks to the other side of *Dewey*. Dean then sits on the step.]

Dean [to *Dewey*]: You don't need that block.

*Dewey*: I need it.

[*Dewey* hits Dean twice.]

Dean: I'm telling, I'm telling.

[Delores says something to Dean.]

Dean: He's fresh.

[*Dewey* walks away. *He* then walks to Ms. Iserman.]

*Dewey* [to Ms. Iserman]: What are you doing?
Ms. Iserman: Damien's going to make a shaker. Have you made one?

[Dean also walks over to Ms. Iserman. *Dewey* tries to grab the truck from Dean.]

Ms. Iserman: *Dewey, Dewey, you* stopped playing with them. Now Dean is playing with it.

[*Dewey* continues talking with Ms. Iserman, then walks over to the table and looks at a gingerbread man made out of paper.]

### Discussion

*Dewey* invites a girl (Delores) who matches *his* FD cognitive style to play (FD activity) with *him*. *He* encounters conflict with the other children, but waits for the teacher to tell *him* what to do. *He* is influenced by the teacher, who in *his* view may be seen as an authority figure.

### FD Child 5: *Dennis*                    Sex: Male

### Observation 1

[*Dennis* is sitting playing with a 3-D puzzle. *He* gets up and walks around the classroom, looks at what other children are doing, walks directly behind Derrick.]

*Dennis*: Derrick, my dad. Derrick, my dad.

[Derrick ignores *Dennis*. *Dennis* walks away, comes back, and slips *his* arm around Derrick.]

*Dennis* [to Derrick]: Hi.

[*Dennis* drops *his* hand down and tries to pinch Derrick on the buttocks.]

Derrick: Don't do that. Don't do that. Don't pull my shirt up.

[*Dennis* smiles and continues to pinch Derrick. They begin to pinch each other.]

*Derrick*: It hurts.

[Derrick punches *Dennis* in the chest. *Dennis* punches Derrick back. Derrick pretends to die.]

Derrick: Ohhh.

[*Dennis* pinches Derrick again.]

Derrick: Stop!

[and holds Dennis's hand. Derrick lets go. Dewey asks Ms. Iserman something.]

**Discussion**

The children (*Dennis*, Derrick, Dewey) match each other's FD cognitive styles. *Dennis* attempts to interact with *his* FD matched peer by trying to get his attention (putting *his* arm around Derrick, pinching him, responding to Derrick's punch). Although *Dennis*, Derrick, and Dewey are disputing, they still seek each other's attention. This may be the influence of the match in their FD cognitive style.

**Observation 2**

[*Dennis* takes a roll of paper towels from the box and walks over to the table with paint on it. Dean is painting his roll. *Dennis* watches Dean. *Dennis* then taps the table and *his* head with the roll, hums into the roll, watches other children for 2½ minutes, and then begins to paint *his* own roll to make it look like a musical instrument.]

**Discussion**

*Dennis* searches for the company of *his* FD matched peer (Dean). *He* engages in a concrete activity as *he* attempts to make a musical instrument. *He* also watches others as *he* completes *his* project to get ideas. Thus, *Dennis* is influenced by *his* peers.

## GENERAL DISCUSSION

These portraits present some of the basic characteristics of cognitive style in young children. The FI children tend to be more idea-oriented than people-oriented. Even when playing with others, these children seem to engage less in activities of a purely social nature. They focus more on the materials and their uses. The social interactions seem less concerned with sustaining social relations than with using the materials.

On the other hand, the FD children tend to be more person-oriented in their play. They engage with each other in social interactions, sometimes for the sake of the interactions themselves. More social conflict is evident in these children, which is not an indication that these children are less socially skilled. At this level, most children lack the skills necessary to negotiate an end to a conflict.

In addition, young children use conflict to make social contact with other children and to sustain that contact.

The portraits also show several FDI characteristics. For example, children typically engage in activities with those peers who match their cognitive styles. FD children engage more in social interactions with their peers and depend on authority. In contrast, FI children depend on their own values, are more assertive with FD children, and encounter conflict with their matched FI peers. The children's FD and FI behaviors are apparent in these children.

Only a few portraits are presented here. They are not a representative sample of how children with varying cognitive styles function. However, they do offer concrete examples of how children with different cognitive styles might function in an early childhood classroom. Thus, they can serve as a baseline for those observing cognitive style differentiation in young children.

## NOTES

1. The children and teachers presented here are identified with fictitious names to protect their anonymity (privacy).

2. The italic letters identify the child who is being portrayed.

Chapter 5

# Students' Learning Behaviors

Cognitive style impacts on the way individual abilities develop. It characterizes consistencies in the use of cognitive processes. All areas of competence are integrated within a person's intellectual processes, but the relationship between cognitive styles and intellectual and social capacities is still vague. Fundamental stylistic variations seem to underlie all of the individuals' differences (Saracho, 1987b). Kalyan-Masih and Curry (1987) found a relationship between preschool students' cognitive styles and their cognitive performances on selected Piagetian tasks. They also found this relationship to be developmental. Younger children were initially more FD and the older slightly more FI. The results support theoretically expected age differentiation in cognitive performance and style and theorize the relationship between the two. This relationship influences the way students process information and perform in school.

## INFORMATION PROCESSING

Learning styles are distinctive qualities of behavior that continue through time, situation, and topic. Learning styles reflect the individual's cognitive and social characteristics. FD and FI students differ in their abilities to use divergent kinds of information (Saracho, 1989d); therefore, they receive and process information differently (Shade, 1989). Hall (1988) examined the relationship between preschool students' FDI and their simultaneous processing. Their results showed that FI preschoolers performed better on simultaneous processing tasks in general. Simultaneous processing is a style of processing information where individuals manage information in a wholistic way. The focus on learning and perceiving processes is consistent with the FDI cognitive style, which emphasizes the way information from the environment is processed.

Cognitive styles are process-oriented and controlled to attain a goal (Brodzinsky, 1982). Students' understanding of characteristics is embedded in a complete view of their social cognitive abilities and in only a relatively implicit understanding of what characteristic terms are. However, the model of the composition of characteristics, associations to research on theory of mind, and the role of social context in determining the function of characteristic terms are still vague (Yuill, 1992). There is a relationship between FDI and performance in proportional reasoning, when relevant-irrelevant information is introduced in a task (Nummedal & Collea, 1981). Proportional reasoning tasks contain field effects (Niaz, 1989b). FD students are influenced by the structure of the perceptual field and lack an articulated conceptual framework. FI individuals can abstract and organize information more spontaneously. For these students, acquisition activities offer them an opportunity to activate this capability and to encode critical ideas immediately (Kiewra & Frank, 1988). The main benefit of acquisition activities is to acquire external storage instead of immediate encoding. FD individuals lack memory (Frank, 1983; Davis & Frank, 1979) and confront a task rigidly. Apparently, the FD student's cognitive style has a debilitating effect during immediate encoding situations, but need not inhibit learning when sufficient opportunity to encode externally stored factual material is available (Kiewra & Frank, 1988; Davis & Cochran, 1982).

FI students usually achieve higher scores on factual and higher-order tests than do FD students (Kiewra & Frank, 1988). Students may have the same learning ability and memory but differ in cognitive styles (Witkin et al., 1977). Stevenson (1954) required young children to search through a box of objects for a particular item. He found an increase in memory for the incidental objects from ages four to six, while Howard and Goldin (1979) showed that under certain conditions, 5-year-olds can attend selectively. To clarify the nature of attention in FD and FI preschoolers, Haynes and Miller (1987) examined the relationship between cognitive style and various components of information processing in preschoolers. They found that reflection (a dimension of cognitive style similar to field independence) related to incidental recall, which increased with age.

The outcomes of the study by Haynes and Miller (1987) may be a function of the requirements of the incidental learning task. Future research could be aimed at the question using more complex visual stimuli in the incidental learning paradigm and requiring more FDI material to be learned, and to discover the role of FDI in different types of learning tasks (Haynes & Miller, 1987). The students' cognitive styles modify their ability to assimilate information and solve problems. Students who have cognitive styles that differ from the cognitive style typically used in their schools and classrooms will have difficulty succeeding, regardless of their level of native intelligence (Cohen, 1969). The success of a particular approach is often context-dependent, but schools usually use FI instructional techniques. Therefore, FI students have an advantage as their strategies are more compatible with those instructional strategies used in the school.

## SCHOOL PERFORMANCE

Several researchers (e.g., Mrosla, Black, & Hardy, 1987; Vaidya & Chanky, 1980; Yore, 1986) indicate that FDI contributes to school performance since the skills required in school tasks and in the school tests include analytical capacity and ability to develop strategies for organizing and restructuring information. FD students do not employ mediators or general principles to process information and need distinctive strategies to succeed with global contexts in perceptually deceptive tasks.

### Subject Areas

Most school subjects require FI strategies that are less developed in FD students. As subject matter becomes more sophisticated, and requires more analytical reasoning, a larger information base is required (Cohen, 1969). FI students possess those analytic skills that facilitate such subjects as science, mathematics, and reading (Davis, 1987; Davis & Cochran, 1990; Witkin, 1978). FI students do better than FD students in subject areas such as Spanish language, mathematics, natural sciences, and social sciences (Páramo & Tinajero, 1990). FD students without analytic skills have high drop-out rates in science and mathematics in the upper grades (Olstad, Juarez, Davenport, & Maury, 1981) and attain low scores on standardized tests (Cohen, 1969) that are abstract in nature, a FI characteristic. These tests rely on analytical-logical reasoning (Cohen, 1969) and reflective response styles (Shade, 1981). The most intelligent nonanalytic FD students may achieve the poorest scores because of their greater reliance on relational strategies and their inability to use the analytic processes (Cohen, 1969).

The study by Páramo and Tinajero (1990) attempted to capture an integral picture by considering all the main academic areas for each group of subjects together. They found that FI students did better in all areas. The advantages of field independence for students is that it allows them to function better within the school environment, even in subjects such as the social sciences that should be more appropriate for the skills and interests of the FD students.

### Academic Achievement

Differences in academic performance have been attributed to personality characteristics. Cognitive style reflects personality characteristics which relate to academic achievement. Martinetti (1994) showed an interaction between cognitive style and academic achievement. Páramo and Tinajero's (1990) study in Spain indicated a significant relationship between field independence and school achievement. In their study, FI children did better than FD children in their overall academic performance. Ismail and Kong (1985) found that Malaysian students in Standard Three (equivalent to third grade in the United States) who were FI had superior academic performance. Traditionally, school achievement has been described in terms of individual differences in intellectual ability.

Academic ability intercedes on intelligence; therefore, the students' cognitive styles can predict their academic performances. Dwyer and Moore (1991) examined the effects that differentially coded (black and white and color) illustrations had on FD and FI students. The outcomes on achievement scores indicated that FI students scored higher than did the FD students. They concluded that field dependency is an important instructional determinant and that, for some types of learning objectives, the process of color coding instructional materials may reduce achievement differences attributed to differences in cognitive styles.

In using criterion measures that are visually oriented and are used to assess visually complemented instruction, Moore and Bedient (1986) found that FI students scored higher with these measures. For the type of learning measured by the identification test, color coding was instrumental in providing the kind of learning structure that enabled the FD students to achieve at a level similar to that achieved by the FI students. The above study is consistent with other studies (e.g., Páramo & Tinajero, 1990) on FDI and performance at school, suggesting that FI students do better than FD students.

Cognitive style qualities influence the students' academic achievement. Important differences in achievement were found between FD and FI students. Saracho (1984d) explored whether FD or FI students had higher levels of academic achievement. She found that first-grade FI students did better than the FD students on a standardized test of academic achievement, but third-grade FD students did not differ from the FI students. The role of cognitive style in relation to academic achievement seems to vary according to grade levels and within academic areas. Additional studies on the relationship of students' cognitive styles to academic achievement can be investigated for different age groups and within specific academic subject areas, such as reading, language, and mathematics.

Older students have been studied in relation to cognitive style and achievement. Older FI students do better in mathematics and reading than do FD students. In a learning situation FI persons use mediators to assist them to use material that is abstract and lacks clear inherent structure. FI students can organize the material in the most useful way for them to learn. FI students function more abstractly and learn material that is in an abstract mode better, but FD students learn material that has social content better.

Studies that compare the FD and FI students' academic achievements in American schools show that FI students outperform their FD peers (Davis, 1987; Davis & Cochran, 1990; Ramírez & Castañeda, 1974). A relationship between cognitive style and academic achievement exists. FI students prefer sciences and mathematics, but FD students prefer social sciences. FD students understand material that is firmly organized, while FI students understand material that is vaguely organized (Saracho, 1988b). Academic disciplines differ in task requirements for students; therefore, FI individuals, who are cognitively abstract, would do better than FD individuals in fields such as engineering and the natural sciences; whereas FD individuals, who are cognitively concrete, would do better than FI individuals in areas within the humanities and social sciences. Performance in these disciplines may be a function of the interaction between cognitive style and task requirements. Then performance interacts between personality (cognitive style) and environment (task requirements). The interactionist approach may be important in the environment in a classroom setting (Saracho, 1988b).

### Environment

In exploring environmental factors, preschoolers were evaluated for FDI and sex-role stereotyping. Boys were more FD and sex-role typecast. Same-sex typing in boys and cross-sex typing in girls were considered predictors of field independence (Chynn et al., 1991). Hertz-Lazarowitz and Sharan (1979) considered self-esteem, locus-of-control, and classroom climate. Their results showed that middle-class children scored higher on personality measures than did lower-class children. However, lower-class children had a more positive perception about the classroom than did middle-class children. Sex and class also made a difference. Middle-class girls scored higher on both personality measures, but they were the ones who had the most negative perceptions about their classroom climate. Conversely, lower-class boys had the most positive perceptions about their classroom social experiences, but they scored lower on the two personality measures. Middle-class boys scored higher on personality questions, but lower on classroom climate. On the other hand, lower-class girls exhibited the opposite behavior.

This seems to show an inverse relationship between personality development and children's perceptions of their social climate in the classroom. Hertz-Lazarowitz and Sharan (1979) drew upon the FDI cognitive style theory to address this relationship. FI persons do not rely on their peer groups for support and gratification, although they count on their peer groups for emotional support. Therefore, they do not belittle their social surroundings. Children from lower social status were more FD. Greater congruence between students' affective development and their social experiences that are promoted in school integrates their psychological development.

According to Páramo & Tinajero (1990), the relationship between FDI and performance in schools is influenced by sex. Both FI girls and FI boys did better than their FD classmates. Sex-linked stereotypes bias the teachers' preferences of students. Several studies of preschool and grade school students show that teachers prefer FI boys to FI girls and FD girls to FD boys. Such preferences are reflected in school marks for the students (Bertini, 1986; Páramo & Tinajero, 1990; Saracho, 1984d). This type of behavior in the study by Páramo and Tinajero (1990) could result from the difference between boys and girls in their cognitive styles, the range of cognitive style scores among girls having been narrower than scores among boys.

Studying techniques are an integrated segment of the students' environment. Annis and Davis (1978) found different effects on two functions of note-taking for their students' study techniques. One group of students received a copy of the lecturer's notes before and after the lecture along with an external memory device, whereas the other group of students recorded their own personal notes and employed them as an external memory device. The students who took notes and then reviewed the material mentally utilized the function of encoding. Students who received a copy of the lecturer's notes both before and after the lecture decoded the lecturer's notes as an external memory device. The encoding function in learning the material was important, and students who encoded their own notes achieved the highest scores on an examination. Appropriate studying techniques are those that (1) encourage students to write their own personal notes because this requires them to recall the material they need to learn, and (2) provide students with an external memory device, which the students personally prepare or is a copy of the lecturer's notes. Students who achieved the highest scores were those who (1) encoded their own notes and (2) then used their notes as well as the lecturer's notes as external devices. Teachers can prepare a summary of their lectures for their students to refer to during their review to increase their students' learning.

Cognitive style theory proposes a conceivable interaction between students' study techniques and cognitive styles. FD persons use the background or environment as a whole without attempting to analyze or locate structure in it. Conversely, FI persons experience items as discrete from their backgrounds and overcome the influence of an embedding context. FI individuals can organize stimulus materials better than do FD individuals. FI persons use their own techniques to separate and engage key elements to process information (Witkin & Moore, 1974). Cognitive style has an impact in the students' study techniques. For example, FD students find taking notes dysfunctional; they need to isolate and analyze the material. In contrast, FI students find that taking notes is most efficient. They can abstract the basics from the material they are reading as well as overlook unimportant information. Studying techniques are only one segment of learning and storing concepts in peoples' memories.

## Concept Development

FD and FI persons differ consistently in the way they learn or memorize knowledge. According to Goodenough (1976), (1) FI persons are more advanced developmentally than FD ones; (2) FD and FI persons employ several learning processes without revealing a different performance; however, FI persons perform more effectively; and (3) if FD and FI persons employ their cognitive processes differently, the effectiveness of their performances will vary under different conditions.

Cognitive style has an impact on cognitive tasks. Hester and Tagatz (1971) used cognitive style as an inherent organismic factor. FD and FI cognitive styles are comparable to the conservative and commonality approaches pertaining to the proportion of dependence on determining the tasks on concept development. The effectiveness of concept development depends on the individual's cognitive style. FI persons psychologically understand the nature of concept development tasks when they are first exposed to the tasks and resolve any expectations within the stimulus field more quickly than the FD persons. FD students learn concepts better when teachers use clarification strategies appropriate to their cognitive styles. FI students learn better than FD students under either matching or non-matching instructional strategies (Hester & Tagatz, 1971). According to Beller (1967), young children who were taught in a way that is comparable to their cognitive styles performed better on a vocabulary test; whereas those who were taught in ways that varied from their cognitive styles (e.g., analytic children were taught using a global technique, global children taught using an analytic strategy) learned less.

FD and FI persons differ in their learning processes with the same performance (Goodenough, 1976). The FD person's memory performance is less than that of a FI person when the task requires him/her to process a large quantity of information. FI persons are more effective than FD persons in remembering information they have stored in their short-term memories (Davis & Frank, 1979).

A review of the literature by Davis and Cochran (1982) included FI persons and *selective attention, encoding,* and *long-term memory. Selective attention* is an information-processing paradigm with dichotic listening, signal detection, and visual search tasks. FD persons cannot attend to irrelevant cues, especially distracting cues. *Encoding* refers to the attentional processes employing tasks that require encoding specificity, digit span, and working memory tasks. FD persons have narrow encoding processes; therefore, they have problems processing information. In contrast, FI persons can process information better than FD persons; consequently, they process a larger quantity of information. *Long-term memory* is the performance on associative learning and memory. Organization processes induce differences in the memory of FD and FI persons. FI individuals' abilities for selective attention, encoding, and long-term memory processes are superior to those of FD individuals. Since individuals' cognitive styles affect their learning modes and outcomes, cognitive styles should be considered in all educational aspects. This is important in early childhood education programs because the focus is on teaching concepts instead of facts alone. Clear cues should provide an assortment of teaching aids with social content (e.g., photographs of peers to teach colors or size). Conversely, FI children learn concepts that are abstract, and they can learn independently without the participation of peers (Saracho, 1988d). They should be provided experiences where they work by themselves, such as working with manipulatives.

## FLEXIBLE COGNITIVE STYLE

Most school situations require FI behaviors and strategies. In these cases, FD children miss the opportunity to perform in their dominant cognitive style. These children find conflict and frustration when they attempt to manage situations where they have to apply a cognitive style that differs from their dominant one. Some researchers (e.g., Ramírez & Castañeda, 1974; Saracho, 1983b; Saracho & Spodek, 1981, 1986) advocate that people learn to use alternative cognitive styles, flexibly applying characteristics of both FD and FI styles. They found that individuals can perform and behave in a cognitive style that differs from their dominant cognitive style. Ramírez and Castañeda (1974), working with adults and children, and Saracho (1983b), working with 5-year-old children, found that individuals can adapt to both cognitive styles. Individuals utilize the cognitive style that is appropriate to a unique situation or task. Ramírez and Castañeda (1974) refer to the described behavioral versatility as *bicognitive development*, while Saracho and Spodek (1981, 1986) refer to it as *cognitive flexibility*.

Ramírez and Castañeda (1974) and Saracho and Spodek (1981,1986) recommend that individuals learn to expand their repertoires of cognitive characteristics beyond those traits and behaviors that conform to their dominant cognitive styles. Children can obtain cognitive flexibility but may experience "cognitive dissonance" (Saracho & Spodek, 1981, 1986). FI persons immerse themselves in activities that require them to become socially sensitive, such as working with a group of children. Social sensitivity is a FD characteristic. In contrast, FD persons immerse themselves in experiences that require them to use FI characteristics, including analytic skills and working alone such as working on a puzzle by themselves. This procedure assists young children to respond better to a wide range of data sources more flexibly in their interactions with ideas and people (Saracho, 1988d; Saracho & Spodek, 1981, 1986).

Many adults and children exhibit characteristics of both FD and FI cognitive styles, thus demonstrating cognitive flexibility without any training (Saracho & Spodek, 1986). They can be either cooperative or competitive, based on the circumstance in which they find themselves, and can solve problems that demand inductive or deductive reasoning, reacting to or disregarding the social environment. These individuals possess a repertoire of strategies they can employ interchangeably in the process of learning and exploring for a solution to a problem (Ramírez & Castañeda, 1974).

Saracho (1983b) supports Saracho and Spodek's (1981, 1986) hypothesis that many individuals exhibit cognitive flexibility. Saracho (1983b) generated a profile of young children (ages three to eight) by mapping their cognitive styles. *Cognitive mapping* is a set of formal, self-descriptive statements. The FD and

FI characteristics and the children's profiles guided the mapping of the children's cognitive styles. The profile depicted thinking, learning, and functioning in reading. Cognitive mapping of 5-year-old children, for instance, demonstrated that they relied on their interpretations of symbols (FI characteristic); analyzed symbols by defining things in order to understand them (FD characteristic); deduced symbols by comparing and contrasting attributes or measurements (FI characteristic); and synthesized some dimensions or events into a unified meaning (FI characteristic). Their interpretations were based on meanings of symbols (FI characteristic), though family members and a few close friends biased their meanings of symbols (FD characteristic).

Under relevant life situations, persons use skills related to both cognitive styles, regardless of their position on the FDI dimension. Persons exhibiting particular cognitive style characteristics with a high degree of regularity are referred to by Witkin and Goodenough (1981) as *fixed*, considering their use of the characteristics identified with a specific cognitive style. Persons who have characteristics of both FD and FI cognitive styles are considered *mobile*. Mobile persons display greater diversity on how persons perform and adapt their cognitive styles depending on the circumstances than those persons with a fixed cognitive style. The person with characteristics of both FD and FI cognitive styles can adapt to a wide array of circumstances, in contrast to those persons who are fixed. Witkin and Goodenough's (1981) mobility-fixity concept manifests a particular perspective for training in cognitive style. This perspective, descending from the bipolarity of the FDI dimension, varies from a perspective inherent in unipolar ability dimensions, where the desirable goal is to support persons to move toward the high end of the dimension. Since each pole of the FDI dimension contains characteristics that can be adapted and extended to those the person already has, a person can have characteristics from both FD and FI cognitive styles. Witkin and Goodenough (1981) believe that it is realistic to train persons to acquire interpersonal skills, although systematic research needs to support this goal. This prospect can assist persons to have a variety of ways to function, cope, and respond to various circumstances.

The potential to have cognitive flexibility (Saracho & Spodek, 1981, 1986), analogous to mobility (Witkin & Goodenough, 1981), is influenced by the person's cognitive style. FI persons are more flexible in selecting effective techniques from the FD or FI cognitive styles to work on a task, solve a problem, or confront a situation. FD persons are challenged more by cognitive style flexibility than FI persons. The distinction between FD and FI persons may be the wider range of alternative opportunities in their background experiences, their willingness to use a range of strategies, and/or their ability to comprehend that a specific technique is more effective (Saracho, 1988d).

Cognitive style flexibility is critical because it facilitates students' learning. A certain cognitive style can be ineffective in a specific context but beneficial in another context. For instance, a FD student can experience frustration in a science activity but may experience success in a social activity (such as a birthday party or family reunion). This student can achieve and perform more appropriately in society if this student's cognitive style is adapted to behave as expected in a more FI fashion. In comparison, FI persons are better in cognitive problem-solving activities but face frustration and obstacles in activities that require them to be socially sensitive, have interpersonal harmony, and use other vital affective experiences (Saracho, 1988d; Saracho & Spodek, 1986).

## CONCLUSION

Individuals learn in a certain manner and develop their own personal learning styles with the aspects of perceptive and cognitive behavior. Their adaptive access to reality and selection of socialization practices vary, based on their cognitive styles.

Learning styles can be studied. Students can describe the conditions in which they learn best. They can also evaluate the match between the instruction and their own learning to respond to a specific teaching approach. Teachers can observe their students to identify their cognitive styles. They can increase their flexibility and the diversity of their teaching methods to better match their students in ways that will help more students to learn (Charlier, 1981). By viewing cognitive style as an information-processing and problem-solving strategy, a pervasive influence on cognitive development and interpersonal competencies of preschool students might be observed.

Cognitive style can be used to evaluate students' progress, and teachers can use the results of such evaluation to plan appropriate interventions. For preschool students, toys and books can be selected and their learning environment can be modified to their interests, styles, and ability levels. Any discrepancies may be the source of communication or behavioral problems (Kalyan-Masih & Curry, 1987). By identifying the students' cognitive styles, teachers can help students increase their educational achievement and efficiency. Teachers can make use of cognitive styles by instructing students with the cognitive strategies and study skills that are appropriate for each student's cognitive style.

Educators need to prepare students to handle a variety of situations. All students have characteristics of both FD and FI cognitive styles that need to be promoted to avoid suppressing students into a specific pattern. Educators need to be flexible in this approach.

Most school tasks require a more FI style. However, FD students can develop the relevant strategies to be successful through appropriate training (Globerson, 1985; Globerson, Weinstein, & Sharabany, 1985). The individuals' cognitive styles affect the way they learn, the strategies they use, and their choice of materials and methods. As Huteau (1987) demonstrates in his work on concept learning, optimal learning requires compatibility between the strategy implemented and the requirements of the task, a concept that has also led to many recent studies on the match between cognitive style and the requirements of school tasks (Federico, 1983; McDonald, 1984; Shade, 1983).

Teachers sometimes make demands on children that are inappropriate for their cognitive strategies. Students at school do not work directly with things, but with their representations, and success at school consequently requires facility in handling symbols. FD students are at a disadvantage in this context, which can be removed when teachers become cognizant of their students' cognitive styles and modify their behavior toward their students accordingly. Society assigns more value to FI instructional strategies (analysis and structural organization) than to FD instructional strategies. In the school environment this probably leads teachers to favor FI students rather than FD students (Bertini, 1986), whereas the latter may perhaps have been favored in a social climate.

The findings in these studies provide important implications for the educational environment. FI cognitive style appears to be an essential prerequisite for success at school; the idea that field dependence is a neutral dimension does not seem tenable (Páramo & Tinajero, 1990). Success in school demands several FI characteristics and behaviors. Saracho and Gerstl (1992) describe the essential characteristics that both FD and FI students need to succeed in a school setting (see Table 5.1).

Teachers can modify their instructional techniques to the needs of different learning styles (Ramírez & Castañeda, 1974; Witkin et al., 1977). They can also facilitate the development of the students' repertoire of strategies by using the individual students' strengths and gradually introducing the students to strategies that differ from their dominant cognitive styles (Ramírez, 1989; Saracho & Spodek, 1981). Successful students are those who can use a more differentiated approach, employing the strengths of both FD and FI cognitive styles as needed in the specific context (Ramírez, 1989; Saracho & Spodek, 1981, 1986; Shade, 1981).

**Table 5.1**
**Successful Characteristics Required of FD and FI Students**

| FD Students | FI Students |
|---|---|
| 1. require structure and organization; | 1. plan and organize their environment; |
| 2. require explicitly defined goals and objectives; | 2. deduce information from distractions; |
| 3. favor social interaction in the learning process; | 3. follow organized time plan; |
| 4. understand material in a social context; | 4. occupy prolonged periods of time executing seat work; |
| 5. like fantasy and humor; | 5. learn in solitary; |
| 6. retain more information with instructional strategies that use concrete and visual examples instead of verbal teaching; | 6. care for learning assignments without social interaction; |
| 7. favor the observer method of learning; | 7. employ analytical reasoning; |
| 8. respond well to praise and poorly to negative feedback; | 8. possess a lengthy attention span; |
| 9. prefer to learn in a cooperative and humanistic setting, where guidance and examples are provided. | 9. manage charts and graphs that stress factual details; |
| | 10. apply trial and error approaches; |
| | 11. understand verbal or written directions; |
| | 12. employ hypothesis testing strategies; |
| | 13. pursue unusual tasks; |
| | 14. react favorably to feedback, even if negative. |

Adapted from Saracho and Gerstl (1992).

Chapter 6

# The Role of Field Dependence Independence in the Early Childhood Curriculum

In educating young children, teachers need to match learning opportunities to the children's developmental levels. Knowledge of child development assists educators to do this. Young children's learning is determined not only by their ability to learn, but also by society's values on what is important for children to know (Spodek & Saracho, 1990).

The content of an early childhood curriculum can be identified and its appropriateness justified in many ways. Teachers must include in the content of early childhood education more than a set of skills that enable children to function adequately and meet the demands of schooling. The content of early childhood education requires diversity in the early childhood curriculum in order that all children learn based on their needs and interests.

Cognitive style influences the way in which individual abilities develop. It describes consistencies in the way they use their cognitive processes independent of cognitive content or cognitive level of performance. As such, cognitive style influences competence in the academic subject areas.

The field dependence independence (FDI) dimension of cognitive style affects how field dependent (FD) and field independent (FI) individuals[1] process information in the academic achievement of the different subject areas. Results from relevant studies will be used to describe this process.

## COGNITIVE PERFORMANCE

Research on children's cognitive performance has been concerned with their adaptation to the world. Contemporary approaches to understanding cognitive performance focus on children's many qualities of mental organization, different styles of cognitive performance, and past experiences. Knowledge about the nature of children's cognitive performance can be obtained by using children's cognitive growth, experiences, and assessments as a frame of reference (Saracho, 1988d). Individual consistencies in cognitive behavior are observed in a wide range of behaviors and strategies that children use in dealing with specific situations, tasks, stimulus-constraints, and purposes for which they are specifically related and appropriate.

The focus of preschool and primary education in recent decades has been on cognitive development. Specific curricula were developed to promote intelligence and achievement. Simultaneously, cognitive development has been receiving the attention of early childhood educators and a great deal of research in the curriculum content areas has been produced.

### Concept Attainment

Cognitive style influences the effectiveness of the cognitive tasks. Hester and Tagatz (1971) found that effectiveness in concept development is contingent on the person's cognitive style. FI persons psychologically grasp the nature of conceptual tasks when they are initially exposed to them. They also identify the implicated elements within the stimulus field faster than FD persons. According to Hester and Tagatz (1971), FD persons learn concepts more effectively when they are taught with techniques that correspond to their cognitive styles. FI persons are more effective learners than FD persons with either matching or nonmatching instructional strategies. In contrast, Beller (1967) found that children who are taught with a method that corresponds to their cognitive style perform better on a vocabulary test while those who are taught using strategies that do not correspond to their cognitive styles (e.g., analytic children are taught using a global technique, global children are taught using an analytic strategy) show negative effects.

FDI affects the person's learning. Goodenough's (1976) review of the literature shows that FD and FI persons differ consistently in the way they learn or memorize information. He concluded that (1) FI persons are more advanced developmentally than FD persons; (2) FD and FI persons utilize several learning processes to achieve the same performance; however, FI persons typically perform more effectively; and (3) if FD and FI persons employ different cognitive processes, the effectiveness of their functioning will differ in each situation.

In teaching concepts to young children, more obvious and socially oriented strategies must be used with FD children than with FI children. This is a major concern in early childhood education programs because the focus is on teaching concepts instead of facts alone. Cues can be made more obvious by using a variety of teaching aids that have social content. For example, photographs of peers can be used to teach colors or size. In contrast, FI children can learn abstract concepts by themselves without the participation of peers (Saracho, 1988d).

### Information Processing

Persons process information as they select the focus of their attention, encode information, and store the information in their memories. Davis and Cochran (1982, 1990) reviewed the literature on FDI cognitive style in relation to *selective attention, encoding,* and *long-term memory. Selective attention* is an information-processing paradigm with dichotic listening, signal detection, and visual search tasks. FD persons encounter problems with irrelevant cues, especially distracting cues. *Encoding* includes attentional processes of tasks that require encoding specificity, digit span, and working memory tasks. FD persons have restricted encoding processes; therefore, processing information is difficult for them. In contrast, FI persons can process information more productively than FD persons; therefore, they are able to process a larger amount of information. *Long-term memory* is the performance on associative learning and memory. Organization processes differ in the memories of FD and FI persons. The selective attention, encoding, and long-term memory processes of FI persons are better than those of their FD counterparts.

FD and FI persons differ in the way they learn but achieve the same performance (Goodenough, 1976). The memory performance of FD persons is less than that of FI persons when the task requires them to process a large amount of information. FI persons can remember information that has been stored in their short-term memory better than FD persons, even if interference occurs. However, if stored information is of poor quality and no interference occurs, both FD and FI persons achieve the same performance (Davis & Frank, 1979; Davis & Cochran, 1990).

Cognitive style affects the children's patterns of processing information. Haynes and Miller (1987) (1) examined the relationship between cognitive style and various components of information processing in preschoolers and (2) described developmental changes in performances on the incidental learning task in preschoolers. FDI and incidental memory increases with age. Analytic thinking (FI) relates to central memory and incidental memory. A FI preschooler has better recall than a FD one. However, cognitive style is not related to memory performance in younger children. Therefore, information processing skills become increasingly interrelated with age (Haynes & Miller, 1987).

### Academic Achievement

The role of the FDI construct goes beyond personality differences to influence academic achievement and success. Martinetti (1994) found an interaction between cognitive style and academic achievement. High achievers scored high on a cognitive style measure, while low achievers' scores indicated the reverse pattern. Differences in the performance of FD and FI individuals may be affected by their ability levels of mental imagery and cognitive flexibility. FI persons respond to relevant cues in their environment, focus on problems to be solved, and seek alternative solutions better than FD persons (Frank, 1983). Frank's research suggests that FD children in academic settings experience difficulty comprehending instructions, recalling and following directions, analyzing problems, and focusing on tasks. Their limited ability to process information may inhibit the cognitive involvement and achievement of FD students in academically oriented classrooms.

FI students are better than FD students in remembering factual information (Frank, 1983), understanding ambiguous material, and retrieving knowledge previously stored in memory. This representation biases the students' achievement. Although Witkin (1978) affirms that both FI and FD cognitive styles should be equally valued in society, research evidence indicates that FD children experience greater levels of frustration and failure in schools as the intensity of the academic experiences increases. This may occur when the FD child's age and grade level increase and when traditionally nonacademic subject areas (e.g., art, music, and movement or physical education) integrate more analytically oriented approaches into the curriculum (Ennis, Chen, & Fernandez-Balboa, 1991).

Studies on the relationship of cognitive style and academic achievement show that FI students prefer sciences and math, while FD students prefer social science. FD students understand material that is tightly organized, whereas FI students understand material that is loosely organized. Each academic discipline requires students to do different tasks. Hammer, Hoffer, and King (1995) found that male liberal arts students were more FI than female liberal arts students. In addition, a disembedding cognitive style predicted success on a cognitive task for architectural students but not for liberal arts students. Pohl and Pervin (1968) found a relationship between cognitive style and academic performance in several fields of academic concentration. Pohl and Pervin (1968) believe that FI persons do better than FD persons in fields such as engineering and the natural sciences, whereas FD persons do better than FI persons in areas within the humanities and social sciences. Since they found that cognitive style did not make a difference in academic performance, the students' performance may be the result of the interaction between cognitive style and task requirements.

### Learning-Teaching Process

The FDI dimension of cognitive style influences the students' preference for learning methods, learning process, and teachers' instructional choices. The degree of FDI influences the way persons learn and their learning outcomes. FD persons are more oriented toward social learning and are easily distracted. In comparison, FI persons are socially detached and prefer to learn in an abstract mode. These characteristics should be considered in planning instruction. Cognitive and attitudinal factors relate to the teachers' instructional approach. Teachers usually follow an academic curriculum that is abstract and requires students to use FI strategies. Students who are familiar with FI strategies may prefer strategies they already know. However, students also may prefer strategies that they lack or perceive to be essential in their academic FI environment, especially since older students may be experiencing a more FI curriculum (Saracho, 1988d).

Students prefer a teacher who manages the classroom and who promotes the learning of the subject matter by being supportive and friendly. These two preferences seem to conflict with each other, but they compliment one another. Teachers select the teaching styles based on their perceptions of the demands of the instructional tasks (Ekstrom, 1976). They assess the requirements of the instructional task to use the appropriate cognitive style in selecting methods, subject areas, and teaching styles based on their perceptions of the demands. Instruction based on grade levels and subject areas also differs in cognitive style. FD and FI second- and fifth-grade teachers determine the requirements for students' grades, subject areas, and classroom management differently (Ekstrom, 1976; Stone, 1976). FD teachers initiate subject-oriented questions and assignments that they want their students to master. FI teachers select analytic questions to present topics and react to students' responses. Teaching methods and subject areas differ for each cognitive style. Teachers instruct the class based upon the subject matter using support and encouragement in the students' task-related activities. They redirect the class away from irrelevant or sidetracking activities.

Teachers must avoid a preoccupation with mastery of subject matters. They must consider the students' individual modes of thinking as well. These factors can assist in predicting students' success and in individualizing educational programs. Students' cognitive styles can be determined early in their school careers in order that curricula and teaching methods are planned and implemented appropriately to the students' cognitive styles (Saracho & Spodek, 1981, 1986).

A thorough assessment of skills and styles can help to select appropriate curriculum materials and instructional methods. Educators strive for this goodness of fit to teach children using their individual strengths. Preferred modalities and styles are used to present basic concepts (Chadwick & Watson, 1986).

## SUBJECT CONTENT AREAS

The need to articulate the content of early childhood education reflects a need to articulate the content of education at all levels. The National Endowment for the Humanities has recently issued a report criticizing elementary and secondary schools for being too involved with "process" and not involved enough with helping children and youth become deeply knowledgeable of the roots of their cultures (Cheney, 1987). This criticism also might be applied to early childhood education programs. Educators need to define the content of early childhood education as something more than a set of skills that will enable children to function adequately and meet the demands of the curriculum for young children.

Defining the content of early childhood education does not require that all children learn the same thing or that there be a single standard for an early childhood curriculum. Indeed, there are many ways that the content of an early childhood curriculum can be identified and its appropriateness justified (Spodek & Saracho, 1990).

Most subjects in school require students to use FI strategies that are less developed in FD students. Riding and Read (1996) found that the nature of school subjects influences how students complete a task. In a school setting, when subject content becomes more sophisticated, more analytical reasoning and a larger information base (Cohen, 1969) are required. FI students have those analytic skills that are used in such subjects as science, mathematics, and reading (Davis, 1987; Davis & Cochran, 1990; Riding & Read, 1996; Witkin, 1978). FI students are better achievers than FD students in subject areas such as Spanish, mathematics, natural sciences, and social sciences (Páramo & Tinajero, 1990). FD students who lack analytic skills often drop out from subjects such as science and mathematics in the upper grades (Olstad, Juarez, Davenport, & Maury, 1981) and achieve low scores on standardized tests (Cohen, 1969) that are abstract in nature, a FI characteristic. These tests require analytical and logical reasoning (Cohen, 1969) and reflective response styles (Shade, 1990). The most intelligent FD students without analytic skills may achieve the lowest scores because of their greater dependence on relational strategies and their inability to use the analytic processes (Cohen, 1969). Páramo and Tinajero (1990) explored the main academic areas and found that FI students did better in all subject areas. The advantages for FI students suggest that this style allows them to function better within the school environment, even in subjects such as the social sciences which should be more appropriate for the skills and interests of the FD students.

New theories of teaching in content areas such as mathematics, science, art, music, social science, and the language arts have been developed and tested. However, the work of individuals in the content areas simply lacks the impact of some psychological factors such as cognitive style.

## Language

Preschool children relate words to objects more effectively when the language program matches their cognitive styles. Children offering descriptive (analytic) responses attain a higher achievement on vocabulary items that require recognition memory, whereas children offering analytic responses score the highest on items that require associative memory. Beller (1967) concludes that in order to promote learning, methods can be modified to match the students' specific cognitive styles. Children who are taught with a method that matches their cognitive style have a positive change in performance on a vocabulary test; while children who are taught with a method that differs from their cognitive style (such as analytic children taught using a global method and global children taught using an analytic method) have negative effects.

Beller's view is supported by other researchers who found the same effects of cognitive style on adult students' and children's learning. Lee, Kagan, and Rabson (1963) presented third-grade boys with three types of concepts (analytic, categorical, and relational) using verbal and pictorial forms. They found that the (1) descriptive (analytic) students are not superior to the relational-contextual or categorical-inferential students in learning analytic concepts either in pictorial or verbal forms, (2) relational-contextual students are not superior in learning the relational concepts, and (3) categorical-inferential students do not excel in learning the categorical concepts. However, analytic students perform better across all concept classes than students with categorical-inferential or relational-conceptual styles. McCain (cited in Cooper & Sigel, 1971) used college students to replicate the study by Lee, Kagan, and Rabson (1963) and achieved similar results. Studies by Coop and Brown (1970); McCain (cited in Cooper & Siegel, 1971); and Lee, Kagan, and Rabson (1963) show that cognitive style has different educational implications for college students and adults than it has for young children. However, these results have been challenged since Kagan, Moss, and Sigel (1963) and Sigel, Jarman, and Hanesian (1967) found parallel results with children and adults.

In relation to learning mode, verbal imagery cognitive style relates to learning performance, that is, the mode of presentation of learning materials and the type of content of learning material. Imagers usually learn best from pictorial presentations, while verbalizers learn best from verbal presentations (Riding & Douglas, 1993). For the type of content in learning the material, imagers recall highly descriptive text better than acoustically complex and unfamiliar text. The opposite pattern is found for verbalizers, who are more active than the imagers (Riding, Burton, Rees, & Sharratt, 1995). A similar study supports these results. Riding and Mathias (1991) found that FD persons prefer the mode that concurs with their verbal-imagery style; verbalizers select text while imagers select pictures. FI persons, in comparison, are evenly divided across the verbal-imagery dimension. On reading achievement and cognitive abilities, the performance of the FD persons is superior by the verbalizers and decreases with increasing imagery style, while FI persons are consistent across the dimension. The best achievement on most tasks may be a blend with the strengths of each style dimension (FD verbalizers and FI imagers), since this merger helps students to analyze and visualize as a whole; but the reverse merger (FD imagery and FI verbalizer) is not as complementary (Riding & Mathias, 1991).

FD children are less able to correctly identify changes in subject object relations in sentence transformations (Tarantino & Loricchio, 1989). Students rated the relative grammar of sentences three times, with sentences presented repeatedly during the first and second judgments. FI students adopted a more stringent criterion on judgments for the second assessment, whereas FD students did not change in criterion. FI students adopted a different strategy during repetition, analyzing primarily the sentential properties of the sentences instead of providing communicative situations for the sentences. When both FD and FI students were negatively reinforced, FD students established a more lenient criterion than FI students. Change in judgments of grammar related to the students' FD or FI cognitive styles (Nagata, 1989).

### Reading

Students with each cognitive style differ in their use of contextual organizers. Instruction is most effective for FD students with illustrative advance organizers and for field intermediate students with illustrative post organizers. Students of three cognitive styles assessed the effectiveness of contextual organizers that differed in information and placement. In addition to the FD and FI groups, treatments included written advance organizers, writer post organizers, illustrative advance organizers, illustrative post organizers, and nontreatment control condition. Illustrative organizers are more effective for FD students; illustrative post organizers are more effective for field intermediate students. Contextual organizers neither helped nor hindered instruction for FI students. Since FI students create structure, contextual organizers may not have had the value for students with this cognitive style. The possible simplicity of the passages for the FI students may have no need for organizers (Meng & Patty, 1991).

Cognitive style interacts with topicalization effects. Davey and Miller (1990) found a cognitive style topicalization interaction on the best title task. FD readers were assisted by a final topic sentence placement. FD readers were particularly affected by the presence of explicitly thematic markers. Davey and Miller (1990) found that this occurred for main idea comprehension, but not for comprehension of passage information. Readers' cognitive styles have their greatest effect on higher-level comprehension processes requiring skills of abstraction, integration, and generalization.

The role of FDI is evident in letter direction during formal reading. FDI influences the (1) detection of silent ''e''s but only slight letter direction of the sounded ''e''s and (2) use of a visual rather than a phonological strategy in letter detection. Although the use of visual strategy affects the detection of silent (but not sounded) ''e''s, the influence of FDI on letter detection performance is not mediated by the use of a visual strategy (Davies, 1988). Instead the effect of FDI was direct, indicating that it is the superior visual disembedding ability of FI persons that is responsible for better detection in reading.

Reading achievement is influenced by FDI, analytic conceptual style, and intelligence. FI students with an analytic conceptual style are better readers. This emphasizes the importance of analytic ability, wherein FI readers pay attention to detail and to reading skills (Roach, 1985).

FI students usually reach higher test scores on both factual and higher-order tests than do FD students. Kiewra and Frank (1988) tested the factual and higher-order achievement of FI and FD students by exposing them to lecture material and promptly testing them without review of notes or by testing them later with reviewing the notes. During the lecture, students participated in (1) personal note-taking, (2) note-taking on a skeletal outline, or (3) listening while examining the instructor's detailed notes. FI students achieved higher scores on factual and higher-order tests than did FD students. When students were tested at a later time, FD students profited more from the storage use of note-taking than from the introductory encoding application. The three learning techniques did not make a difference on achievement after the immediate factual test. However, when the detailed notes were reviewed and the test was delayed, the students gained higher achievement scores. Apparently, all three techniques grant a comparable encoding purpose, while reviewing the instructor's detailed notes provides an exceptional external storage use. Factual achievement suggests cognitive style differences on immediate testing but not on delayed testing after review. Cognitive style differences seem most pronounced under conditions concerning immediate and instant encoding of the stimulus into memory, and are reduced when more time is provided during review to encode what is externally stored. Such performance differences do not consider observable note-taking behaviors, but are compatible with the styles that these groups characteristically display when undergoing learning and memory tasks, and perhaps in their attempt to take notes (Kiewra & Frank, 1988).

The students' cognitive styles interact with the strategies and affect performance on comprehension of prose. Adejumo (1983) tested the effects of cognitive style on the performance of four groups who used different strategies to comprehend prose. FI students perform better overall. Specifically, FI students who are provided with factual and inferential questions as study aids perform better than the FD students. The difference in performance by the FD and FI students is in the kind of strategy. FI students who receive inferential questions as study aids perform better on factual and inferential items while the FD students who received factual questions as aids performed better in the factual items. This finding justifies Witkin's (Witkin et al., 1977) observation that, when instructions are explicit in problem-solving strategies, FD students learn more; but when the students are required to use their own mediators or draw inferences from a situation, FI students perform better than FD ones. Inferential questions as aids for comprehending prose require students to go beyond the literal content of the text. It also forces students to restructure the text. Students use a hypothesis-testing approach when using inferential questions as aids. This finding is consistent with the observation of Witkin et al. (1977), who conclude that FD students learn better from the teacher's structured plan for a lecture, but that the FI ones provide themselves with mediating structural rules in addition to the structured plan to facilitate their learning.

The way children learn to read and how their reading progress develops is an educational problem. The advancement of reading is important in achieving literacy. Cognitive style may relate to success or failure in reading. Drane, Halpin, Halpin, vonEschenbach, and Worden (1989) found a relationship between reading proficiency and FDI. Second-grade children's silent reading comprehension, sight vocabulary, recognition of vocabulary in context, and the use of word-part clues relate to their cognitive styles. FI children are more proficient readers. Stone (1976) supports the notion that FDI relates to reading achievement among elementary school children. It has been theorized that the FDI functions as a mediating variable to make a difference in how children learn instead of how much they learn. The outcome that FI students are more proficient readers in the separate skills areas of reading was found by Davis and Frank (1979), who noted that the learning process is accomplished more effectively by FI students. Davey (1990) found that FI readers outperform FD readers on tasks with high memory demands and with requirements for efficient restructuring skills. FI students are more successful than FD students on free response questions under the condition of no reading.

A review of the literature by Davis (1987) indicates that FI children are more efficient readers than FD children and that FD children develop more severe reading problems. He submits that the effects of FDI occur most during the initial acquisition of many reading skills. Beginning readers need to be actively analytic, sensitive to relevant graphic cues, skilled at segmenting and blending sounds, able to structure information, and flexible in their hypothesis-testing routines, although persons differ widely in these processing style dimensions.

Complex interactions between FDI and several elements in learning to read have been found (see Davey & Menke, 1990 for a comprehensive review of the literature). Usually, FDI relates to aspects of reading skill acquisition, including both word recognition skills (such as letter naming, phonemic awareness, concepts of print) and comprehension processes (such as recall organization, hypotheses-testing behaviors, use of context, identifying important information). FI children are more successful overall with these components during initial acquisition of reading skills, although the consequences of this effect appear to lessen as children progress to phases of more fluent, automatized behaviors. Currently, research suggests that explicit training and task instruction reduce the differences between FD and FI children in beginning reading activities.

### Second Language

The relationships of cognitive style, personality, and sociocultural variables to performance on language tests may be potentially important in second-language acquisition (L2) (Chapelle & Green, 1992). Elliott (1995) showed that field independence is important for language acquisition/learning. FI students did better in pronunciation accuracy. However, when subject attention emphasized ''communication'' and not specifically pronunciation, FD students provided a correct pronunciation. Therefore, FDI must be considered in second-language instruction. Jamieson (1992) believes that evidence indicates a positive relationship between FDI and selected linguistic tasks. The results from the study by Jamieson (1992) show that FDI positively relates to proficiency in English as a second language. FI students do better than FD students in subject areas such as Spanish (Páramo & Tinajero, 1990).

The cognitive analytic qualities of the FI students facilitate their focus on the language stimuli related to the language learning task. The personality dimension of FDI may influence how students interact in L2 situations. The FI students depend on internal frames of reference; therefore, they are more confident language learners, actively speak out in class, and take risks, thereby receiving more of the teachers' attention. In acquiring language, FD students prefer social interactions through contextualized practice with native speakers (Chapelle & Green, 1992).

A review of the literature on FDI cognitive style and second-language learning led Griffiths and Sheen (1992) to conclude that FDI does not have any relevance for second-language learning. However, Chapelle (1992) disputes their argument and proposes a future research agenda exploring the relationship between L2 and the FDI construct. She also identifies the value characteristics of the FDI construct. Griffiths and Sheen's (1992) analysis of the L2 literature determines that those who first introduced FDI consider Witkin and his associates' work sufficient justification for the hypothesis (Sheen, 1993).

### Mathematics

Social interaction in the classroom is being emphasized in teaching mathematics. Social interactions encourage alternative points of view that stimulate cognitive growth (Hiebert, 1992). This type of learning may assist FD students to achieve better in mathematics, especially since research shows that FI students are better mathematics achievers than FD students. Roberge and Flexer (1983) examined the effects of FDI and the level of operational development based on the total mathematics achievement test scores and those scores on subtests of computations, concepts, and problem-solving. FI students did better than FD students on mathematics as a whole, and on concepts and problem-solving tests. The results are further supported by other studies (e.g., Kornbluth & Sabban, 1982; Mrosla, Black, & Hardy, 1987; Vaidya & Chansky, 1980). Kornbluth and Sabban (1982) found that an aptitude treatment interaction (ATI) exists between cognitive style and a study method on mathematical achievement. FI students perform better than FD students. Such achievement may have been because FI students are better at analyzing and imposing organization on poorly organized stimuli, and ignoring distracting cues. Mrosla, Black, and Hardy (1987) compared high-achieving and low-achieving students in a geometry course. FD students were those with low achievement. Vaidya and Chansky (1980) support these results using elementary school children. Apparently, the FI cognitive style relates to mathematics achievement at all grade levels.

The relationship between a FI cognitive style and mathematics achievement emphasizes the importance of individualizing instruction based on the student's cognitive style. Teachers should understand how cognitive styles influence the learning of mathematics. FD students may do as well in those areas which focus on their abilities to deal with concrete and social situations.

## Computers

More than 150,000 microcomputers were available in the schools a decade ago (Chadwick & Watson, 1986). Many more are available today. Microcomputers in the classroom enhance the possibility of providing individualized instruction for all students. Thus, microcomputers assume an important role in relation to cognitive style. They provide drill and practice for "overlearning" that is important for some students. Tutorials introduce new concepts through step-by-step presentations, variable pacing, immediate feedback, and additional examples (Chadwick & Watson, 1986). *Logo*, a computer language for children (Papert, 1980) enhances some cognitive styles (Clements & Gullo, 1984). Simulations and graphics also promote interactive and nonverbal approaches in students' learning. Interactive software can be used to teach science and mathematical concepts. Advanced technological features in the microcomputer can expand simulation experiences through the use of touch screens, voice synthesizers, and storage of large amounts of relevant information for the students (Chadwick & Watson, 1986).

Some computers have an assessment and prescription process that provides directions on what and how students can be taught. Content (what) is suggested from scores on an achievement test, while approaches (how) are suggested from an assessment on learning styles and modalities. Saracho's (1982b) study on Computer Assisted Instruction (CAI) suggests that the students' cognitive styles influence the ways they respond to different kinds of instruction. For example, FI students prefer instruction that is independent, impersonal, and indirect, whereas FD students prefer instruction that requires dependence and social interaction. She assumes that students who use the CAI program prefer the more dependent, personal, and direct instruction that justifies their positive attitudes toward the CAI program.

## Science

Science requires students to extract critical attributes related to specific concepts from a reasonably diverse experience to formulate the desired concept. Science also stresses cognitive skills other than direct recall and requires the application of knowledge in a different context. The science teaching/learning modes usually focus on intellectual activities that require extraction, restructuring, and application in a different context (Wollman, 1986). The use of rules rather than traditional instruction helps students become better achievers. The organized rules method is slightly better, although the elaborative rules approach is better for two groups who were found to be weak in science: females and FD students (Ross, 1990).

Chemistry teachers differ in the way they use rules, relationships, examples, and questions. FI teachers present topics and answer students' answers using questions, but FD teachers assess the students' learning using questions. FI teachers use questions within the context of a lecture as a discovery strategy. The FI teachers' questioning patterns of verbal teaching behaviors may be similar to teacher directiveness (Moore, 1973).

Fifth-grade students learn science concepts better through inquiry than through conventional ways; but fourth- and sixth-grade students infer and categorize their responses when they are taught in a conventional way. Therefore, fourth- and sixth-grade students can learn better through the use of different cognitive styles (Scott & Sigel, cited in Cooper & Sigel, 1971). Wollman (1986) found that FI students achieve higher science scores than do FD students. Niaz (1989) explored the effect of FDI cognitive style upon the ability to solve chemistry problems. The study showed that FI students obtain better performance in solving chemistry problems than FD students. These results support the results reported by Witkin et al. (1977).

Cognitive preference tests originate with the idea of detecting cognitive styles within the framework of certain disciplines such as science or even more specific disciplines such as biology, chemistry, and physics. Tamir (1975) investigated the cognitive style preferences of high school biology students and the cognitive preferences as related to specific subject matter areas in the field of biology. Tamir's (1975) study dealt with cognitive preferences in biology. Yet, biology itself may be divided into different subject matter areas (e.g., botany, zoology, human biology, evolution, microorganisms, and biochemical processes). The patterns integrate a variety of topics that differ from each other. The students' preference for the application of fundamental principles concerning human biology certainly considers the readiness and willingness of students to apply what they learn in relation to themselves, whereas the distinctly low position of critical questioning of principles in that area is also highly possible. Tamir's (1975) findings suggest the existence of a remarkable dependence of cognitive preference styles on specific subject matter areas. This implies that some students may have specific cognitive preference patterns for one subject matter area but simultaneously the same student may have different cognitive preference patterns concerning another subject matter area even within the same discipline.

### Social Studies

During social studies lessons, FD student teachers use discussion rather than discovery approaches. FI teachers employ both lecture and discovery methods as a form of instruction to facilitate and guide the students' learning or provide them with information (Wu, 1968).

The student's cognitive style is an important factor in determining the student's achievement in geography. Grieve and Davis (1971) found that extreme FD males who receive expository instruction encounter difficulty acquiring and applying the knowledge presented, whereas FI males are more successful.

The structure of concepts in a social studies unit (content structure) shows that although the configurations for FD students indicate that cultural diffusion is not perceived as related to other concepts, both FI students and FD students structure concepts differently. FI students have fewer concepts per cluster, refining perceived relationships as a result of social studies instruction. In comparison, FD students have concepts that often appear in more than one cluster. FD students overlap concepts, indicating a less differentiated view of the concepts (Cox & Moore, 1976).

## Art

One study of the relationship between cognitive style and student achievement in art appreciation shows that FI students do better than FD students in an art appreciation class. However, in this study, Copeland (1983) did not consider the teachers' methods of instruction, students' attitudes, and the interactions between the students and teachers. The outcomes in the art appreciation class do support that cognitive style affects academic achievement.

### Movement (Physical Education)

An analytical focus demands mental energy, memory storage/retrieval capacity, and cognitive flexibility that are especially challenging for FD children. FI children enjoy both the physical and the cognitive challenge of the games. FD children understand the physical aspects of the games better than the cognitive strategies of the games. Both FI and FD children enjoy the strenuous physical activity of the game; they laugh and shout as the game becomes more competitive and children are eliminated. In exploring the FDI cognitive style differences exhibited in second-grade children in analytically oriented movement education curricula within the natural school context, Ennis, Chen, and Fernandez-Balboa (1991) found that FI children experience success more than FD children. FI children succeed academically and socially, although FD children succeed socially. FD children are as successful as FI children when the academic category involves motor performance of a well-learned skill. However, FD children do not succeed as well when academic performance involves a novel motor task or a cognitive response.

On motor skill activities (e.g., striking, throwing skills) FI children focus on the teacher's description of the activity, respond to questions on movement analysis, and use movements correctly to obtain strategic advantage. They learn and memorize the directions and practice for prolonged periods, even when the task is repetitive and monotonous. FD children succeed the most when the teacher's directions are concrete and precise. They enjoy the movement itself, especially when they believe they are expected to achieve product-oriented objectives, ignoring the technique or quality of the performance (Ennis, Chen, & Fernandez-Balboa, 1991).

In cross-examining the teachers, studies found that teachers select FI children to respond and to demonstrate motor tasks more frequently than they do FD children. Teachers allow FI children to respond to questions and participate in demonstrations more frequently than FD children. They also discuss the FD children's behavioral responses to complex problem-solving situations (Ennis, Chen, & Fernandez-Balboa, 1991).

In activities where they learn striking skills using bats and balls, FD children have trouble focusing on the task for a prolonged period of time, especially if it requires them to listen to directions and skill feedback. FD children throw the bat in the air, tap it on the ground, and practice swinging it several times. Essentially, they incessantly move, look out of the door or window, and jump or spin while they wait for an activity to begin. More passive FD children direct their attention within themselves, absentmindedly untie and tie their shoe laces, or sketch lines on the floor with their feet or hands. If their attention is refocused to the activity, they quietly participate until the next set of directions that requires them to wait for the activity to begin (Ennis, Chen, & Fernandez-Balboa, 1991).

When FD children encounter challenging problems, they become passive and uninvolved, pursue social relationships with children who are successful problem solvers, or express frustration with failure through disruptive behavior (e.g., Ennis & Chepyator-Thompson, 1991). Limitations in memory storage and retrieval ability, cognitive flexibility, and mental energy contribute to the children's success and failure with analytical tasks. This has been supported by researchers on reading comprehension (Davis, 1987), concept formation (Ohnmacht, 1966), musical analysis (Schmidt & Lewis, 1987), and motor skill acquisition (Ennis, Chen, & Fernandez-Balboa, 1991).

## SUMMARY

No straightforward statement can be made about the consequences of cognitive style and education (such as the cognitive style of the FDI curriculum). Teachers may inadvertently design and implement techniques that stifle the students' learning. Teachers must know all the possible biases and become proficient in teaching methods that are productive for both FD and FI cognitive styles. Classroom activities should be designed to meet the needs of both FD and FI cognitive styles. Developing cognitive flexibility should be part of the early childhood curriculum to extend the students' cognitive style repertoire. Children can engage in individual projects (such as in learning centers) and in group projects that foster personal relationships with others (e.g., teacher, teacher aide, peers). Teachers can learn to use cognitive style assessment techniques, to determine the children's cognitive styles, and to provide instruction that is responsive to both FD and FI cognitive styles. Teachers must consider individual differences in learning and thinking styles, because these differences can have serious ramifications for teaching and learning.

Cognitive style biases the teachers' decisions in the curriculum content and program process. Cognitive style also sets the rate on the quantity and genre of information the students accumulate, how they acquire it, and how they use it. Educational programs must develop a repertoire of teaching and learning alternatives to be able to meet individual differences in both FD and FI cognitive styles.

## NOTE

1. Refer to Chapter 2 for a description of FD and FI individuals.

Chapter 7

# Field Dependent Independent Characteristics in Young Children's Social Behaviors

As noted in Chapters 1, 2, and 3, cognitive style is a variable affecting several areas of human function, including the individual's socialization. One element of cognitive style is the field dependent independent (FDI) dimension, which influences the individual's social functioning. It is possible to differentiate between field dependent (FD) and field independent (FI) individuals by their social characteristics.

The most current form of the FDI theory (Witkin & Goodenough, 1981) emphasizes the value-neutral quality of each cognitive style. However, FD persons are socially oriented, while FI persons are socially detached. FI children are able to solve problems (often spatial in character) that require the structuring or reorganization of any information that is presented, while FD children display a social sensitivity that provides them with good interpersonal skills (Kogan, 1987). This chapter describes the FDI characteristics in young children's social behaviors, such as social interaction, social orientation, and cognitive-social play.

## SOCIAL INTERACTION

Peer interactions promote young children's cognitive and social development. The socialization process includes learning to live with other people and accepting their beliefs, customs, mores, traditions, social controls, experiences, emotions, and language. The socialization process requires young children to become aware that others may differ from them in their feelings, attitudes, and needs. They learn to understand the feelings of others, wait their turn, cooperate with others, share materials and experiences, and become satisfied through others. The goal in social development is to get along with others in our society (Saracho, 1986a).

A model of the socialization process was proposed by Dodge et al. (1986). This model describes the sequence of social interaction; this model can provide a framework for empirical research. The model presents the cyclical relationship between social behavior and social-information processing, using five major units of social interaction: (1) social cues or stimuli; (2) the child's social information-processing of those social cues (encoding, interpretation, response search, response evaluation, and enactment); (3) the child's social behaviors that take place as a result of the child's processing of social cues; (4) peers' judgments about the child's behavior; and (5) peers' social behavior toward the child. Dodge et al. (1986) tested their model in two studies. These studies, in combination, provide support for the use of this reciprocal effective model in relation to social information-processing and children's social behavior.

Information-processing influences children's cognitive development. In a longitudinal study, Lytton, Watts, and Dunn (1986) examined the social characteristics of male twins (from age two until age nine) in relation to cognitive development. Although none of the children's individual social characteristics show total stability, the child characteristics that were identified by age two predicted 63 percent of the variance of the composite variable, cognitive competence. Some researchers (e.g., Haight & Miller, 1992; Park, Lay, & Ramsay, 1993), however, have found stability in the behavior of preschool friends over a one-year period. Children's social interactions with other children contribute to their cognitive development, which includes children's cognitive styles and play behaviors (Saracho, 1986a).

Research shows a relationship between cognitive style and social interaction. FD persons have an advantage in the social realm. They have an interpersonal orientation (e.g., they are comfortable with others and seek to be with others) as compared with FI persons, who typically lack interpersonal skills. FD persons depend on authority figures or a peer group to form their attitudes on an issue (Deever, 1968). FD persons identify themselves as part of the setting and depend on external referents in psychological functioning (Jacobs, 1985–1986). FD students engage in a greater number of social interactions during instruction than do FI students (Jacobs & Gedeon, 1982). Reflecting their use of external sources of information for self-definition, FD persons are selectively attentive to the human content of their environment. For instance, when they interact they look at the person's face (Konstadt & Forman, 1965; Nakamura & Finck, 1980; Ruble & Nakamura, 1972). The face provides a major source of information to understand the person's feelings and thoughts. For example, the eyes and mouth may open to express shock, a frown might mean puzzlement, and a raised eyebrow may express disbelief. FD persons also are better at recognizing persons' faces (Messick & Damarin, 1964). Since they always look at the persons' faces when they are talking to them, FD persons can remember persons' faces better.

This social focus allows FD persons to attend to and recall verbal messages with a social content better than FI persons (Goldberger & Bendich, 1972).

In contrast, Kogan and Block (1991) report that FI persons are verbally fluent, attentive, competent, reflective, and use and respond to reason. They also have high performance standards, are persistent, plan and think ahead, and become involved in tasks. Kogan and Block (1991) characterize FI children as creative, curious and exploring, and possessing unusual thought processes; but they consider FD children as seeking others to affirm their self-worth, showing an eagerness to please, manipulating individuals by ingratiating themselves, and being suspicious of others. They are also jealous and envious of others; they are easily offended and look to adults for help (Kogan & Block, 1991). FD persons cope with their social world with a sense of anxious vulnerability. These attributes are consistent with Witkin et al.'s (1954/1972, 1981) descriptions of FD and FI children. The FD persons' special awareness and their adaptation to the social surroundings help them to have a repertoire of highly matured social skills (Witkin, 1976).

## SOCIAL ORIENTATION

While the relationship of social orientation to FDI has mostly been studied with older children or adults, it does have implications for early childhood education. The results are similar to the few social orientation studies conducted with young children.

FD persons are sensitive to social elements in the social environment. FD persons are more socially oriented than FI persons (Saracho, 1985b). FDI cognitive style has the form of people versus object orientation in young children (Kogan, 1987). The contrast may be more like task versus social orientations, which Ruble and Nakamura (1972) found with second and third graders. In working with object-assembly and concept-attainment problems, they found that FD children were particularly alert to social cues emitted by the examiner (e.g., gesture of the head); while FI children focused their attention on less personal cues (e.g., hand movements of the examiner modeling an assembly task). Both examples indicate the person's use of specific cues based on his/her cognitive style. Thus, social cues are more effective for FD children, while impersonal cues are more effective for FI children.

In a later study, Nakamura and Finck (1980) observed the effectiveness of task and social orientations of 9- to 12-year-olds. They found that low-social, task-effective children were more FI, while FD children were more socially oriented. Evidently, field dependence is related to social sensitivity. However, it has not been determined if at the elementary school level, FD children are more socially competent or effective (Kogan, 1987; Kogan & Block, 1991). For example, Saracho (1991a) examined young children's social competence and found that the more FI children were better able to assume a social role and solve a social problem than FD children.

In another study, Saracho (1991b) observed several social correlates of FD and FI kindergarten children. She found that teachers perceived (1) the more FI children as more socially competent and (2) FD pairs of children where one child is accepted and the other is rejected as more socially competent. She also found that both FD and FI children who were rejected as playmates by other children engaged in more social play. In a different study, Saracho (1991a) established that teachers perceive the more FI children as more socially competent. The FI children may indeed be more socially competent. The teachers' assessments were validated by the children's social play and their peers' selection to engage in social play with their FI counterparts. FI children participated more in social play and initiated their own play activities more often than did FD children. Both FD and FI children selected FI children more often as playmates. Also, FI children attained higher scores on a popularity test (Saracho, 1991a).

Gullo's (1988) study supports these results. He found that reflective children, who have similar characteristics as FI children, were perceived as more socially competent. Black (1992) found that children's communication in social pretend play is a function of social status. These children negotiate the creation of a dialogue, distribute roles, and enact pretense in episodes of social play.

Although play is a form of social behavior (Saracho, 1984a), its complexity may require children to use FI strategies. FD persons may be interpersonally oriented, but Kogan and Block (1991) believe that their study provides no indication that social orientation translates into actual interpersonal skill.

These results may be supported by the FDI theory. According to Saracho and Spodek (1981, 1986), FI persons can solve problems confronted in a variety of contexts. The bipolar FDI dimension represents analytic and global field approaches reflected in the way persons resolve problems or understand experiences. FDI also describes the person's ability to reason and process information. Since problem solving requires persons to use analytic thinking, those who have the basic capacity to analyze problems can solve problems with greater ease. Cognitive styles include stable attitudes, choices or habitual strategies of perceiving, remembering, processing, thinking, and solving problems. General stylistic differences underlie most of the individuals' unique traits (Saracho, 1988e, 1988c).

### Cognitive-Social Play

Cognitive-social play occurs when children transform objects and roles in their play into something other than what they are. They simultaneously become aware of the original identity and performance of the object. The objects then become symbols. The complexity in children's symbolic play develops their ability to substitute language for play actions and objects (Saracho, 1986a). Rubin (1980) refers to these processes as social-cognition.

Young children's participation in play reflects their cognitive style. Haight and Miller (1992) report that pretend play occurs predominantly with another person. During play, young children respond to the variety of social situations they meet in their play experiences. Such situations require them to learn to cooperate, assist others, share, and solve social problems in an appropriate manner. These social skills make children think about their social world, considering the others' point of view, making moral judgments, and acquiring conceptions of friendship (Saracho, 1987a).

Play is composed of several constructs (i.e., cognitive, creative, language, social, and manipulative constructs) that direct children toward themselves and their world (Saracho, 1986a). Children's play experiences provide them the opportunity to capture and refine new information and generate new ideas; comparing and contrasting the new information with familiar information; and generating and testing their hypotheses to refute, accept, confirm, expand, or modify their knowledge (Spodek & Saracho, 1987). Young children's play experiences allow them to become active learners to form and store knowledge. FI children use their analytic skills for these processes (Saracho, 1991a). However, young children's sociability may relate to their cognitive style. Since FD children are strongly interested in people and are also sensitive to the expressed needs of others, this style may assist them in acquiring social skills.

When children engage in play, their cognitive style promotes their understanding of the social process. The greater social interest of FD children compared with FI children is evidenced in the studies of play preferences among preschool children (Coates, 1972; Coates, Lord, & Jakabovics, 1975; Saracho, 1987a; Steele, 1981). Coates (1972), Coates et al. (1975), Saracho (1991a, 1991b), and Steele (1981) found that preschool FD children engage more in social play than do FI preschool children. FD preschool children are more often socially oriented in their play, while FI preschool children are more often involved in solitary play. Saracho (1985b, 1986a) suggests similar relationships between the children's cognitive styles and their play; however, few studies have examined the relationship between these two areas. The study of play behaviors by Renninger and Sigel (1987) shows that young children display a stylistic style performance in their choice of strategies and processes as they cognitively arrange and understand tasks.

Over time, young children identify specific patterns that they perceive as appropriate to them. They constantly implement strategies unfolding an organizational pattern. Once such an organizational pattern is employed with a type of task, then the children's range of strategies develop a particular style level. The children's play behaviors become consistent and deliberate in their performance. Coates et al.'s (1975) study had similar results. They show that FD children prefer social play areas such as the doll corner and the block corner, while FI children prefer to play with blocks and at table tasks. Thus, social play is related to a more FD cognitive style while solitary activity is related to a more FI cognitive style, regardless of the presence of others. Those children who preferred activities requiring social participation instead of solitary activities were more FD. Those children who chose solitary play activities such as working alone on projects were more FI. According to Saracho (1987a), FD children engage in parallel, cooperative, or associative play, while FI children, who appear socially detached but have analytic instead of social skills, prefer solitary play.

Solitary play relates to impersonal objects such as puzzles or pegboards, while social play relates to objects or events with a human referent such as those found in dramatic play (Saracho, 1985b). Coates (1972) conducted two studies measuring the relationship between children's play behaviors and their cognitive styles. Her first study, conducted with children ranging in age from three to five years, demonstrated that preschool FD children cooperate more with their playmates in social activities, while FI children, who periodically interact with other children, engage in more nonsocial activities. Her second study showed a relationship between children's play behaviors and their cognitive styles. She provided three play options to each of the children: block building, playing house, or other activities (e.g., painting, making collages, or working with puzzles). Her results are consistent with studies of older children that show that persons with low analytic ability are more socially oriented than persons with high analytic ability. Jennings (1975) reported a stronger relationship in this direction, although these two elements of play are different. The results reflect the FDI theory of people versus object orientation in young children (Coates et al., 1975; Kogan, 1987; Saracho, 1985b, 1989c, 1989g).

Only a few studies on social orientation and FDI have been conducted to date with preschool children in natural settings. Halverson and Waldrop (1976) investigated the relationship of fast-moving, vigorous, high-active behavior to the development of cognitive and social behavior in young children. They observed the social behaviors (e.g., high-active, vigorous, impulsive) that children exhibit when they engage in free and unrestricted situations. High-active behaviors were positively correlated with field independence. FI children were highly active, while during play FD children were less active. In this longitudinal study, differences in social behavior of young children were related to cognitive style differences. A primary focus in the Halverson and Waldrop study was their belief that children's high levels of activity and impulsiveness would affect the development of cognitive and social behaviors. Thus, the children's high levels of vigorous and intense play activity may block their cognitive thinking and limit their ability to select alternatives in new situations. These results support Kagan's (1971) suggestion that a child's tempo of play, as indexed by variations in play levels, has important consequences for his/her social and cognitive functioning.

In relating social behaviors to cognitive functioning, Steele (1981) investigated the relationship between young children's cognitive styles and their play behaviors (e.g., pretend play events, talkativeness, playfulness, sense of humor, acts of aggression). In observing children, more acts of aggression were observed in FD children and fewer in FI children.

Young children's play behaviors relate to their cognitive styles. Saracho (1987a, 1989c, 1989g, 1990c, 1991a, 1991b, 1992, 1994) conducted a series of studies to explore the relationship among 3- to 5-year-old children's cognitive styles and their play. Saracho (1987a, 1992) found that FI children engaged in more play than FD ones. She also found differences in FD and FI young children's play behaviors (e.g., ability and creativity to communicate ideas, social levels of participation, and capacity to lead in their play). Although there were differences, FI children displayed more play behaviors and played more often than FD children. The least observed play behavior in both FD and FI children was their ability and creativity to communicate, while the most observed behavior in both FD and FI children was cooperative play (Saracho, 1987a).

Studies examining preschool children's cognitive styles and their social orientations showed that (1) FD children more than FI children played more in the different play areas (Saracho, 1991a, 1991b); (2) FI children favored physical and block play more than FD children (Saracho, 1990c, 1991a, 1991b, 1994); (3) FI children engaged more in manipulative play (Saracho, 1991a, 1991b, 1994), which had more effects than the other types of play (Saracho, 1994); and (4) FI children exhibited more play behaviors (e.g., ability and creativity to communicate ideas, social levels of participation, and capacity to lead in their play) than did FD children, although the children's frequency of play did not have a large difference (Saracho, 1992).

FI children engaged more in social play than did FD children, who are considered to be more warm, socially oriented, and nurturant than FI children. This suggests that the play behaviors could be interpreted in the two-dimensional manner as reflecting both field independence cognitive style and social orientation. Further understanding of this phenomenon may be gained with further studies.

Social factors related to cognitive style have been identified in children's play. Saracho (1989g) reported two dimensions of play behaviors for each group of preschool children: (1) social relations and (2) concrete objects for FD children, and (1) role-playing ideas and (2) block-building activities for FI children. Saracho (1989c) showed that FD children participate more in activities with others and with concrete objects, while FI children are more involved in restructuring the environment (Table 7.1). For example, FD children engage in moving with others and using play equipment, reflecting FD characteristics. FD persons are interested in others (Saracho & Spodek, 1981, 1986) and normally learn concrete and structured information. In comparison, FI children generate ideas and initiate their own play activities. Even when FI children engage in social roles, they propose acting out different roles or delineate the roles, reflecting FI characteristics. According to Saracho and Spodek (1981, 1986), FI persons solve problems that are introduced and restructured in various contexts and act independently of authority. However, some FI children display some FD characteristics, such as participating in social roles and communicating with others in manipulative play. Although social roles and communicating with others are

**Table 7.1**
**Descriptive Factors for FD and FI Girls and Boys**

| Children | | FD Children | FI Children |
|---|---|---|---|
| **Age** | **Sex** | | |
| 3 | Girls | Organized social roles | Directed social roles |
| 3 | Girls | Influenced by others | Developed ideas |
| 3 | Boys | Used play equipment | Planned activities with others |
| 3 | Boys | Engaged in various activities | Began activities with others |
| 4 | Girls | Structured social roles with others | Developed social roles through movement |
| 4 | Girls | Began various activities | Defined social roles |
| 4 | Boys | Conveyed social ideas | None |
| 4 | Boys | Duplicated motor activities | None |
| 5 | Girls | Managed objects in social roles | Talked with others |
| 5 | Girls | Used objects in movement | Integrated objects with body movement with others |
| 5 | Boys | Depicted social roles in movement | Used motor skills |
| 5 | Boys | Employed objects to generate ideas | Used objects in social roles |

FD characteristics, two ambivalent inferences may be considered: (1) manipulative and physical play, FI types of play, may have focused on FI activities, and (2) children's cognitive style and play, behaviors may be more complex than has previously been assumed.

In a later study, with a larger population, Saracho (1992) identified those factors underlying the play of FD and FI preschool children. Two dimensions of play behaviors were found for each group of children: (1) communicating ideas using dramatic, manipulative, and physical activities, and (2) communicating ideas in physical and block activities for FD children; and (1) communicating ideas in all forms of play, and (2) engaging in block and physical play for FI children.

The existence of these differences received additional support in an earlier study that investigated the relationship between play behaviors and FDI in a natural setting. Coates et al. (1975) provided 4- and 5-year-olds with an opportunity to select the activity they preferred during free play. Activities were categorized according to their primary focus: (1) social interaction (such as playing in the doll corner, playing formal games, and playing with others in the block corner) and (2) nonsocial interaction (such as constructing with blocks and playing at the task table making paintings and collages, working with puzzles, stringing beads, weaving pot holders). FD children were socially oriented in their play, while FI children favored solitary activities. Saracho (1987a) reports that the children's cognitive styles regulate their play behaviors. FI children play more than FD children. Both FD and FI children display the play behaviors that characterize their cognitive styles. When young children engage in group play, they develop their private symbolism into communicable configurations within play episodes. Their maturity in language and cognitive skills encourages them to engage in solitary play (Saracho, 1986a). Rubin, Watson, and Jambor (1978) showed that some children prefer to take part in solitary play. Children who participate in parallel play prefer the company of their peers, since children who consider the points of view of their peers take part in associative and cooperative play (Rubin, 1976; Saracho, 1985b). These characteristics and others provided by researchers of cognitive style (e.g., Saracho, 1983a, 1984c, 1985b, 1986b, 1989a; Saracho & Spodek, 1981, 1986) present a convincing connection between cognitive style and play.

## Age Differences

Differences in children's ages have been explored in the relationship to cognitive style and play, with conflicting results. Although some studies have indicated age differences, other studies did not find them. Saracho (1994) tested 3- to 5-year-old children's cognitive styles and their play preferences but did not report age differences in the children's selection for the different types of play. Other studies that have examined age differences in relation to children's play behaviors and cognitive styles support these results, including those studies of children ranging in age from three to four (Renninger & Sigel, 1987; Steele, 1981), three to five (Saracho, 1989g, 1990c, 1991a, 1991b, 1992, 1994), three to five years, ten months (Coates, 1972), and four to five (Coates, 1972; Coates et al., 1975). However, Steele (1981) reported age differences for only part of her study, while Saracho (1987a, 1989c) did find age differences in several of her studies.

Steele (1981) did not find any age differences among 3- and 4-year-olds in relation to their cognitive styles and play behaviors (pretend play and playfulness), but did find age differences for 5- and 6-year-olds. Saracho (1987a) reports that older (age five) FD and FI children played more, were better able to communicate and create ideas, engaged more in cooperative play, and were better able to lead in play; although FI 5-year-old children exhibited all of the behaviors with more frequency.

Different social factors have been identified in children's play for the different age groups. Saracho (1989c) interpreted two dependent dimensions of play behaviors for each age group of FD and FI children (see Table 7.1). Evidently, FD 3-year-olds engaged in social play and used play equipment; FD 4-year-olds generated social roles and engaged in activities with others, conveyed social ideas, and imitated motor activities; and FD 5-year-olds used objects in social roles to generate ideas and depicted social roles in movement. In contrast, FI 3-year-olds directed social roles, generated ideas, and initiated and directed activities with others; FI 4-year-olds developed and defined social roles; and FI 5-year-olds interacted with others, used body/motor skills and used objects in movement with others, and manipulated objects in social roles.


## Sex Differences

Several studies have found sex differences in relation to children's cognitive styles and play. Coates (1972) discovered that girls were slightly more FI than boys and that sex differences existed in cognitive styles and play. Most of the FD girls played house and a few of them worked on other activities. In a sharp contrast, all of the FI girls selected activities other than house play. These results suggest that (1) most FD girls preferred a social activity requiring the cooperation of several children such as playing house and (2) most FI girls preferred to work on nonsocial activities by themselves, although they periodically interacted with other children. Coates et al. (1975) also found that FD girls played in the doll corner, while FI girls played with blocks. FI boys played at table tasks, while FD boys engaged in social play in areas such as the doll corner and the block corner.

Other studies support these results. Saracho (1987a, 1990c, 1994) found sex differences in several of her studies. Saracho (1987a) showed sex differences in the children's frequency of play. Boys played more than girls in the different play areas. In Saracho's (1994) study: (1) boys played more than girls in all areas, (2) boys engaged more in physical play and less in manipulative play, and (3) girls engaged more in dramatic play and less in block play. Saracho's (1990c) earlier study supports these results. She found that (1) FD and FI boys engaged more in physical and block play than did the girls, (2) boys engaged more in all forms of play than girls, and (3) order of preference for play differed between boys and girls. Boys preferred physical, block, dramatic, and manipulative play; while girls preferred dramatic, physical, manipulative, and block play.

In exploring social factors in children's play related to cognitive style, Saracho (1989c) discovered that FD girls developed social roles with others, initiated activities, and used objects in social roles; while FI girls generated ideas, developed social roles, interacted with others, and used both body and objects in movement with others. On the other hand, FD boys used play equipment, participated in different play activities, engaged in social roles, conveyed social ideas, reproduced motor activities, and used objects to create ideas; while FI boys directed and initiated activities with others, exercised motor skills, and used objects in social roles.

## SUMMARY

Young children's social behaviors relate to their cognitive style. This relationship has important implications for research and education. Saracho (1985b, 1986a) suggests that a relationship exists between the cognitive style and young children's play behaviors. Several studies have investigated this relationship. These studies (see Table 7.2) show that (1) FD preschool children are more socially oriented in their play and FI children engage more in solitary play; (2) FD children are more aggressive than FI children; (3) FI children play more than FD children; and (4) both FD and FI children display the play behaviors, but FI children, who are considered less socially oriented, engage more in play and display more play behaviors. Studies with conflicting results should not discourage researchers from exploring the possibility that a relationship exists between cognitive styles and social behaviors.

Supporting and conflicting results should inspire an unbiased inquiry of any relationship between cognitive styles and children's social behaviors, which should contribute to the knowledge about cognitive style. Since the children's cognitive styles may influence their choices and modes of play, it is especially important to explore if cognitive styles relate to the quality of the play. Research questions also may be asked in reverse, namely, which play behaviors display the children's cognitive style.[1] Studies can assess young children's cognitive styles and search for the social factors found in their play based on their cognitive styles. Sex and age differences can be included in these studies.

The studies reviewed provide a knowledge base about children's cognitive styles and social behaviors, which can be associated with theories of early childhood development and learning such as those suggested by Piaget (1962) or Bruner (1972). Researchers and educators who become aware of these relationships can propose teaching strategies that integrate both cognitive style and play. Teachers can design their educational goals and then consider learning alternatives that integrate both cognitive style and play. They can observe and evaluate their educational goals, engaging in children's activities according to their cognitive styles and play to make learning more effective.

## NOTE

1. Chapter 3 describes how children's play can be used to assess cognitive style.

**Table 7.2**
**Social Orientation Studies with Young Children**

| Scholars | Date | Children's Age | Outcomes |
|----------|------|----------------|----------|
| Ruble & Nakamura | (1972) | 7-8 | FD children were alert to social cues emitted by the examiner (e.g., gesture of the head); while FI children focused their attention on less personal cues (e.g., hand movements of the examiner modeling an assembly task). |
| Coates | (1972)+ | 3-5 | FD children cooperated with their playmates in social activities; while FI children, who periodically interacted with other children, engaged in more nonsocial activities. |
| Coates | (1972)+ | 3-5 | FD children who have a low analytic ability are more socially oriented than FI children who have a high analytic ability. |
| Coates et al. | (1975)+ | 4-5 | FD children prefer social play areas such as the doll corner and the block corner; while FI children preferred to play with blocks and at table tasks. |
| Jennings | (1975) | 4-5 | More people-oriented children were considerably more peer directed than other children, while more object-oriented children were more adult directed. |
| Halverson & Waldrop | (1976) | | During play, FI children were highly active while FD children were less active. |
| Nakamura | (1980) | 9-12 | FI children were low-social, task-effective, while FD children were more socially oriented. |
| Steele | (1981)* | 3-6 | More acts of aggression were observed in FD children and less in FI children. |
| Renninger & Sigel | (1987) | 3-4 | Young children display a stylistic style performance in their choice of strategies and processes to cognitively arrange and understand tasks. Over time, young children's cognitive arrangement manifests specific patterns that they perceive as appropriate to them, or with great interest. Children constantly implement strategies unfolding an organizational pattern. Once such an organizational pattern is employed with a type of task, then the children's range of strategies reaches a stylistic level. |
| Saracho | (1987a)*+ | 3-5 | FI children engaged more in play than FD ones. FI children displayed more play behaviors and played more often than FD children. |

**Table 7.2 (continued)**

| Scholars | Date | Children's Age | Outcomes |
|---|---|---|---|
| Saracho | (1989c)*+ | 3-5 | FD children participated more in activities with others and with concrete objects, while FI children were more involved in restructuring the environment. |
| Saracho | (1989g) | 3-5 | Dimensions of play behaviors for FD children were (1) social relations and (2) concrete objects; while for FI children were (1) role-playing ideas and (2) block-building activities. |
| Saracho | (1990c)+ | 3-5 | Results were (1) FD and FI boys engaged more in physical and block play than did the girls, (2) boys engaged more in all forms of play than girls, and (3) order of preference for play differed between boys and girls. Boys preferred physical, block, dramatic, and manipulative play, while girls preferred dramatic, physical, manipulative, and block play. |
| Saracho | (1991a) | 3-5 | FI children were more able to assume a social role and solve a social problem than the FD children. |
| Saracho | (1991b) | 3-5 | Teachers perceived (1) the more FD children as more socially competent, (2) FD pairs of children where one child was accepted and the other was rejected as more socially competent, (3) both FD and FI children who were rejected as playmates by other children were found to engage in more social play. |
| Saracho | (1992) | 3-5 | Dimensions of play behaviors for FD children were (1) communicating ideas using dramatic, manipulative, and physical activities and (2) communicating ideas in physical and block activities, while for FI children were (1) communicating ideas in all forms of play and (2) engaging in block and physical play. |
| Saracho | (1994)+ | 3-5 | FI children favored physical and block play more than FD children, while FI children engaged more in manipulative play. |

*Studies showing age differences.
+Studies showing sex differences.

# Part III

# Teachers' Instruction

Chapter 8

# Portraits of Field Dependent Independent Teachers

## BACKGROUND

The observations reported here have roots in an approach to personality theory that expresses itself through studies of individual differences in adaptive modes of organizing and experiencing the stimulus world. The focus of these observations has been upon personal organization. The person's behavior corresponding to his/her cognitive style field dependence independence (FDI) is congruous and pervasive. Teachers cull teaching strategies, manage their classes, and present patterns of instructional behavior according to the predominance of their field dependent (FD) and field independent (FI) characteristics.[1]

## DESCRIPTION OF TEACHERS

These observations illustrate how teachers differ in the ways they instruct their classes according to their particular cognitive styles. Examples of differences between FD and FI teachers are depicted in the following portraits, which identify more clearly the characteristics of FD and FI teachers. The examples include teachers who are teaching different subject areas (e.g., mathematics, reading, science, art) and a range of age levels (e.g., nursery school, kindergarten, primary grades).

Extreme FD and FI teachers were identified using tests of cognitive style, including the Group Embedded Figures Test (Oltman, Raskin, & Witkin, 1971), Articulation of the Body-Concept Scale (Witkin et al., 1962/1974), and Goodenough-Harris Drawing Test (Harris, 1963; Saracho, 1984c, 1985a, 1986b). Children in these teachers' classrooms were also administered the appropriate forms of these cognitive style tests, such as the Children's Embedded Figures Test (Karp & Konstadt, 1971). These tests are described in Chapter 3.

Based on scores on the cognitive style tests, five extreme FD and five extreme FI teachers were selected to be portrayed. Classroom observations of these teachers were recorded. These observations provided examples of instructional strategies and content used by teachers with different cognitive styles. Transcriptions per teacher were randomly selected for inclusion in the portraits.[2] Teachers and students who were considered more FD were assigned a name beginning with the letter D, while those who were considered more FI were assigned a name beginning with the letter I. This process helped to identify the teachers' and students' cognitive styles when their behavior was described. The following are descriptions of FD and FI teachers and their interactions with FD and FI students.

## Portraits

Five extreme cases were chosen as samples of teachers who gave FD or FI performances in a classroom setting. After each case, the teachers' behaviors are discussed. At the end of all the portraits, the teachers' behaviors are summarized.

## Field Dependent Teachers

**FD Teacher:** *Ms. Dailey*[3]

**Level:** Nursery School                 **Subject Area:** Reading

### Observation

*Ms. Dailey* sat on the floor with four children (2 FD [1 FD girl and 1 FD boy] and 2 FI girls) in the corner of the room. She took a gray puppet from a bag and asked the children, "Do you know what this is?"

The children knew immediately that it was an elephant. "But," *Ms. Dailey* asked, "what is different about this elephant than those that you have seen in books or at the zoo?"

Isabelle jumped up and said, "Its trunk is funny."

"That's right, Isabelle," *Ms. Dailey* said. "Look. Its trunk is short. Don't elephants usually have long trunks? Can everyone stand up and pretend to be an elephant?" *Ms. Dailey* stood up first, bent over, put her arm way out in front, and used it as a trunk.

The children followed her lead.

"O.K. Let's sit down because I have another animal that I would like to show you." The children quickly sat down and looked as *Ms. Dailey* brought a green animal out of her bag. "What do you think this little creature is?" *Ms. Dailey* asked.

"It's a crocodile, like in Peter Pan," said Ida.

"Wow, that's great," said *Ms. Dailey*. Now, these two animals are puppets, and I am going to need two of you to be my puppet holders during the story. All of the children jumped up, reaching out for the puppets. *Ms. Dailey* asked them to sit quietly as she gave the elephant to Don and the crocodile to Debra.

"I want you all to listen carefully while I tell you a story about how the elephant got its trunk. We said this elephant doesn't have a trunk. But the story I am about to tell you will explain how all the elephants got their trunks. Now Don, make sure you have that elephant on your hand real tight, and Debra, you put that crocodile on your hand and get ready to help me tell the story," *Ms. Dailey* requested.

And *Ms. Dailey* began her story about the elephant that asked too many questions, but the one question that he asked more than any other was, "What does the crocodile eat for breakfast?"

"Don," *Ms. Dailey* asked, "Can you hold up your elephant and ask the question?"

Don raised the elephant in the air and said in a loud voice, "What does the crocodile eat for breakfast?"

"Finally," *Ms. Dailey* continued, "one day a bird told him to go to the river and ask the crocodile what he eats for breakfast. So off the elephant went. And what do you think he said when he found the crocodile?" *Ms. Dailey* asked.

Don moved his elephant right next to Debra's crocodile and said, "What do you eat for breakfast?"

"Well," *Ms. Dailey* continued, "do you know what the crocodile said? What would you say, Debra?"

"I don't know. Maybe I eat people for breakfast or Captain Hook!!!!"

"Well, if you've been watching Peter Pan, you're right. But this crocodile said, 'Come closer and I'll tell you.' Can you say that to the elephant, Debra?"

So Debra said, "Come closer and I'll tell you."

Don moved the elephant close to the crocodile.

*Ms. Dailey* continued with the story. "Well, the crocodile kept telling the elephant to come closer and closer until, guess what, he grabbed hold of the elephant's face and would not let go. Can you do that, Debra?"

Debra grabbed the elephant. The children laughed and squirmed. Don pulled his elephant away.

*Ms. Dailey* said, "That's exactly what the elephant did. He pulled and pulled and pulled until finally the crocodile lost his grip. But guess what?" When he got up on his feet and looked down, he had this long, long, long nose. Guess what we call that long, long, long nose?

"A trunk!!" all the children shouted.

"Do you think the elephant liked his trunk?" *Ms. Dailey* asked. "He did," she continued. "He liked it very much. He could spray water all over himself with it and catch bugs. He liked it so much that he went home to all of the other elephants and told them to go down to the river and ask the crocodile what he eats for breakfast so they too could get a trunk."

### Discussion

*Ms. Dailey* provides teaching experiences that are congruent with her cognitive style such as

1. interacting with a small group of children,
2. using concrete objects (such as when she presented objects and pretended to be an elephant),
3. reinforcing their responses,

4. modeling for children (such as when she led the children to imitate the elephant walk and used her hands as a trunk rather than having the children create their own imitation and when she expected them to use her dialogue verbatim rather than letting the children create their own) and

5. giving them direct directions as to what to do first, second, next, etc. She also gave more attention to her matched students (Don and Debra), which is supported by some literature (see Chapter 10 for a discussion of the match of teachers and students).

**FD Teacher:** *Ms. Dainis*

**Level:** Kindergarten                          **Subject Area:** Language Arts

**Observation**

"On Friday, we are going to have a picnic in our classroom," *Ms. Dainis* begins, as the students sit in a circle on the floor in front of her. "Today we are going to discuss how to prepare a picnic basket," *Ms. Dainis* continues.

The students smile as *Ms. Dainis* continues. "But before we begin our book today, let's do some thinking. Everyone please close your eyes and place your hands in your lap. I'd like you to imagine that you are going on a picnic and that you are in charge of packing the picnic basket. What will you bring? Use your senses to help you remember the things that you will need. Maybe you are standing in the kitchen. What do you see that must be included? Is anyone reminding you that you must bring certain things?

The students think quietly for a minute or two before *Ms. Dainis* asks them to open their eyes. "Everyone will have a chance to respond so there is no reason to raise your hands. I will call on each one of you, and when I do, please tell me one thing that must be included in your picnic."

As *Ms. Dainis* listens to each response, she records it on the chalkboard. By the end of the responses, the list looks like this:

| | |
|---|---|
| fruit | ice cream in a bowl |
| pizza | coke |
| orange | lollipops |
| banana | pears |
| apple | |

"Great," *Ms. Dainis* says, as she sits down in her little chair in front of the circle of students. "Now I have something to show you. I have packed a basket for my picnic and I would like to show you what's inside." She places a large picnic basket in front of the students and takes out the first item. "I have packed one tablecloth." *Ms. Dainis* holds it up so the students can see it, and then continues revealing the contents of her basket.

"I have packed two carrots.

I have packed three rolls.

I have packed four pickles.

I have packed five oranges.

I have packed six napkins.

I have packed seven cookies.

I have packed eight cookie cutters.

I have packed nine cups.

I have packed ten Hershey kisses."

The students identify the pattern by about number five and begin counting with her. After her basket has been emptied, *Ms. Dainis* asks, "Now, let's pretend that we have arrived at our picnic site and started to set up. What could possibly happen that would cause us to leave?"

Isaac answers, "Rain!"

Darron says, "We have to go to the potty."

Ivan says, "Storm."

Dennis adds, "We might run out of food."

*Ms. Dainis* praises the students for their good thinking, and then announces that it is time to read a big book. "And guess what the name of the book is—THE PICNIC. And we're going to find out what they have packed and what causes them to leave their picnic."

## Discussion

*Ms. Dainis* exhibits several FD characteristics including:

1. working in a group to encourage interpersonal relationships and interactions among the students;

2. giving direct instruction in sequences such as close your eyes, place your hands in your lap, and imagine you are on a picnic;

3. expecting them to depend on authority, such as when she says that she will call on each of them to tell her one thing to include in the picnic basket;

4. providing concrete information by recording the responses on the chalkboard, presenting a real picnic basket, showing the tablecloth, and revealing the contents of the basket;

5. praising the children as a form of feedback; and

6. setting up standards for them by telling them what to say in their selection of items to be included in the picnic basket (e.g., expressing these items verbatim as she told them). For example, "I have two carrots and I have nine cups."

**FD Teacher:** *Ms. Dalton*

**Level:** Grades 1, 2, and 3                    **Subject Area:** Music

### Observation

The students are seated in a large circle, as *Ms. Dalton* sits at the piano that is at the front and center of the room.

"Today," *Ms. Dalton* begins, "I have an echo song for you. Who can tell me what my echo would say if I said 'Hello'?"

Irwin quickly says, "It has something to do with sound."

"Yes, that's right. Now who can raise their hand and give me more information about an echo?"

Irene raises her hand and responds, "Hello."

"Very good! An echo has to do with sounds and it repeats a sound. Today we are going to sing a kind of song that is called an echo song. I'll sing it for you the first time:

| | |
|---|---|
| "Who has the penny? | I have the penny. |
| Who has the key? | I have the key. |
| Who has the thimble? | I have the thimble. |
| Please let me see. | Please let me see." |

*Ms. Dalton* explains that she will sing the first line and the student will sing the echo. *Ms. Dalton* demonstrates and then explains, "Now this isn't a perfect echo because we're changing 'who' to 'I' each time."

The students practice the song a few times. Then *Ms. Dalton* gets up from the piano and shows the students that she has a penny, a key, and a thimble. "Do you know what a thimble is?" *Ms. Dalton* asks. Everyone sits quietly, so she explains that a thimble is used in sewing to protect fingers.

"Now," *Ms. Dalton* says, "I am going to give out the penny, the key, and the thimble and this time when I ask who has the penny, I want the person who has it to stand up and sing, 'I have the penny'."

*Ms. Dalton* hands the penny to Donna, the key to Dean, and the thimble to Derrin.

*Ms. Dalton* returns to the piano and begins singing, "Who has the penny?"

Donna jumps from her chair and screeches, "I have the penny."

"Who has the key," *Ms. Dalton* sings.

Dean stands up sheepishly and quietly sings, "I have the key."

Then *Ms. Dalton* sings, "Who has the thimble?"

But this time, no one answers so *Ms. Dalton* sings again, "Who has the thimble?" Still no answer, so *Ms. Dalton* gets up from the piano and asks Derrin to sing, but he refuses. She then asks Derrin to give back the thimble and she quickly hands it to another student.

*Ms. Dalton* returns to the piano and continues with the song.

### Discussion

*Ms. Dalton* exhibits the following FD characteristics:

1. working in a group (several students in a circle) to encourage interpersonal relationships and interactions among the students;

2. giving specific directions rather than letting them develop a plan and act on it;

3. presenting concrete objects, such as a penny, a key, and thimble, to help children understand what she is teaching; and

4. requesting very specific responses, such as asking, "Who has the thimble?" and child responds, "I have the thimble," rather than allowing the child to create his/her own dialogue.

She also gave consideration to her matched students (Donna, Dean, and Derrin) by giving them the objects that were supposed to be returned to the teacher as they sang the song. This behavior is supported by some recent literature (see Chapter 10 on the match of teachers and students).

**FD Teacher:** *Ms. Damron*

**Level:** Kindergarten                    **Subject Area:** Art

**Observation**

*Ms. Damron* leads at circle time. She introduced a craft activity planned for that day. "It's a very funny one." *Ms. Damron* then put out a finished work on the board with a magnet. It was a cut paper picture of a man wearing black boots, holding an umbrella, which covered up his head. The umbrella, the lower part of the coat, and a pair of boots were cut out from three pieces of paper, respectively, and then glued together. *Ms. Damron*'s introduction of the craft project was composed of six specific steps:

1. showing the finished craft work,

2. initiating talk about the work,

3. labeling every part of the picture,

4. explaining how it was made,

5. modeling the process, and then

6. sending children to different tables to start doing the project on their own.

Part of the talk went like this:

*Ms. Damron*: Why is this such a funny picture?

Inez: It's funny because he has no head.

Ida: It's so funny because it has an umbrella on it, instead of a head.

Dean: He bent down to make a mushroom.

*Ms. Damron*: Which part do you think is the jacket?

*Ms. Damron*: OK, let's see how you are going to make this silly guy. How many pieces are you going to get to work today?

We're going to have double cutting here.

Every part has to be cut out from a folded piece of paper with half of the figure on it. *Ms. Damron* showed the children how to cut on the line and had a child go to the front of the room to open it up. The children were amazed when the figure got opened. *Ms. Damron*: "I'm going to have Donald open it up."

When children did not put the parts of the picture the way *Ms. Damron* expected, she cued them with Yes-No questions, such as "You want to ... or you want to cover it up a little bit? "Do you want to put the boots ... or do you want to put them underneath it?

After the demonstration, which took about ten minutes, the children were sent to different tables. On each table, the teacher had placed several pairs of scissors in the middle and three pieces of folded paper with half of the figures on them.

*Ms. Damron* then walked to one of the tables, and stayed there for the rest of the time. Children started working right after they went to their seats. Children were eager to show *Ms. Damron* what they had done, and *Ms. Damron* commented with replies such as "Oh, look at how neat that is!" Denny was working at the table where *Ms. Damron* stayed and finished cutting the pictures in less than three minutes. Denny was the one who first finished the whole project.

*Ms. Damron* then encouraged him to help clean up by saying, "Do you see something that we don't need on the table?" In fact, most of the children finished the project in less than five minutes and went to the centers to play.

Ira put the umbrella upside down and showed it to *Ms. Damron*. *Ms. Damron* asked Ira why it was that way; Ira laughed, as the other children did, and said "Because he wants to fall down." *Ms. Damron* then told Ira, "Be sure to tell your mom why it is like that." Most of the boys went to play with Legos, and most of the girls went to play at the dramatic play center.

**Discussion**

*Ms. Damron* displayed FD characteristics. Her cutting and pasting activity required specific directions. The only creativity allowed in this activity was the children's interpretation of the picture and of their own work.

*Ms. Damron* provided a model for the children to follow. Two children chose to paste the pieces together in a different way. *Ms. Damron* accepted their minor transformation but apparently did not expect or encourage it. This might be described as a simple exercise of hands (FD) but not of minds (FI).

*Ms. Damron* also gave more attention to her matched students (Dean, Donald, and Denny), which is supported by some recent literature (see Chapter 10 on the match of teachers and students).

**FD Teacher:** *Ms. Danco*

**Level:** Grade 3                                    **Subject Area:** Art

**Observation**

The students entered the classroom in order. Those who arrived earlier went to stand around the table where the materials for the new project were displayed and unfinished work of the previous project was displayed. Some children went to the table, picked up their unfinished work, and started working on it. It was a weaving project. Students used a big needle to weave out lines with yarns of different colors or sew on buttons of different sizes. When all the children arrived (about 10 minutes later), *Ms. Danco* explained the new activity. After the explanation and demonstration, some students continued the new project while some worked on the unfinished one. Twenty minutes later, *Ms. Danco* walked around the room, commented on what students were doing, and provided guidance and helped them by saying, ''Oh, you've got it, very nice.'' Sometimes, *Ms. Danco* got some materials that a student asked for. The students were free to move around and talked to their peers about the project, the difficulties they confronted, or the solutions they came up with.

At the end of the art period, the teacher gave the following explanation:

*Ms. Danco*: If you're not finished yet, make sure you complete your project Try real hard to finish it today. And I really don't want you to do it on another day. It's been enough time for this project.

After a while the teacher added:

*Ms. Danco*: Now, I would like for everybody to stop working on their project for just a few minutes. Some people who are finished now and other people who will be finishing later. We need to talk about our next project. Look up here, sit, and see what I do. All right, we're going to do a crayon with this project. Can you tell me, somebody remember what that is?

Irma: A vase.

*Ms. Danco*: You draw with a crayon and then you be what?

Irma: Watercolor.

*Ms. Danco*: Right. Exactly. There are two different ways you can use watercolor, that's one. One is doing the way we're doing, to separate colors with the crayon, the wax, so you do not mix. The other way is to use the wax and to have colors lay on top of each other, which is very nice, too, but it takes a very long time. And some artists do it purposely. It's a very nice effect for sunrises, sunsets, and you have colors on it and it's very beautiful. All right, since this is spring, we're going to do the vase of your choice at the bottom and you add flowers. It's going to fill out the whole, entire page. Now, there's a couple of things that I want you to do, when you're doing it. I want you to think about the flowers as the main part of the design, not the vase. Therefore, you don't want a very, very tall vase. It does not have to be like this. It could be a narrow vase. Have you seen the vases in the stores? What are their shapes? Are they the same on both sides?

Illene: Did you do anything for the vase?

*Ms. Danco*: Vases are of a football shape. They made vases for every occasion. Do anything you want to. When you're doing the flowers, I want you to think about balance. Is this balance, Dwayne, what would you say?

Dwayne: Yeah.

*Ms. Danco*: Why?

Dwayne: You put a flower on one side, you have another flower on the other side. Every time you have a flower on one side, the flowers go on the other side.

*Ms. Danco*: Right. Now, it's not exactly balanced, but, in art, you can have a purple flower here, and I put another purple flower over here. On the larger vase the purple flower is in the middle but it's not exactly in the middle. Nothing has to be exactly alike. The best way of doing this is to do the flowers first, don't think about the leaves and stems, leave those for the end. . . . I'll like you to decorate the vase, too.

### Discussion

*Ms. Danco* displayed several FD characteristics. For example:

1. While students drew vases of different shapes and flowers of different kinds, all of them followed the teacher's perspective. All of them portrayed the facade of the vase with the flowers. Students were not allowed to set their own standards and create their own work.

2. The teacher set up a model to be followed. *Ms. Danco* drew a sketch on the chalkboard. Students were constrained to think of it as a two-dimensional object. Some students even went to sit close to the chalkboard so they could easily "copy" *Ms. Danco*'s drawing. Another student successfully imitated *Ms. Danco*'s drawing or at least included everything that appeared in it.

3. *Ms. Danco* wanted students to "try very hard" to finish the previous project so they could move on to the next one. The point seemed to be just moving on to the next thing, to a different project. There was little connection between the two projects, in form or content. Those who had not finished the previous project did get the point. Some of them worked on it when *Ms. Danco* was explaining the new one.

## Field Independent Teachers

**FI Teacher:** *Ms. Idelberg*

**Level:** Grade 1                                    **Subject Area:** Art

### Observation

Students returned to the classroom from the gym. *Ms. Idelberg* was already in the classroom waiting for them. She had all the children gather at the central area of the classroom, which was surrounded by five tables, and started to explain the project. After the explanation, *Ms. Idelberg* demonstrated the project by drawing on the blackboard opposite to where she initially sat. Two minutes later, *Ms. Idelberg* sent the children to sit at the tables. A student helper distributed paper and *Ms. Idelberg* passed out brushes to every table. Students worked on the project. *Ms. Idelberg* then moved around to provide extra materials, assistance, or answered the questions raised by the students.

Students talked to each other about the projects or simply chatted about other things unrelated to the ongoing project. Some just worked quietly.

The following are examples of part of the "talk" that was going on in this art activity.

Darzelle: Oh, cool.

*Ms. Idelberg*: Now let everybody be quiet, I know some of you have done this before, ok? But for those of you who have never done this before, be quiet so everyone can hear me, ok? All right. Today we're going to make this. And then next week, we're going to put it on a rack and dry it. We're going to make this into a butterfly. Ok?

Daphne: Oh!

*Ms. Idelberg*: This is why I have this black strip down the middle, the body, you know when you draw a butterfly, you make a body here; what can you guys tell me about the wings? What's this like?

Students are silent.

*Ms. Idelberg*: Anybody know what's a white dot in the pattern? Right. If there's a dot on this wing, is there a dot on this wing?

Darzelle: Yeah.

*Ms. Idelberg*: Yeah. Ok. They are symmetrical just like we are. We have one arm or what do we have?

Isiah: Two arms.

*Ms. Idelberg*: We have two arms. So on your pattern, say you want to make, um, diamond coming down and you make a diamond.

Darzelle: Yeah.

*Ms. Idelberg*: Yes. Ok, so remember that when we put the paper down. You make it exactly the same on each side. Now, just a minute. I'm going to draw on the board just a second 'cause I want to show you something. Then I'll have you each do it.

Students are talking.

*Ms. Idelberg*: So, the first thing you're going to do is to have these little tissue squares. You're going to get the middle of the paper and you're going to put the squares right down the middle of the paper, ok? In the dark color, ok? and overlapping. Black, brown, dark blue, purple, whatever, so that when it's done, it looks like what?

Isiah: The body.

*Ms. Idelberg*: The body, ok? Then you're going to make wings like this (drawing on the blackboard), ok? So, if you put spots here, what do you do here?

Isiah: Spot there.

*Ms. Idelberg*: Ok, if you put spatter like this, you put one over like this?

Darzelle: Yeah.

*Ms. Idelberg*: Ok. That's the only thing I want you to remember. You just put this side then put the same thing over here. So, you make all things black here. If you put a pink square here, you put a pink square here, too. Ok? You put a blue square here, you put a blue square here, too. So you're going to do two at a time. I don't care what you do with this part, anything you want to make, ok? Any color combination you want to make, whatever.

Inga: Is the paper hard, or do you make it hard?

*Ms. Idelberg*: What do you mean?

Inga: The paper is hard.

*Ms. Idelberg*: Oh, it gets hard cause you're going to use glue mixed with water. So as it dries, it gets harder. So what you're going to do, I'm going to show you in just a minute.

   All right, turn back again.

Darzelle: (Loudly) Ahhhhhh!

*Ms. Idelberg*: This is a hard one. (Showing students how to put the glue on the tissue paper). See, that's all you do. Each person gonna get glue, you gonna get paper. Ok? You all set? All right, say, I wanna make this part might get green so here's what I'm going to do. Say I want light green, so the next one, I might do one square at a time, and that's what happens if you don't. You get all muddy and yucky. You cover it with glue, one at a time. Are there any questions?

Isiah: No.

*Ms. Idelberg*: You want to try it?

Darzelle: Yeah!

*Ms. Idelberg*: Ok. (Passing out materials)

*Ms. Idelberg* talked as she walked around.

*Ms. Idelberg*: Do you know how to overlap? (She held up a blue and pink tissue paper, overlapped them, and made a purple tissue.)

Dale: How do you make this? (He pointed at a color in *Ms. Idelberg*'s picture.)

*Ms. Idelberg*: I have blue, yellow, and I have green. [She overlapped the blue and yellow tissues to get a green tissue.

*Ms. Idelberg*: It looks pretty, you guys are doing a really good job.

## Discussion

   *Ms. Idelberg* displayed several FI characteristics. For example:

1. *Ms. Idelberg* stressed that squares have to be balanced on the two sides. She assumed that children needed to have the instructions repeated.

2. Although groups of students could interact with each other, *Ms. Idelberg* had them working by themselves. She demonstrated the art project and then asked the children to work by themselves.

3. *Ms. Idelberg* seldom interacted with the students, even though the art project provides numerous opportunities.

4. The art project was rather abstract (square tissues), which is typical of FI individuals.

5. *Ms. Idelberg* lectured them on how to make their art project.

**FI Teacher:** *Ms. Impett*

**Level:** Kindergarten                    **Subject Area:** Play

**Observation**

*Ms. Impett* is seated at her desk in the corner of the room. Most of the students are seated at their desks, finishing an assignment. One by one, *Ms. Impett* calls each student to her desk to assess his/her progress on the day's assignment.

However, four students are seated in an open area in the opposite corner of the room. Ingrid and Ivey sit amid a pile of blocks, quietly building structures and knocking them to the ground.

Igor and Ivan are standing with large orange squares, pretending to be pizza delivery men. Igor, holding a stack of four to five letters in his hand, says to Ivan, "Here are all your pizzas." He then drops them on the ground.

Ivan picks them up and tosses them back at Igor. They repeat this routine again, only this time the two girls, Ingrid and Ivey, notice the fun that they are having and consequently decide to join them.

All four of the students now have four to five orange blocks and begin tossing them at each other. They no longer mention pizza, but instead they are just tossing the blocks back and forth, chatting and laughing as they play.

*Ms. Impett* notices their behavior and asks them to use the supplies properly. Ingrid and Ivey move away from Ivan and Igor, and return to building structure with blocks. Ivan and Igor sit down quietly, trying to straighten up the orange blocks.

**Discussion**

*Ms. Impett* displays FI characteristics in her behavior. For example:

1. *Ms. Impett* is impersonal as she calls students to her desk to assess their progress. She seems socially detached and does not get near the students.
2. *Ms. Impett*'s activities are abstract (FI). Her FI children are the ones who are engaged in these activities with blocks and letters.
3. *Ms. Impett*'s FI children are engaged in other activities while most of the other children are finishing the assignment.
4. *Ms. Impett* reprimands the students rather than using her social skills to encourage them to complete their work.

**FI Teacher:** *Ms. Ikenberry*

**Level:** Kindergarten                    **Subject Area:** Math

**Observation**

The students gather in a circle on the floor as *Ms. Ikenberry* sits in front of them in a small chair. "We're going to continue talking about money today. What did we say our fingers represented yesterday?"

Irving raises his five fingers and says, "Pennies."

*Ms. Ikenberry* affirms his answer and then raises her ten fingers and says, "Each one of my fingers represents one penny. How many pennies do I have? Let's count."

As *Ms. Ikenberry* points to each finger, the students count, "One, two, three, four, five, six, seven, eight, nine, ten."

Then *Ms. Ikenberry* begins to ask the students to show their pennies. "I am going to ask you to use your fingers to show me how many pennies you have. Before you put up your fingers, I want you to figure it out in your lap first. When I say 'show me,' then put up your fingers."

"Show me nine pennies," *Ms. Ikenberry* requests. "First think, then do it in your lap." *Ms. Ikenberry* waits a few seconds. "Now, show me."

All of the students raise their hands in the air, showing their nine pennies. *Ms. Ikenberry* asks Doris to come to the front of the class. Doris shows eight pennies instead of nine. The class counts her fingers together. When they only count eight, *Ms. Ikenberry* asks Dorris what she needs to do. Doris puts up one more finger. "Good!" exclaims *Ms. Ikenberry*. "You only need to keep one finger down! Thanks, Doris."

"This time I want you to show me five cents. Figure it out in your lap first," explains *Ms. Ikenberry*. She allows a few seconds to pass. "Show me," *Ms. Ikenberry* announces.

*Ms. Ikenberry* checks for understanding. This time, all of the students get it right. "Great!" she praises. "Now we are going to do magic on our fingers. I will say the magic word—Abracadabra—and change my five cents into a nickel." As she says the magic word, she folds her five fingers down to make a fist. Holding up her fist, she says, "This is a nickel. And how many pennies are in a nickel?" One by one, *Ms. Ikenberry* unfolds each finger, counting, "One, two, three, four, five. There are five pennies in a nickel."

"If you need to know how many pennies are in a nickel, all you need to do is shake your fist loose, and look at what you have." The teacher demonstrates, shaking her fist loose and the students shout, "Five!"

"Now it is time for you to show me if you understand," says *Ms. Ikenberry*. "I would like you to show me ten cents. Think first and then figure it out in your lap. Now show me." *Ms. Ikenberry* looks around the room and then calls three students to the front of the class. When the students show their ten cents, they each have a different show of fingers.

David shows two fists. Ismael shows one fist and five fingers. Delores shows ten fingers. *Ms. Ikenberry* has the students explain why each answer is correct.

At the end of the lesson, *Ms. Ikenberry* gives each student a ditto with a picture of a nickel on it and asks her/him to return to his/her table to color the picture. She also places real nickels at each table so the students can examine them.

**Discussion**

*Ms. Ikenberry* displays the following FI characteristics:

1. She instructs students in an impersonal way: the students sit in a circle while she sits in front of them.

2. She emphasizes abstract subjects, mathematics in this case.

3. She is academically oriented.

**FI Teacher:** *Ms. Ickes*

**Level:** Grade 1                              **Subject Area:** Math

#### Observation

*Ms. Ickes* moves to the front of the room near the chalkboard. The students are at their desks, clearing books and supplies. As the students finish clearing their desks, they sit with their hands folded and eyes focused on *Ms. Ickes*. One by one, the students are called to the front of the class, where they sit in a small carpeted area. *Ms. Ickes* announces that today's lesson will be on subtraction. "What do we do when we subtract?" she asks.

"We take away," answers Ilse.

Then *Ms. Ickes* writes a subtraction problem on the board:

$$6 - 3 = \underline{\hspace{1cm}}$$

*Ms. Ickes* instructs all the students to solve the problem. After a few minutes, she asks Ismael for the answer. After Ismael gives the correct answer, *Ms. Ickes* asks, "How did you think to solve that problem?"

Ismael explains, "I think that $3 + 3 = 6$."

"Good!" Did everyone hear what Ismael said?" *Ms. Ickes* asks. She then repeats his answer.

These steps are repeated several times with more problems. Eventually, *Ms. Ickes* sends the students back to their seats.

Once the students are seated, *Ms. Ickes* distributes sets of linking cubes to each student. "Now," she explains, "I would like you to solve some problems using the cubes." She turns on the overhead projector and writes down the problem:

$$5 - 4 = \underline{\hspace{1cm}}$$

The students work independently, using their cubes. *Ms. Ickes* moves throughout the room, watching each student solve the problem. She talks quietly with Dwight, who does not solve the problem correctly. *Ms. Ickes* says, "Show me five cubes." Dwight puts five cubes on the desk.

Then *Ms. Ickes* says, "Now take away four of the cubes."

Dwight follows her directions. "Now, how many cubes do you have left?"

Dwight places one cube on the desk. *Ms. Ickes* smiles and moves on to check the next student.

#### Discussion

*Ms. Ickes* displays the following FI characteristics:

1. She instructs students in an impersonal way, such as, the students are at their desks.

2. She emphasizes abstract subjects, mathematics in this case.

3. She is academically oriented.

4. She has students working independently using their cubes.

5. She is socially detached, moving through the room, watching students solve problems, and having only minor interactions with them.


**FI Teacher:** *Ms. Innis*

**Level:** Nursery School                          **Subject Area:** Science

### Observation

*Ms. Innis* begins by asking the children what they do at home to care for birds in the cold winter time. Many hands go up around the room.

Daphne says, "My mommy puts sunflower seeds in a feeder almost every day."

Dexter answers, "My daddy says it's not good to feed the birds in our front yard because they make a mess."

Derrick answers, "We made a tree just for the birds in our yard. We put peanut butter on the tree."

*Ms. Innis* listens to all the answers and then announces that today in class everyone will make a special gift for birds in the winter. "Why do we need to help feed the birds during the winter? What happens to many of the seeds and worms that they normally eat?" she asks.

"It gets cold and the worms disappear," answers Indiva.

"Yes, that's right, the ground gets cold and the worms stay underground so the birds can't find them. What about seeds from plants?" asks *Ms. Innis*.

"They're gone in the winter," answers Imogene.

"When will they be back so the birds will have their food sources again?" questions *Ms. Innis*.

"Soon," says Damien.

A few students chuckle at Damien's answer. A little boy (Irving) adds, "They'll be back in the summer when it's hot."

"That's right, and in the spring," adds *Ms. Innis*.

*Ms. Innis* then begins to give instructions. "I would like each of you to leave our circle and move to your working tables. You will notice that they are covered with newspaper. Please be careful not to push the newspaper off the tables.

As the students seat themselves, *Ms. Innis* and an aide distribute a pine cone to each student. At the top of the pine cone is a string for hanging the pine cone onto a tree. "Now I'd like all eyes on me. I will demonstrate the project that you are about to make. Each of you will receive a small cup of peanut butter, a small cup of bird seed, and a popsicle stick. The first thing you should do is spread the peanut butter all over the pine cone. When you have used all of your peanut butter, then you can sprinkle your cone with the bird seed. It's just like sprinkles on an ice cream cone," explains *Ms. Innis*. "And the more seeds you get on the cone, the more the birds will like it!"

The students chatter among themselves. *Ms. Innis* adds, "If you have any seeds left on your newspaper when you are finished, you can roll the cone around to see if you can get them to stick."

The students seem anxious to begin working on their projects. As *Ms. Innis* and the aide pass out the supplies, the students begin talking about where they will hang their bird feeders. *Ms. Innis* reminds them to choose a very safe place for the feeders, away from hungry cats and squirrels.

### Discussion

*Ms. Innis* displays the following FI characteristics:

1. She instructs students in an impersonal way, lecturing and asking them questions.

2. She emphasizes abstract subjects, science in this case.

3. She is academically oriented.

4. She has students work independently at their tables.

5. She is socially detached, having minor interactions with students.

**FI Teacher:** *Ms. Irish*

**Level:** Grade 2                    **Subject Area:** Science

### Observation

The students are seated at their desks as *Ms. Irish* begins a large group discussion about the skill of "observing." She asks the question, "What does it mean to observe?"

Destinee raises her hand and answers, "It means to look at things."

Derek also raises his hand and responds, "It means to touch things too."

*Ms. Irish* uses these responses to further elaborate on the skill of observing. "We can use all of our senses when we observe. We can touch, smell, taste, listen, and see. Right?"

*Ms. Irish* then asks the students to work with their assigned partners to complete an observation activity. She hands each pair of students a brown lunch bag that has many different kinds of pasta inside the bag. She explains to the students that they are to observe the pasta in any way they think is appropriate.

One pair of students immediately calls out: "One looks like a bow tie!" *Ms. Irish* responds affirmatively, but then asks the students to work quietly with their partners.

*Ms. Irish* walks around the room, listening to student responses. After several minutes have passed, she calls the students' attention to the front of the room. "Please share with me and your class members what you have observed about your bag of pasta," *Ms. Irish* requests of the students.

The students are anxious to share their observations. "All of our pasta is hard," says Debbie.

"We have red pasta, green pasta, and yellow pasta," announces Dale.

"Not us! We have a bag of orange pasta!! YUCK!!!" says Inga.

*Ms. Irish* listens to several responses that have to do with what the students have seen before she asks, "Did anyone use your sense of taste to observe the pasta?"

One little girl (Diane) in the back of the class says, "Yes, we tried to eat our pasta, but it tasted yucky."

"What do you mean by yucky?" asks *Ms. Irish*.

"Well, it was boring and kind of didn't taste like anything," responds Diane.

"Did anyone smell the pasta?" *Ms. Irish* asks.

No one responds so *Ms. Irish* asks them all to smell their pasta. "Well," she asks, "how would you describe the smell?"

Danny says, "It smells like noodles."

Isidro disagrees. "I don't think it smells at all."

*Ms. Irish* praises the students for being such good observers and then explains that she is now going to ask them to do some heavy thinking.

"What would happen," *Ms. Irish* asks, "if we placed our bags of pasta in hot water?"

One little boy's (Ira) hand shoots up and he shouts, "It will turn into macaroni and cheese."

*Ms. Irish* says, "You're on the right track. Tomorrow we are going to put our pasta in hot water and then observe the changes that have occurred. What senses do you think we will want to use?"

Dale says, "When it's cooked, I'll want to taste it."

"That's a good idea," says *Ms. Irish*. "And we will also want to smell it, touch it, and look at it, too. Maybe some of you will want to listen to it while it is cooking."

**Discussion**

*Ms. Irish* displays the following FI characteristics:

1. She instructs students in an impersonal way (e.g., the students are at their desks during a discussion).

2. She emphasizes abstract subjects, science in this case.

3. She is academically oriented.

4. She is socially detached as she moves around the room listening to student responses and having minor interactions with them.

## GENERAL DISCUSSION

These observations show that teachers can be characterized in consistent ways when they conduct a variety of adaptive tasks. The observed differences are notable, in spite of the fact that teachers seem to be a homogeneous group.

From the point of view of theory construction and as an economical method of checking hypotheses about the teachers, it will be important to compare their performances in the presented observations with their approaches to tasks developed in the same classroom setting and from the same general matrix of thinking about perceptual phenomena and personality theory. The FD teachers used FD instructional behaviors while the FI teachers consistently used FI instructional behaviors. Although some instructional behaviors of their dominant cognitive styles were evident, there were more and most frequent instructional behaviors of their dominant cognitive styles. While the observations were focused on the teachers' behavior, the students in the teachers' classrooms also responded using characteristics of their dominant FDI cognitive styles.

Observations of the teachers were used as aids in formulating the hypotheses about the meaning of a particular kind of cognitive style preference. It was assumed, for instance, that teachers at the extremes of the dispersion relate themselves to the world about them in quite different ways in their preferred modes of teaching, in their ways of "knowing" the external world, and in their modes of affective response to their students.

## NOTES

1. Chapter 2 provides comparisons of the individuals' FD and FI characteristics.

2. The names of all teachers and children described have been changed to protect their privacy.

3. The *italic* letters identify the teacher who is being portrayed.

# Chapter 9

# Teachers' Instructional Behaviors

In ancient Greece, Plato used questions and dialogue to teach his students, while Aristotle created his model of imagery and associations as the foundation for learning and memory. They were great educators. Recently, attention has been focused on the competence criteria for teachers. Educators and researchers aim to explain how students learn as a result of teaching.

One of the things we have learned is that an optimal approach to instruction involves attention to each student on a personal level. Individual instruction allows for the transfer of information in a guided, supportive, and useful way. It reinforces the students' cognitive and affective learning and nurtures information-processing and integration. This chapter reviews the impact of the teachers' instructional behaviors in maximizing student involvement in learning.

Each early childhood teacher has his or her own personal instructional style. This may reflect the specifics of their preparation, their instructional situation, and the way they process information. Individual teachers also have their own ways of responding to their students. Learning style is broadly considered a subset of cognitive style. De Bello (1990) defined learning style as the way people absorb or retain information. Keefe (1986) broadened the definition, encompassing more than cognitive processes and also focusing it on affective and physiological behaviors that aid learners to perceive, interact with, and respond to the learning environment. Such a cognitive approach to teaching improves some of our basic concepts about teaching and its effects upon learning. A cognitive approach to teaching is cognitive style.

A teacher's cognitive style influences his/her preferred teaching style, developing a "format preference." It is assumed that a bias exists for most teachers that contributes to the unique characteristics of each teacher (Riding & Read, 1996). Effective teachers use a range of teaching strategies and choose those

**Table 9.1**
**Comparison of Field Independent and Field Dependent Teachers' Instructional Behaviors**

| Field Independent Teachers | Field Dependent Teachers |
|---|---|
| 1. are analytical; | 1. are global; |
| 2. use lecture as a means of instruction; | 2. use discussion as a means of instruction; |
| 3. assign tasks where students work by themselves; | 3. assign tasks where students work in groups; |
| 4. allow students to set up their own values and standards; | 4. set up values and standards for the students; |
| 5. are impersonal and socially detached with their students; | 5. have a strong interest in their students, respond to their emotional expressions, and like to have them around them; |
| 6. provide assignments where working with others is not essential; | 6. provide assignments which require involvement with others such as cooperative learning; |
| 7. focus on impersonal abstract subjects such as mathematics and science; | 7. focus on subject areas which relate most directly to people, such as social studies; |
| 8. teach using abstract content. | 8. teach using concrete content. |

most appropriate to tasks and content (OFSTED, 1993) based on their cognitive styles.

The field dependence independence dimension (FDI) of cognitive style differentiates the way field dependent (FD) and field independent (FI) teachers select their instructional strategies, materials, and interactions. Table 9.1 compares the teachers' instructional behaviors. Teachers and students continuously interact in a classroom setting. During this interaction, teachers negatively or positively influence the students' learning through their behavior. FD teachers focus on socialization goals. Conversely, FI teachers take a direct approach (Saracho, 1993). FI teachers employ intercessors during instruction when they abstract from their experiences and rely on general principles.

## CLASSROOM INSTRUCTION

Research shows that teacher personality may predict selected global teaching behaviors (e.g., Bush, 1986; Erdle, Murray, & Rushton, 1985; McCutcheon, Schmidt, & Bolden, 1991). For example, DeNovellis and Lawrence (1983) found that global (FD) classroom indicators (such as teacher-centered behaviors) related to those persons who focus on their own inner worlds, preferring to understand the world before experiencing it and to those individuals who become practical by accepting and working with what is "given" in the here and now. The students'-centered classroom behaviors, including making decisions, were based on person-centered values. Nonverbal, negative behaviors were given to those individuals who valued imagination, inspiration, new possibilities and ways of doing; to those individuals who made decisions based on person-centered values; and to those individuals who preferred flexibility and spontaneity.

Friction between teachers and students usually disturbs the teaching/learning experience. Such friction is often attributed to differences in personality between teachers and students. The difficulties experienced between teachers and students may be overcome if instructors and students are more similar in personality or if instructors modify their teaching styles in relation to their students' personalities (McDonald, 1984). Learning theorists have acknowledged the effects of personality in education. As early as 1932, Wheeler and Perkins (1932) noted that the teacher's personality was the means through which the students overcame those topics that they perceived as irrelevant.

Peoples' cognitive styles interact in interesting ways. The individuals' cognitive styles affect the behavior of others toward them. For example, psychotherapists may apply more understanding procedures to their FD patients than to their FI patients (Greene, 1972; Karp, Kissin, & Hustmyer, 1970). They utilize quite a different series of interpersonal relationships for FD and FI patients. Karp, Kissin, & Hustmyer (1970) also found different treatments for two kinds of alcohol patients. Therapists employed insight psychotherapy for FD patients and drug therapy for FI patients. Insight psychotherapy addresses a generally quick treatment where therapists advise their patients to capture insight into their problem. In contrast, drug therapy deals with an ongoing treatment where therapists prescribe to patients various kinds of drugs, mainly tranquilizers and antidepressants.

In regard to teaching, FD and FI teachers select different teaching strategies, conduct their classes differently, and exhibit different patterns of instructional behavior, based on the predominance of their FD or FI characteristics. Major differences are observed in the way teachers use lectures or discovery approaches, elicit questions or responses, facilitate the teaching or learning process, manage their classrooms, and interact with students.

### Lectures versus Discovery Approaches

The role of teachers' cognitive styles is important in the teaching-learning process (Emmerich, Oltman, & McDonald, cited in Witkin et al., 1977). Lyons (1985) found that the teachers' behaviors in teaching reflect their cognitive styles. Cognitive style stimulates the teachers' classroom behaviors, which compel either a more social or more personal orientation. Teachers' cognitive styles simulate the way they interact with others and select a more social or a more abstract curriculum content (Saracho, 1989f). FD and FI teachers' instructional behaviors represent cognitive style differences in actual classroom teaching. FD teachers interact with their students in small groups and individually, while FI teachers initiate academic interactions with their students as a whole class (Mahlios, 1981, 1990). Saracho (1987c) found that the teachers' cognitive styles can influence their instruction in a kindergarten classroom. The FD teacher studied provides simple, short, and concrete activities, whereas the FI teacher studied provides self-explanatory and self-corrected activities. The FD teacher taught in smaller groups than did the FI teacher. FD teachers believe in a student-centered approach, whereas FI teachers usually focus on teachers' standards.

The relationship between both cognitive style and the method of instruction and its relation to student performance in geography was examined by Grieve and Davis (1971). Eleven hours of instruction were provided to ninth-grade students, using one of two methods of instruction: discovery or exposition. In the discovery method the teachers presented the generalization to be learned as the initial step of the instructional sequence. They found that neither cognitive style nor method of instruction impacted on the students' acquisition of knowledge. However, FD males, who received expository instruction, had difficulty in gaining and applying the knowledge presented. In contrast, FI males were more successful.

Cognitive style influences both the cognitive and social elements in teachers' instructional styles. During instruction, FD teachers use discussion as a means of instruction, whereas FI teachers lecture as a means of instruction. Mahlios (1990) found that FI teachers use lecture and discovery techniques, while FD teachers use class discussion accomplished in private dyadic interactions. FI teachers use direct questioning techniques with students more than do FD teachers. In addition, FI teachers are less accepting and are more critical of students' answers than FD teachers.

These differences have important implications for early childhood teachers. It is assumed that young children need instruction that conforms to a more social and personal orientation. The teachers' cognitive styles influence whether teachers interact with others (peers or students) and their selection of a more social or a more abstract curriculum content.

Witkin et al.'s (1977) review of cognitive style research suggests that FD teachers create sensitive and personal learning atmospheres and motivate their students to generate their own personal goals to focus their learning. In contrast, FI teachers emphasize cognitive instructional elements instead of focusing on the social elements. Consequently, FI teachers offer instructional conditions that may be less sensitive to student needs and more impersonal. FD teachers utilize class discussion as an effective instructional strategy to reinforce learning. This strategy encourages social interaction and gives students the opportunity to establish their classroom status. For example, Wu (1968) discovered that FD student teachers used discussion rather than discovery approaches during social studies lessons. FI teachers use both lecture and discovery techniques as a form of instruction to facilitate and direct the students' learning or provide them with information. The teachers' instructional behaviors manifest that FD teachers personally interact with their students, while FI teachers are impersonal and focus on abstract cognitive elements.

### Questions versus Responses

Lecturing is an impersonal instructional strategy. According to Mahlios (1990), FI teachers use questions to introduce topics following students' answers. Moore (1973) found that chemistry teachers differ in the way they use rules, relationships, examples, and questions. FI teachers introduced topics and responded to the students' answers through questions, whereas FD teachers evaluated the students' learning after instruction through questions. Consequently, FD teachers used questions as a major means of assessing their students' learning after completing an instructional phase. FI teachers used questions within the context of a lecture as a discovery strategy. Their limited verbal interaction and student responses did not permit them to use discovery or discussion strategies. The FI teachers' questioning patterns of verbal teaching behaviors may be similar to teacher directiveness.

Emmerich, Oltman, and McDonald (cited in Witkin et al., 1977) determined that FD teachers used class discussions over teacher lectures and engaged their students in structuring the learning activity. In contrast, FI teachers used questioning to introduce new units, and responding to students' answers. The teacher's type of reinforcement is also related to his/her FDI. Mahlios (1990) found that FI teachers asked FD students a greater proportion of product-level questions. On a test, FD teachers used multiple-choice questions.

FD teachers focus on learning by initiating subject-oriented questions and assignments that they require their students to master. FI teachers utilize analytic questions to present topics and react to students' responses. Saracho (1987c) also found differences in the FD and FI teachers' reactions to their kindergarten students' responses. The FD teacher did not explicitly assess the students' responses. She rejected wrong responses and ignored correct responses by continuing to the next question. The FI teacher allowed her students plenty of time to respond to her questions, provided them with prompts, and facilitated their inferences to accurate replies. She proceeded to the following question only if students had trouble responding to the initial question (Saracho, 1987c). Witkin, Lewis, and Weil (1968) explained this dissimilarity in relation to a greater sense of separate identity of FI individuals; whereas FD individuals relied on others for self-definition.

According to Saracho (1987c), the way teachers use reinforcement relates to teacher directiveness. FI teachers correct the students' mistakes and tell them why specific responses are wrong, to reinforce their learning. FI teachers assume that corrective feedback provides students enough information to help them improve their performance. FI teachers employ feedback as an instructional technique to organize and direct the students' learning. FI teachers believe that negative assessment (e.g., expressing displeasure if a student achieves below his/her ability) is a productive instructional strategy. FI teachers focus on both corrective feedback and negative assessment when they criticize their students. FI teachers employ corrective feedback to show students their mistakes by telling them why they made a mistake. They believe this is an effective instructional technique. FI teachers criticize their students and make negative judgments of them (Saracho, 1988a). In spite of such criticisms, FI teachers may not express or feel hostile toward their students. Mahlios (1981) also notes that FI teachers use corrective feedback to improve their students' learning performance and criticize those students who are performing below their capability.

FD and FI teachers differ in how they respond to students' wrong answers (Jolly & Strawitz, 1984; Mahlios, 1981). Mahlios (1981, 1990) found that FD teachers interact more with their students in small groups and individually, while FI teachers introduce more academic interactions with their students as a whole class. FD teachers ask more factual questions, whereas FI teachers ask more analytic questions. FI teachers also solicit more academic questions than do FD teachers. Consequently, FI teachers stimulate their students to use principles in answering questions. FI teachers also correct the students' wrong responses and conceptually elaborate after the students have answered correctly. Apparently, FD and FI teachers vary in how they interact with their students in situations, in context, in conceptual level of instructional activity, and in the type of feedback they give to their students. The techniques the teachers employ in classroom teaching are based on the teachers' cognitive styles.

### Teaching-Learning Process

A component that accounts for most of the discrepancy in achievement is the student's conception of success in school. Students believe that good teachers are warm, friendly, supportive, and communicative; while at the same time orderly, highly motivating, and in charge of classroom discipline. They yearn for a teacher who manages discipline, but one who also promotes the learning of the subject matter by being supportive and friendly. These two characteristics seem to conflict with each other, but they are compatible. These characteristics influence how the teacher directs the class based on the subject, with teacher support and encouragement for the students' task-related activities. They guide the class away from irrelevant or sidetracking activities (Wittrock, 1987). This interpretation influences the students' achievement.

FI persons have a major interest in the abstract, the theoretical, and in structure. FI teachers are perceived by their students as encouraging them to apply principles, while FD teachers are perceived as teaching facts (Emmerich, Oltman, & McDonald, cited in Witkin et al., 1977; Mahlios, 1981).

Differences exist between FD and FI kindergarten teachers' cognitive styles and classroom instruction, including amount of time spent in activities (e.g., sharing time, small group instruction, individual instruction, independent work, seatwork, learning centers, outdoor play, and leaving the room for recess and lunch), instruction, schedule, learning centers, evaluation, and classroom management (Saracho, 1987c). The FD teacher exercises overt social control by requiring that students pay complete attention when she is talking, whereas the FI teacher controls the students by focusing on the rhythm of the students' activity and changing activities when the students are ready to change. The FD teacher has simple, short, and concrete activities, while the FI teacher has self-explanatory and self-corrected activities. Small group instruction is observed more in the FD teacher's classroom than in the FI teacher's classroom. The FD teacher has more learning centers than the FI teacher, but she provides more space and materials in each center. These kindergarten teachers differed in many ways, based on their cognitive styles.

Fifth-grade teachers use instructional techniques of explanation, discussion, and more sustained questioning. Fifth-grade FD teachers use mild social control techniques, such as redirecting, to manage their classes. Several of the performance characteristics of second-grade FD teachers are similar to the fifth-grade FI teachers (Ekstrom, 1976).

### Classroom Management

FI teachers' classrooms are more confined and less democratic, whereas FD teachers use less restricted classroom practices and focus on democratic procedures (Ohnmacht, 1967a, 1967b, 1968; Victor, 1976)). The classroom management techniques used during instruction time are related to teachers' cognitive styles. FD and FI kindergarten teachers identify appropriate classroom management as their major instructional goal; but they differ in their approaches to classroom management. In one study, the FD teacher closely supervises an activity with her students, more than the FI teacher. Both FD and FI teachers monitor their students' behavior, but the FD teacher circulates more around the room to provide a "tighter" supervision. According to the FD teacher, students need to be "watched closely" to keep them from getting out of control; whereas the FI teacher believes that interesting activities do not need supervision. FI teachers use a classroom structure where students work independently of the teacher. The FD teacher exercises overt social control by requiring the students' complete attention when she is talking. The FI teacher maintains control over the students by focusing on the rhythm of the students' activities and changing activities when the students are ready to change (Saracho, 1987c). Others have found that FD teachers are more concerned with maintaining behavioral control in the classroom than are the FI teachers (Ekstrom, 1976; Stone, 1976).

Apparently, the ways in which FD and FI teachers conduct their classes and perform in teaching situations differ in relation to their degrees of FDI. Stone (1976) found that FD teachers are more suitable for teaching in the lower grades. FD teachers use more direct instruction, practice, or review of skills and facts, and use more concrete instructional materials. Their instruction is frequently the spot check, question and answer type, and they use interactive techniques to redirect and manage their classroom environments.

## TEACHER-STUDENT INTERACTIONS

It is important to consider the interaction of the teachers' and students' cognitive styles in the classroom and the effects on the teaching-learning process.

### Teacher-Student Congeniality

An old but newly rekindled alternative method to studying teaching is to explore how teaching influences the students' thinking, which, in turn, influences their achievement. To understand teaching and its effects upon learning, researchers have developed and used different ways to relate teaching to student achievement.

The cognitive style of the teacher is as important as the cognitive style of the student in determining the outcome. Saracho (1991d) examined whether FD and FI students would systematically reflect a greater preference for task-oriented or socially oriented characteristics of teachers. She found that different characteristics are selected based on the cognitive style of the teacher. The interaction of the teachers' cognitive styles and the FDI teacher characteristics indicated that:

1. FD teachers should teach students about abstract topics such as stars and experiments.
2. FD teachers should like teaching.
3. FD teachers should be more impersonal and socially detached.
4. FI teachers should play and work more with children.

The results of Saracho's (1991d) study encourage teachers to acquire characteristics that are beyond the repertoire of their dominant cognitive style. She found that students preferred more FI teacher characteristics for FD teachers but students also preferred FD teacher characteristics for FI teachers. However, studies with older children promote FI characteristics. Fourth-grade FD and FI students prefer a FI cognitive style to a FD one in relation to conceptual performance (Thornell, 1977). Students favor FI strategies. Most teachers follow an academic curriculum that is abstract and requires students to use FI strategies. Students may be used to FI strategies, and their familiarity with these FI strategies may encourage them to select something they already know. However, students also may select a strategy that they themselves lack or perceive as one to be successful in their academic FI environment, especially since older students may be experiencing a more FI curriculum.

The variation of eleventh- and twelfth-grade students' perceptions of the "ideal" teacher (task-oriented or socially oriented teacher characteristics) indicates that FI students prefer the FI characteristic "conducts informative lectures'' and FD students prefer two of the task-oriented characteristics (''well-organized'' and ''clearly explains directions for assignments''). FD students value task-oriented teacher characteristics more highly than do FI students (Coward, Davis, & Wichern, 1978). When students designate the person possessing such cognitive style as a ''good teacher,'' FI teachers receive the highest evaluation. Dor-Shave and Peleg (1989) conclude that FI teachers are better liked than the FD teachers.

The teachers' cognitive styles affect their students' judgments of them. FD teachers receive more positive ratings than do FI teachers. In one study, FD teachers are better for FD students, whereas FI teachers are better for FI students (Packer & Bain, 1978). A series of studies show that the teachers' cognitive styles make a significant difference in the students' learning. For example, Saracho (1993) found that 5-year-old students of FI teachers achieve higher gains on a standardized achievement test over a one-year period. FI teachers have higher expectations for their FD students than do FD teachers. Therefore, the FI teachers' students achieve higher gains on a standardized achievement test than do the students of FD teachers (Saracho, 1980, 1991d, 1991e; Saracho & Dayton, 1980; Saracho & Spodek, 1981, 1986), which may have been affected by the expectations of the teacher (Rosenthal & Jacobson, 1968).

Higher expectations may enhance higher achievement scores. Teachers' expectations can bias student outcomes (Good, 1987) and can become self-fulfilling prophecies (Rosenthal & Jacobson, 1968). Some students sense that teachers have different expectations for the high-achieving and the low-achieving learners. Students' self-concepts prevail upon the teachers' expectations of their performance (Weinstein et al., 1982). Teachers need to understand that low expectations can induce some students to generate low academic self-concepts and refuse to attempt to succeed in school. On the positive side, high and sensible teacher expectations can entice some students to persist with hard but attainable school assignments and to raise their achievement. Teacher praise of students' academic performance should be utilized carefully to achieve these beneficial kinds of teacher expectations. More precisely, praise for successful completion of a simple assignment usually suggests that the teacher has low expectations for that student or a low estimate of that student's competence. Praise for success at a demanding assignment denotes a high estimate of the student's competence. Further, the teacher needs to be sensitive to the ways students receive and interpret feedback. The interpretation, not the teachers' meaning, affects achievement (Wittrock, 1987).

Teachers' instructional behaviors toward individual students depend on the expectations they form for them. The students' responses are influenced by the teachers' performance, requirements, and expectations (Brophy & Good, 1972, 1986; Saracho, 1991d). Teachers instruct students in relation to their expectations of their students' competence. Teachers' high expectations for students, interest in them, and regard for those students promotes their learning performance. However, when teachers have low expectations and an elusive interest, the performance of those students diminishes. The teachers' low expectations negatively influence their students' achievement. Teachers present these students with learning opportunities that disregard their abilities and provide them with negative feedback about their academic work and classroom behavior. In contrast, for those students for whom teachers expect high achievement, they offer conditions and alternatives that only support the high achievers' learning (Saracho, 1991d; Weinstein, 1983, 1985; Weinstein et al., 1982). Students acquire refined interpretations (Weinstein, 1983) of their teachers' behaviors, attitudes, expectations, and differential treatment toward them (Brattesani, Weinstein, & Marshall, 1984), which may reinforce or reduce the students' self-concept and classroom performance. Teachers improve the students' academic performance when they provide a high quality of teacher praise.

Persons differ in their abilities to learn and perform. Their unique differences must be considered in teaching and learning. This study examined individual differences in the FDI dimension which underlie two different modes of cognitive functioning. FI teachers were more effective than FD teachers (Saracho & Dayton, 1980). FI teachers perceive their FD students more positively, while FD teachers perceive their FI students more negatively (Saracho, 1980). Consequently, FI teachers' expectations were higher for their FD students than the FD teachers' expectations for their FD students. The teachers' perceptions of their students according to teacher-student cognitive style affect the students' academic success. Saracho and Spodek (1981) suggest the following assignments (in order of priority) for second- and fifth-grade students:

1. FI teachers–FI students

2. FI teachers–FD students

3. FD teachers–FI students

4. FD teachers–FD students

Since FI students perform better than do FD students with FI teachers, Frank and Davis (1982), Jolly and Strawitz (1984), and Packer and Bain (1978) recommend similar assignments as those suggested by Saracho and Spodek (1981). Although FI students may be taught by and may achieve equally well with either FD or FI teachers, FD students are more successfully taught by FI teachers than by FD teachers.

The teachers' perceptions of their students based on teacher-student cognitive style suggest important relationships among the cognitive styles of teachers and students and the students' gender (Saracho, 1982a). See Table 9.2 for a comparison of the teachers' perceptions of their male and female students based on the teachers' and students' cognitive styles. Saracho's (1982a) study shows the following:

**Table 9.2**
**Comparison of the Teachers' Perceptions of Their Male and Female Students Based on the Teachers' and Students' Cognitive Styles**

| Cognitive Style of Teachers | Cognitive Style of Students | Teachers' Perceptions of Males | Teachers' Perceptions of Females |
|---|---|---|---|
| FD | FD | – | – |
| FD | FI | – | + |
| FI | FI | – | similar to rest |
| FI | FD | + | – |

*Legend*:
– = Underestimated
+ = Overestimated

1. FD teachers underestimate both FD male and FI female students.
2. FD teachers underestimate FI male students but overestimate FI female students.
3. FI teachers underestimate FI male students and assess their FI female students according to their scores on a standardized achievement test.
4. FI teachers overestimate FI male students but underestimate FI female students.

Evidently, the best situation is FD male students with FI teachers and FI female students with both FD and FI teachers. The following assignments may be a disadvantage for students:

1. FD teachers with FD male and female students.
2. FD and FI teachers with FI male students.
3. FI teachers with FD female students.

These results suggest that the teachers' perceptions of students are influenced by both cognitive style and gender. Such perceptions can have important educational consequences.

Teachers' cognitive styles and their perceptions of their first- and third-grade students differ according to cognitive style and grade level. First-grade FD and FI teachers underestimate both their FD and FI students. Third-grade FD teachers overestimate both FD and FI students, but third-grade FI teachers perceive both their FD and FI students according to their scores on a standardized test (Saracho, 1983d). Preschool teachers categorize their FD and FI students into four characteristics: attachment, indifference, concern, and rejection. FD teachers are more concerned for their students than are FI teachers.

FD teachers are more "satisfied with" and "enjoy more" their students, give their students higher grades, and perceive their students as exerting "more meaningful effort." FD students are sensitive to some differences related to teacher style, and they find their interactions with FD teachers more satisfying and enjoyable (Renninger & Snyder, 1983).

## Identifying Students' Cognitive Styles

Educators are perpetually pursuing innovative instructional techniques to improve learning. Students refine information and accumulate abilities in numerous diverse modes. These variations fluctuate from realms in individuals' intelligence, drives, abilities, and achievements as well as personal, family, and cultural influences. Acknowledgment and acceptance of the students' individual characteristics in motivation, intelligence, interests, and needs add personal and social adaptation through activating several styles in the learning process. A determinant in effective teaching is the proficiency to identify and understand these variations and to plan instruction and materials that are appropriate to the students' learning needs.

Students learn better and enjoy learning more when teachers use the students' own learning styles in implementing their instructional strategies. Teachers need to implement an optimum diversity of instructional strategies, materials, and activities in order to employ a variety of the students' cognitive styles to give them an opportunity to succeed. Students enjoy the learning process when their learning styles are used in planning what they have to learn and how it should be evaluated. Learning can be enjoyed when students can use their learning styles to express themselves and when they are encouraged to determine the more acceptable learning styles. Fulfillment is gained from learning pursuits when a student realizes that his/her learning style is respected by peers and teachers (Bhasin, 1987).

Teachers can recognize students' cognitive style characteristics through observation. They can then diagnose the students' cognitive styles to plan their instruction. There is a relationship among instructional strategy, cognitive style, and learning performance. Business and industrial trainers communicate with trainees more effectively by identifying learning styles with appropriate strategies for teaching and learning (Ash, 1986).

Educational outcomes can be improved when instruction is designed to accommodate the students' learning needs and their cognitive styles are considered a worthwhile characteristic (Trout & Crawley, 1985). Kolb (1984) argued that different learning environments require different skills of learners. Hodges and Evans (1983) cited studies to support their contention that learning is more proficient when students are presented with information that matches their cognitive styles. However, Halphin and Peterson (1986) debated the recommendation that the learners' stylistic characteristics facilitate the planning of individualistic instruction. Teachers make choices and decisions about instruction that are guided by three major considerations: the learning process, knowledge of the learner, and knowledge of the content (Rink, 1985). Although teachers cannot force students to learn or achieve success in school, they can manipulate the elements that affect learning. Teachers' behavior, selection of materials, and manipulation of the environment influence the students' learning. Teachers can give individual students experiences that will permit them to achieve their fullest potential (Pettigrew & Buell, 1989).

## SUMMARY

At this point, sufficient evidence exists to support the concept that FD students learn more from a didactic instructional approach, where rules and principles are explicitly stated rather than induced. Teachers may optimize the learning of subject matter at the price of neglecting individual differences, providing FD students with various learning alternatives whereby students learn to use a discovery approach in an educational setting. Teachers must avoid the exclusive preoccupation of concentrating on mastery of subject matters. They must consider the students' individual modes of thinking as well. Education must be responsive to the individual differences of students to provide more educational opportunities to all students, regardless of their strengths and needs.

Chapter 10

# Matching Teachers and Students

Individuals differ in the ways in which they process information from the environment. Educators and researchers have acknowledged the need to adapt instructional situations and strategies to students' learning characteristics.

Differences in the teachers' instructional behaviors and students' learning relate to their degree of field dependence independence (FDI). The teachers' and students' cognitive styles prompt their choices of specific instructional strategies. The interaction of these individuals' cognitive styles in the classroom affects the teaching-learning process. Classroom interactions generate differences in student and teacher behaviors in connection to their field dependent (FD) and field independent (FI) cognitive styles. Thus, their cognitive styles direct their understanding of the teaching and learning experience. For example, FD teachers and students choose situations that compel independently generated problem-solving strategies. FI teachers and students are content-oriented, though FD teachers and students distribute a greater interpersonal orientation (Witkin et al., 1977). Consequently, the content orientation preference of the FI students is probably not well accepted by FD teachers and the interpersonal orientation of the FD students is probably unproductive in the classroom of a FI teacher. The situation may be similar to learning and memory tasks. Teachers who devise and implement instructional strategies that are compatible with their own cognitive styles alter learning in a positive or negative manner based on their students' cognitive styles.

Teachers respond differently in their instructional approach based on their cognitive styles. FD teachers employ more discussion and discovery approaches to foster interpersonal relations. In contrast, FI teachers employ more lecturing, a direct approach that diminishes interpersonal interactions. Both teachers' and students' cognitive styles and their effects on the teaching-learning process must be considered. Both teachers and students have their own cognitive styles and favor specific strategies. Teachers' and students' interactions will vary when teachers and students match or mismatch in cognitive style. Such interactions will be discussed based on an educational matching model.

## THE MATCH

A "match" suggests harmony between a specific person and his/her environment. Learning style theory considers the uniqueness of individual differences while focusing on a variety of conditions, modes, and environments that each individual may prefer. Proponents of learning style suggest that matching students' learning styles with instructional styles facilitates students' learning (Pettigrew & Buell, 1989). Hodges and Evans's (1983) review of three instructional styles contends that learning is more productive when students are presented with information that matches their cognitive styles. Halphin and Peterson (1986) recommend that it is theoretically sound to consider the stylistic characteristics of learners' individualistic instruction. The issue concerning the "matching hypothesis" was proposed several decades ago by Witkin (1965). He speculated that "when students are matched with their preferred instructional mode, achievement and satisfaction with learning will be enhanced" (Hudak, 1985, p. 405). An effective match needs to satisfy and stimulate students (Saracho, 1990b) and be contemporaneous and developmental (Hunt, 1971, 1978). A contemporaneous match assists individuals to employ the skills they have in their repertoire, disregarding new concepts or strategies to manage environmental demands. A developmental match, on the other hand, requires the development of new concepts and strategies.

Researchers differ on the way they define the "match." Some have found that the students' cognitive styles should be matched (1) to teachers with similar cognitive styles (DiStefano, 1970; Mahlios, 1990; Saracho, 1984b, 1988e, 1990b; Stasz, Shavelson, Cox, & Moore, 1976); (2) with those teachers who have cognitive styles that foster the students' learning (Saracho, 1988e, 1990b; Saracho & Dayton, 1980; Saracho & Spodek, 1981, 1994); (3) with matching achievement styles to instructional environments (Ross, 1980); (4) with teachers' cognitive style responses to teaching skills (Winnie & Marx, 1980); and (5) to teachers' preferred teaching styles (Reiff, 1982; Saracho, 1991d). Different matching strategies describe the FDI cognitive styles of teachers and students.

### Educational Desirability

Underlying the concern for teaching and learning styles is the belief that adapting the teachers' approach to instruction to the students' approach to learning leads to (1) better individual learning (achievement) and/or (2) higher teacher ratings (satisfaction). The teachers' approaches to their students' relationships may be influenced by their way of building rapport and facilitating interaction in the educational setting. The suggestion that there is an interaction between teaching and learning styles is compelling. Learning competence supports the capacity for learning style, which depends partially on the ways students are treated in school and how the students respond to that treatment (Bhasin, 1987). Meredith (1985) found a relationship between instructors' teaching styles and students' learning styles.

Generally, researchers match teachers and students to examine their perceptions of each other. Positive and negative effects relate to a match that should improve student learning (Witkin et al., 1977). The literature on teaching styles acknowledges a range of outcomes and considerations. Moran (1991) believes there are two reasons for these differences: (1) the hypothesis is vague and (2) studies on the matching hypothesis do not control for possible differences in *ability* between the students involved. In addition, Witkin et al. (1977) concede that "for certain kinds of learning content a contrast in styles between teacher and student may be more stimulating than similarity" (p. 36), because heterogeneity generates a diversity of viewpoints. Saracho and Dayton (1980) advocate the "mismatching" view. They found that while a cognitive style match is beneficial to FI students, a mismatch is useful to FD students. However, studies that fail to control for possible differences in *ability* between the students involved are difficult to interpret.

Cognitive psychological research (e.g., Campione, Brown, & Bryant, 1985) demonstrates that higher-ability students monitor their own learning better than lower-ability cohorts. Contrasts in "metacognition" (i.e., our awareness and knowledge of our own mental skills) influence the appropriateness of people's self-reported selections for different learning environments. Thus, learning styles may be confused with abilities (metacognitive abilities). The current status of this hypothesis should be to match students to what is educationally advantageous for them.

The educational desirability of matching teachers and students according to cognitive styles is supported by several researchers (e.g., Witkin et al., 1977; Saracho, 1980, 1988e; Saracho & Spodek, 1981, 1986, 1994). *Identical matching style* and *performance matching style* are two major configurations in matching teachers and students (Saracho, 1988e).

*Identical matching style* is an appropriate and effective matching style. Teachers and students with identical matching cognitive styles have similar content and psychological structures. Their instructional strategies are congruent with their students' internalized modes of thinking and problem solving (Saracho, 1990b). When teachers with the same cognitive styles as their students teach concepts, they are able to define and extend when they teach concepts. Both FD teachers and students discriminate less among concepts than do FI teachers and students (Stasz et al., 1976).

Individuals with identical cognitive styles see one another in a highly positive manner, while individuals who differ in cognitive styles perceive one another in a negative manner (DiStefano, 1970; Folman, 1973; Greene, 1972; Mahlios, 1990). Extreme FD and extreme FI male teachers and students who match in cognitive styles perceive each other more favorably when assessing their personal characteristics (e.g., potency, activity, rationality, uniqueness, sociability) and cognitive competence (DiStefano, 1970).

Matching produces a positive effect on interpersonal attraction (Mahlios, 1990). The positive and negative assessments of teachers and students are influenced by both the individuals' personal and cognitive characteristics. Mahlios (1990) and James (1973) found greater interpersonal attraction with teachers and students who were matched in their cognitive styles. Extremely FI teachers rated all three of their FI students higher than their three FD students. Conversely, extreme FD teachers assigned the three highest grades to their three FD students (James, 1973). The DiStefano, James, and Mahlios studies strengthen the idea that a teacher-student match in cognitive style promotes greater interpersonal attraction than does the mismatch.

The teachers' higher assessments of their matched students may promote better student performance. However, since only teacher assessments of the students were reported, this possibility is still based on subjectivity. When teachers and students are matched in cognitive styles to teach and learn mathematical concepts, the FD and FI match is more effective in the teaching-learning situation. FD teachers are better for FD students, and FI teachers are better for FI students (Packer & Bain, 1978). Apparently, an identical cognitive style match is important where FD teachers match their FD students and FI teachers match their FI students. Saracho (1984b) reports that identical matching in cognitive styles is better with young children. However, a FI match is better than a FD match with an identical cognitive style match (Saracho, 1980, 1984b; Saracho & Dayton, 1980; Saracho & Spodek, 1981; 1986, 1994). McDonald (1984) concludes that matching students and instructors by FDI traits would be beneficial for only a small proportion of students' greater academic success. Apparently, FD teachers are better than FI teachers for FD students; although FI teachers are better for FI students.

The conclusions on identical matching on cognitive style can be argued. A few studies exist from which to generalize on the importance of identical matching in cognitive style. A match may be appropriate for some situations such as when it is important to be supportive and provide comfort. However, it may lack motivation to succeed. Pettigrew and Heikkinen (1985) propose ''style expansion,'' that is, broadening the individual's learning styles. Such an approach emphasizes the need for an eclectic approach to teaching. Different learning environments require different skills of the learners (Kolb, 1984). The mismatch of cognitive styles may provide enrichment, challenge, and stimulation for both teachers and students. Therefore, the mismatching of cognitive styles may become a performance-matching style, as described in the next section.

*Performance matching style* refers to the assignment of students with a certain cognitive style to a teacher who has a particular cognitive style that will foster the student's learning. The matching hypothesis increases the promise to improve educational outcomes if instruction is adapted to the students' learning

**Table 10.1**
**Matching Teachers' Cognitive Styles to Their Students'**

| Students' Age | Teachers | Perceptions |
|---|---|---|
| 3 | FD | underestimated M and MM students |
| 3 | FI | underestimated M and MM students |
| 4 | FD & FI | overestimated M and MM students, but assigned MM students higher values |
| 5 | FD | perceived in a negative way MM students |
| 5 | FI | perceived in a positive way MM students |

*Legend*:
M = matched
MM = mismatched

needs based on their cognitive style characteristics (Trout & Crawley, 1985). According to Ash (1986), a relationship exists among instructional strategies, cognitive styles, and learning performance. She describes how business and industrial trainers are able to reach trainees more effectively by using appropriate strategies for teaching and learning. According to McDonald (1984), instructors should evaluate their own personality type (FDI) and be knowledgeable as to its impact on students' academic achievement.

Pettigrew, Bayless, Zakrajeck, and Goc-Karp (1985) compared students' assessments of teaching performance to those whose selection for learning styles is specifically matched and specifically mismatched with their instructors' favorite teaching styles. There were consequences of combining different matched and mismatched dyads: two FI, two FD, or one FD and one FI (Oltman et al., 1975). After the dyads had settled a dispute between them, individuals evaluated the extent to which they liked each other. FI dyads disputed in reaching a solution and differed more than FD dyads, whereas FD dyads constantly changed their minds. FI individuals made most of the decisions in mixed dyads (FD/FI). After the session, FI dyads liked each other less than FD or FD/FI dyads. Frank and Davis (1982) found that matched dyads with FI students were more effective than matched dyads with FD students. The interactions of teachers and students in an educational setting predict a variety of consequences based on their cognitive styles. According to Packer and Bain (1978), the students' feelings about their teachers relate to their teachers' cognitive styles, with the more FD teachers receiving more positive ratings than the more FI teachers.

Cognitive style and teacher-student compatibility make a difference in an educational setting. This difference describes the comparable satisfaction and performance both perceive. Saracho (1988f) reports the following results on the teachers' cognitive styles and the importance of matching students (ages three to five). Table 10.1 shows the teachers' perceptions of their matched and mismatched students. Saracho (1993) found that the matches of FI 5-year-old students had the highest scores on a standardized achievement test. A year later, both matched and mismatched students of FI teachers achieved higher scores than those of the FD teachers. Saracho's (1983d) study found similar results with first- and second-grade teachers. Both first-grade FD and FI teachers underestimate their matched and mismatched students, whereas third-grade FD teachers overestimate their mismatched students, and third-grade FI teachers assess their matched students similarly to a standardized test. The teachers' perceptions of their matched and mismatched students are also influenced by the students' genders. FD teachers underestimate both their matched male and female students but underestimate their female students more. In a teacher-student mismatch, FD teachers overestimate their female students but underestimate their male students more so than they do with both their matched male and female students.

In contrast, FI teachers' assessments of their matched female students are comparable to their scores on a standardized achievement test but lower for their matched male students. However, FI teachers overestimate their mismatched male students and underestimate their mismatched female students (Saracho, 1983d).

When FI teachers and FD teachers exhibit their different instructional behaviors, students can concentrate on the use of respective teaching styles within the classroom and select the characteristics they prefer in an ''ideal'' teacher. FD and FI students' preferences for some characteristics of their ideal teachers support performance matching style. FI students do not favor teachers with socially oriented characteristics, whereas FD students show more of a preference than do FI students for teacher characteristics reflecting a FI cognitive style (Coward, Davis, & Wichern, 1978; Saracho, 1990b). Matched dyads with FI students perform better than matched dyads with FD students in a communication task (Frank & Davis, 1982). Students of FI teachers attain greater achievement gains than do students of FD teachers (Saracho & Dayton, 1980; Saracho & Spodek, 1981, 1986, 1994). Packer and Bain (1978) recommend that the importance of cognitive style matching in relation to student achievement must be explored further.

Differences in the teachers' expectations of their matched and mismatched students are related to their cognitive styles. FI teachers have been found to have higher expectations for their mismatched students (Saracho, 1980, 1991c; Saracho & Spodek, 1981, 1986) and FD teachers expect more from their matched students (Saracho, 1991d). Teacher expectations, however, can vary with age. Saracho and Spodek (1994) found that FD teachers underestimate their matched 3-year-old students but underestimate their 3-year-old mismatched students even more; whereas FI teachers underestimate their matched children more than they underestimate their mismatched children; FD and FI teachers overestimate 4-year-old students in both groups, but rate their mismatched 4-year-old students higher; and FD teachers perceive their 5-year-old mismatched students more negatively than their 5-year-old matched students, although FI teachers perceive their mismatched 5-year-old students more positively than the FD teachers.

Higher expectations are related to higher achievement scores. Teachers' expectations have been found to bias student outcomes (Good, 1987). Teachers' expectations can become self-fulfilling prophecies (Rosenthal & Jacobson, 1968). When individuals know what others expect of them, their behavior conforms to this pattern. Thus, what the teacher expects in the classroom influences the students' behavior. Teachers who expect certain students to improve their academic performance will find that those students will perform well; whereas teachers who do not expect certain students to perform well academically will find that those students will perform poorly (Rosenthal & Jacobson, 1968; Saracho, 1991c).

Teachers treat individual students based on the expectations they form for them. The students respond according to the teachers' performance demands and expectations (Brophy & Good, 1972, 1986; Saracho, 1991c). Teachers instruct students in regard to their expectations of their students' ability (Dusek, 1975). When teachers' expectations for students are high, they develop an interest in them and attend to those students; but if the teachers' expectations are low, their interest in those students diminishes, depreciating their performance. The teachers' low expectations negatively affect their students' achievement. Teachers offer these students learning opportunities that are nonchallenging and provide negative feedback in relation to their academic work and classroom behavior (Weinstein, 1983, 1985; Weinstein, Marshall, Brattesani, & Middlestadt, 1982). On the other hand, for those students on whom teachers project high achievement expectations, they provide situations and choices that nourish the high achievers' learning (Weinstein, 1983, 1985; Weinstein et al., 1982). The teachers' behaviors indicate to students the differential treatment and their teachers' expectations (Brattesani, Weinstein, & Marshall, 1984), providing students with refined interpretations of their teachers' expectations (Weinstein, 1983). The teachers' attitudes may enhance or diminish the students' self-concepts as well as their classroom performance. Students who receive a high level of teacher praise improve their academic performance, but those who are ignored or criticized do not achieve as well.

FI students can achieve equally well in biology either with teachers who match or mismatch their cognitive styles, but FD students obtain a higher achievement with a teacher who mismatches their cognitive style (Jolly & Strawitz, 1984). FI teachers are more effective than FD teachers with both FD and FI students. Thus, Frank and Davis (1982), Jolly and Strawitz (1984), Saracho (1980), Saracho and Dayton (1980), and Saracho and Spodek (1981, 1994) support matching students based on their performance style; that usually means providing them with a FI teacher. Data from these studies suggest that for achievement purposes, the performance cognitive style match is better than the identical cognitive style match. Perhaps, in these studies, FD students benefited from some of the FI teachers' skills. According to Coward et al. (1978), FD students may acknowledge or be conscious of their lack of the obvious characteristics that they need to consciously counteract their own weaknesses. For example, Marshall (1985) found that in counseling situations clients choose counselors whose counseling strategies either coincide with or differ from their own learning styles. Some clients select the counseling technique that does not match their learning style. However, clients who are more abstract learners choose either the rational or the behavioral strategies, although clients who are more concrete learners choose client-centered or experiential strategies. According to Humphries, Elam, and Metzler (1988), a student may prefer one learning style but has the ability to use other styles. Likewise, the instructor may have the ability to switch teaching styles for different students.

The performance cognitive style matching should not be considered as "opposite characteristics attract." It may be, as discussed earlier, a result of students choosing those characteristics that they yearn for themselves or of the reality that schools are academic-oriented rather than socially oriented. Their success requires them to possess FI characteristics (Saracho, 1990b). However, Doebler and Eicke (1979) believe the interpersonal relations between teachers and students can be improved without any type of matching. Beyond the demand of the educational structure, student outcomes may be improved through activities regarding questioning skills and evaluating students' performance. Teachers are responsible for providing a diverse, rich environment from which students select activities or for strategically merging activities into each lesson to meet the students' needs as well as to stimulate them to improve an area of their preference (Turner, 1993).

Challenging students to think should be integrated in their education. An analytical (FI) instructional strategy stimulates the students' capacity for critical thinking (Humphries, Elam, & Metzler, 1988). Teachers also need to be concerned for the individual students' feelings and learning goals. Teachers can provide instruction that is appropriate for and interesting to their students. They can be informed of the educational consequences of the students' unique cognitive styles. In addition, the possibility still exists that teachers and students do better under either identical matching style or performance matching style conditions. When grouping teachers and students, teachers may in fact do better with students with an identical matching cognitive style, while students may learn more effectively with a performance matching style (Saracho, 1990b).

## SUMMARY

From the educators' point of view, FD or FI students may be at a disadvantage in a particular classroom if they are with a teacher who has the cognitive style characteristics that do not reinforce their learning. Individual differences in the FDI characteristics bias the understanding of the students' satisfaction, which can impact on their classroom performance (Renninger & Snyder, 1983). Acknowledgment of such divergences and some recognition for their consequences merit attention in any effort to design classroom learning experiences. Instructional schemes and the interpersonal classroom environment can profit from sensitivity to the influence of students' and teachers' cognitive styles. The concept that a person's learning style is the result of deeply embedded structures suggests that a person's learning style is somewhat stable (Lyons, 1985).

Practitioners and researchers generate a perplexing structure of relationships in an attempt to improve the students' learning performance and/or attitudes utilizing cognitive style matches between teachers and students. The cited studies explain that the matching relationship is subtle. The perplex structure of the match is represented in such studies as Grieve and Davis (1971), Saracho (1980, 1990b, 1991c, 1991d), Saracho and Dayton (1980), and Saracho and Spodek (1981, 1986, 1994). The conflicting results in the studies make it an obstacle for researchers to generalize, though these results stimulate them to continue exploring this important area and for educators to consider the match effects in their curriculum planning.

The present challenge is to recognize the characteristics and competence that are unique to FD and FI persons and the importance of identical cognitive style matching or performance cognitive style matching; becoming aware of the educational ramifications of the different cognitive styles can enrich the relationship between teachers and students (Doebler & Eicke, 1979). Knowledge of cognitive style can facilitate the teachers' decisions in determining which cognitive style is more appropriate in certain situations. It is also important to foster an appreciation of each cognitive style, along with teaching interests, strategies, content, and materials to capitalize on the characteristics of the teachers' and students' different cognitive styles (Saracho, 1990b).

# Part IV

# Future Directions

Chapter 11

# Preparation of Early Childhood Teachers

Early childhood educators and researchers of cognitive style have suggested that FD persons are better teachers of younger children because of their warmth, nurturance, and social skills, providing them with a warm relationship to enhance young students' learning. However, when academic achievement is the major goal in the early childhood education program, FI teachers are more effective teachers of young children. Possibly, if socialization is the major goal, FD teachers may be more effective (Saracho & Spodek, 1981, 1986).

The ways teachers and students interact in the classroom can either promote or stifle students' learning. FD persons are strongly interested in people and in social affairs. Thus, FD teachers concentrate on social affairs and social goals in the classroom. In contrast, FI teachers are socially detached, impersonal, and oriented toward active striving. Their focus in the classroom is cognitive achievement.

Since teachers' cognitive styles influence their students' learning, it is important that cognitive style characteristics be considered in selecting and preparing teachers. McCutcheon, Schmidt, and Bolden (1991) identified specific teaching behaviors (e.g., demonstrates knowledge in the subject area being taught, uses procedures to gain initial class attention, emphasizes feedback to provide specific information for improvement) that are associated with personality type. These findings shed light on who are best suited for the different specialties in the teaching profession. Future research on personality and successful classroom performance may yield information that can be used to refine admission and advising practices for early childhood teacher education programs. Selection policies must be related to the goals of the early childhood education programs. For example, if social goals are the major foci, FD teachers might be selected; but if academic goals are the major foci, FI teachers might be selected.

Most early childhood education programs combine social and academic goals. Thus, the selection of only FD or only FI teachers cannot be justified. Social and academic goals can be merged by training teachers to achieve what Saracho and Spodek (1986) refer to as "cognitive flexibility."

## INSTRUCTIONAL STRATEGIES

FD and FI teachers typically use different instructional strategies. While FD persons are competent with social interactions, the application of theory in actual teaching situations and the ability to analyze problems are difficult because FD persons are restricted in their ability to perceive items without being influenced by the background environment (Partridge, 1983). However, teachers can implement different instructional strategies to facilitate learning for children with different cognitive styles. For example, observational learning experiences incorporate the spectator tendencies of the FD person.

FI persons can understand theoretical knowledge and apply it to several situations. Teaching strategies should emphasize situations that stimulate students. For instance, allowing the FI students to physically manipulate unfamiliar materials and demonstrate their use as they actively imitate the learning process instead of just observing or listening.

FD teachers more often use questions to assess students' learning after finishing an instructional phase (Moore, 1973). They also use class discussions instead of lectures (Emmerich, Oltman, & MacDonald, cited in Witkin, Moore, Goodenough, & Cox, 1977). FD teachers use mild social control strategies, such as redirecting to guide their classes (Stone, 1976). FD and FI teachers prefer different classroom interactions and provide different kinds of feedback to their students. FD teachers interact with individual students and in small groups, whereas FI teachers interact in an academic way with their students as a whole class (Mahlios, 1981, 1990). FD teachers engage their students in structuring the learning activities, but FI teachers do not. FI teachers use questions as instructional tools to introduce new units and to respond to students' answers (Emmerich, Oltman, & McDonald, cited in Witkin et al., 1977). FD teachers ask factual questions, but FI teachers ask analytic and academic questions (Mahlios, 1981, 1990). FD teachers prompt their students to apply theoretical principles.

The degree of reinforcement varies with FD and FI teachers. FI teachers use feedback to correct the students' errors (negative assessment) and explain underlying errors to promote the students' learning (Emmerich, Oltman, & MacDonald, cited in Witkin et al., 1977). If students cannot provide correct answers, FI teachers respond with corrective feedback statements. If students provide correct answers, FI teachers conceptually elaborate on their answers as part of their feedback.

**Table 11.1**

**Instructional Approaches of FD Teachers and FI Teachers**

| FD Teachers | FI Teachers |
| --- | --- |
| 1. design warm and personal surroundings; | 1. design socially detached surroundings; |
| 2. encourage students to set up their own goals and direct their own learning; | 2. initiate and focus students' learning; |
| 3. employ discussion to encourage students' learning; | 3. employ lectures to foster students' learning; |
| 4. interact with their students; | 4. teach in situations that are impersonal in nature; |
| 5. focus on concrete instructional elements; | 5. focus on abstract instructional elements; |
| 6. struggle on affective components. | 6. struggle on cognitive components. |

Adapted from Saracho (1989f).

In relation to classroom control, FD teachers emphasize behavioral control in the classroom (Ekstrom, 1976). FD teachers practice more control in the classroom for instruction, classroom management, evaluation, activities, and supervision of classroom. In contrast, FI teachers promote more freedom in the classroom (Saracho, 1987c). FD and FI teachers vary in the ways they provide instruction for the different grade levels and subject areas. They select the teaching styles that are appropriate in meeting the requirements of the instructional task (Ekstrom, 1976). Differences in approaches to instruction between FD and FI teachers are summarized on Table 11.1.

Teachers tend to use instructional strategies that they feel most comfortable with and believe to be more effective. Research on teachers' cognitive styles indicates that teachers select instructional methods that are consistent with their cognitive styles. Cognitive styles influence the persons' cognitive *preferences* (their likes and situations), *motivation*, and *personality* (Good & Stipek, 1983). Cognitive style affects *how* teachers teach rather than *how effectively* they teach.

## LEARNING STRATEGIES

The choices and decisions that teachers make about instructional strategies must be guided by three major considerations: the learning process, knowledge of the learners, and knowledge of the content (Rink, 1985). Teachers cannot coerce students into learning or promise that students will succeed in their learning, even if they do control the elements that stimulate students to learn. Saracho (1991d, 1993) found that the cognitive style of the *teacher* made the most difference in the students' outcomes, rather than if the teacher and students were matched in cognitive style. Teachers' behaviors, selection of materials, and command of the environment influence the students' learning. Thus, teachers have the responsibility to offer each of the students experiences that will provide them the opportunity to learn to their fullest potential (Pettigrew & Buell, 1989). Teachers need to know the learning strategies of FD and FI students and promote their learning based on the students' cognitive styles.

### FD Learning Strategies

Recognizing and implementing FD persons' strengths and identifying problem areas are essential for effective performance. FD teacher candidates develop a strong, therapeutic, interpersonal relationship with those students who have learning problems. Thus, they become effective in assisting students to gain interest and self-management with learning changes such as engaging in a social role or social studies assignment. However, such a student may have difficulty implementing and analyzing the new, different skills that are required to solve mathematical problems; both the interpersonal and monitoring components are essential for the students' care. Teachers must recognize the effective interpersonal interactions and help the students to devise a work flow sheet or schedule to monitor tasks. The self-devised work flow sheets can serve as concrete, external referents for information processing (Witkin et al., 1977). These teaching strategies help FD students to organize their work in the classroom.

Guided discovery learning can provide FD persons with the structure they need without stifling creativity and analytic abilities. FD persons can use a checklist to guide them in performing a physical assessment or reviewing a student's chart to obtain information. Finally, repeated practice to identify details from the "global picture" of a situation helps FD persons to consciously change their perceptual abilities and to maximize their learning experiences (Ismeurt, Ismeurt, & Miller, 1992).

Clearly delineated evaluation measures (e.g., checklists with performance objectives) help FD persons. FD students need structured environments, but they need to be involved in establishing goals for satisfying and successful outcomes. Before a formal evaluation, both educators and students can periodically and informally assess the students' performance to guide the FD persons' progress and maximize the learning experience (Ismeurt, Ismeurt, & Miller, 1992).

### FI Learning Strategies

FI persons need guidance to develop therapeutic interpersonal skills, since they are more impersonal and socially detached from others. A FI teacher can completely and accurately assess students to plan appropriate instruction, but he/she may fail to interact with and discuss the instructional play with the students. The teacher can facilitate interpersonal interactions by discussing with the students several alternative strategies for learning. The students can then independently select a strategy that they feel is more comfortable.

FI persons are less influenced by feedback. Self-assessments should be used to present useful information and to provide a reference point for discussion. Goals should be mutually established with FI students to ensure appropriate challenge and to provide an outlet for creativity and self-direction (Garity, 1985). FI persons give greater credit to internal referents (Witkin et al. 1976a). Internal referents may be inaccurate in a new environment that can confuse students when they test their ideas. Therefore, teachers can encourage FI students to verbalize and share their ideas before implementing them to verify accuracy.

## INSTRUCTIONAL AND LEARNING STRATEGIES

Teachers have both FD and FI students in their classrooms. They must be conscious of the strengths and needs of each. Both FD and FI teachers must be conscious of other individuals' actual needs and strengths. Teachers can become sensitive to the students' cognitive styles. In a study by Doebler and Eicke (1979), fifth-grade teachers in an experimental group were provided with information about their students' degree of FDI, and teaching strategies to use with FD and FI cognitive styles, but teachers in a control group were not given any information. The outcomes showed that students who were in the classrooms with the teachers who had knowledge of the students' cognitive styles had better self-concepts and attitudes toward school.

Teachers can determine the students' cognitive styles by observing them in a variety of situations. (Chapter 3 describes several assessment techniques.) Then they can use those instructional strategies that facilitate each student's way of learning (Pettigrew & Buell, 1989). FI teachers can cultivate positive personal relationships with their students. They must stimulate and compliment their students to foster their success, although they must be objective and sympathetic as they correct their students' mistakes. FD teachers communicate indirectly with FI students, but they need to learn to communicate directly with them. FD teachers must be tolerant with those FI students who are negative or reject the teachers' warmth or praise. FD teachers need to also respect the FI students' preferences for privacy and distance. They must not be penalized for their low social involvement (Saracho, 1989f).

The teachers' understanding of the students' cognitive styles makes teachers aware of how students are motivated. This understanding helps teachers to integrate more diversity in their instructional strategies than they otherwise would. For example, if teachers realize that (1) only a proportion of bright students benefit from a fast-paced questioning style, (2) several students like to work by themselves, or (3) other students prefer to work with their counterparts, they can arrange the class accordingly. Flexibility in using instructional strategies, concepts, and content must be developed. While research and theory cannot prescribe particular instructional strategies, they do suggest that strategies should be adjusted to meet the unique needs of the students.

## TEACHER PREPARATION PROGRAMS

FD and FI learning styles offer content to prepare teacher candidates and are valuable for in-service programs. Even experienced and competent teachers must be knowledgeable of the FD and FI learning styles. This type of program encourages self-evaluation and self-assessment for greater individual enhancement and accountability. It also offers new modes and avenues for self-growth. The enhancement of teaching techniques helps staff and/or students acquire effective teaching and learning strategies for teaching that incorporates a variety of procedures or changes in their daily activities. Also, participants from this in-service program can identify mentors that help facilitate changes.

Teacher education programs can use knowledge of cognitive style in their preparation of practitioners. This integration can take place in a series of steps. Information about learning styles should be integrated in the curriculum of professional preparation programs (Pettigrew & Buell, 1989). First, teacher educators must know, understand, and respect the FD and FI cognitive style characteristics and design instruction that is appropriate for these unique cognitive styles. Teachers learn to respect these individual differences by acquiring knowledge about both FD and FI orientations of the FDI construct and by having experiences compatible with different cognitive stylistic choices, including those that differ from their own. Teaching methods that are consistent with the teacher's cognitive style are learned first, then methods different from the individual's dominant cognitive style are learned next.

Teacher education programs can be developed where FD teachers learn analytic skills and independence, while FI teachers learn social skills and sensitivity to the others' needs (Saracho, 1989f; Saracho & Spodek, 1981, 1986). A teacher education program also can teach its students to perform in both FD and FI cognitive styles, becoming flexible in their thinking. After the teacher candidates have acquired knowledge of cognitive style, then they learn the instructional and learning strategies of FD and FI persons and ways in which they can acquire cognitive flexibility.

## COGNITIVE FLEXIBILITY

Proponents of cognitive style suggest that matching students' learning styles with instructional styles facilitates students' learning. Conversely, Pettigrew and Heikkinen (1985), Ramírez and Castañeda (1974), and Saracho and Spodek (1981, 1986) propose "style expansion." They believe that modifying the persons' cognitive styles facilitates or stifles the students' learning. One type of cognitive style may be limiting in one specific instructional context but may be an advantage in another. For instance, a FD student may encounter difficulty with formal instruction in mathematics, a FI activity. However, this FD student may be able to learn the same concept using a social experience, such as in dramatic play. When a FD student's cognitive style is modified, he/she is able to learn FI material such as abstract mathematical concepts and is able to acceptably perform in a FI manner. Conversely, when the FI student's cognitive style is modified, he/she can solve cognitive problem tasks and is able to perform tasks that demand social sensitivity, interpersonal harmony, and other important affective skills (Saracho, 1989f; Saracho & Spodek, 1981, 1986).

Teachers can help students to learn more effectively by using appropriate strategies. In order to do this effectively, a teacher education program must consider the inclusion of cognitive style in its curriculum to meet the students' needs.

A teacher education program could provide teacher candidates with guided experiences to assist them to recognize the students' learning styles. Such experiences can include development of observational skills and the utilization of assessment methods (Pettigrew & Buell, 1989) in cognitive styles. Observing and interacting with both FD and FI persons can provide specific information that can be used to facilitate learning (Ismeurt, Ismeurt, & Miller, 1992). This component should also be part of the introductory course. After the material has been learned in the introductory course, the different ways to assess cognitive style should be taught. This information and any observation guides or checklists that teacher candidates might have developed are kept, to be used in their teaching methods during the semester.

Cognitive flexibility is important for teachers. Saracho (1983b) offers evidence on the value of cognitive flexibility. Her study supports the evidence that the cognitive styles of persons (such as teachers) can be adapted to the appropriate cognitive style that is required in each situation. Thus, teachers can learn to use the characteristics of both FD and FI cognitive styles, regardless of their own dominant cognitive style. Ramírez and Castañeda (1974) found that persons can develop the ability to use both FD and FI cognitive styles. They characterize this process as "bicognitive development," concluding that persons can manifest a repertoire of cognitive style approaches to solve problems.

Teacher candidates need to increase their repertoires beyond their own dominant cognitive styles to embrace those characteristics and behaviors that differ from their own cognitive styles—to develop "cognitive flexibility" (Saracho & Spodek, 1981, 1986). Humphries, Elam, and Metzler (1988) also believe that a student may have one preferred learning style, but have the ability to employ other styles. Likewise, teacher candidates need to learn to shift teaching styles. That way they can present students with a variety of learning alternatives.

The teacher candidates can learn to function in both FD and FI cognitive styles. After the teachers' FD or FI cognitive style is identified, the range of their cognitive style behaviors is expanded. They can be provided with experiences that increase their repertoire of cognitive style behaviors. First, individuals are provided with experiences that are comparable with their own cognitive styles. Such experiences will help them to feel comfortable and secure in the educational program. Then these individuals are introduced to experiences that differ from their cognitive styles. Individuals may encounter some degree of "cognitive-style dissonance" that will help them to shift from their dominant cognitive style to a different cognitive style whenever it is necessary. For example, a FI person can function with a group in a social activity. Social skills, a characteristic of FD individuals, are used in this experience. Alike, a FD person can work independently on a mathematics problem. Since it requires analytic skills, it is considered a FI activity. Hence, FD teachers can extend their repertoires with FI-oriented experiences. Assignments that use analysis and theory are useful for FI experiences. Conversely, FI teachers can extend their behaviors by working on assignments where they have to use social skills and obtain social information (Saracho, 1989f). Teachers need to develop cognitive flexibility to be able to adapt instructional behaviors that differ from those which are exhibited by their dominant cognitive styles to provide a variety of learning alternatives to their students.

While FD students are relatively competent with social interactions, the application of theory in actual everyday situations and the ability to analyze others' problems may be more difficult because of limited ability to perceive items without being influenced by the background environment (Partridge, 1983). However, teachers can implement instructional strategies that facilitate learning for the FD persons. The teacher can use open-ended and nondirected questions such as "What do you think?" or "How could this situation be resolved?" to stimulate hypotheses formation and to test the FD students. For instance, observational learning experiences combine the spectator tendencies of the FD persons. Additional guided practice in a structured environment may help solidify motor skills with varied new equipment and procedures capitalizing on the trial-and-error methods found effective for students with varying cognitive learning styles (Edwards & Lee, 1985; Ismeurt, Ismeurt, & Miller, 1992).

Researchers and educators are concerned with providing students with appropriate instruction. Several schools of thought exist concerning the educational implications of learning styles for curriculum and instruction (Keefe & Farrell, 1990). Instruction should not conform solely to the students' cognitive styles (Cronbach & Snow, 1977; Good & Stipek, 1983; Ramírez & Castañeda, 1974; Saracho & Spodek, 1981, 1986). Initial instruction should match the students' cognitive styles. Then students should gradually be provided with instruction that differs from their cognitive styles to ultimately be able to modify the students' cognitive styles and help them become flexible. Cognitive flexibility, the extent to which persons can transform their information processing techniques by using the precise activities, is an important educational goal (Saracho, 1989f; Saracho & Spodek, 1981, 1986).

## Integrating Cognitive Style in Teacher Education

The teacher education program that considers cognitive style characteristics could incorporate a mixture of recommendations by Saracho (1989f), Saracho and Spodek (1981, 1986), and Witkin et al. (1977). Knowledge of cognitive style may be presented in an introductory course[1] where teacher candidates learn the characteristics of cognitive style, the impact of cognitive style on the teaching-learning process, and ways to change their own and their students' cognitive styles. Historical information and discussions on the topic can be generated. FDI cognitive style and its characteristics can be defined, explained, described, and discussed with specific examples. Relevant research findings on cognitive style and its educational implications are taught. Knowledge of cognitive style can be taught before students are enrolled in their methods courses. This knowledge becomes more relevant to the teacher candidates when they are enrolled in their observation course, methods classes, and student teaching experience.

### Assessing Cognitive Style

The teacher candidates can experience several ways to assess the individuals' cognitive styles[2] including formal and informal assessment. First, they can evaluate a standardized test of cognitive style as recommended by Anastasi (1988). Table 11.2 provides directions for this evaluation. This will allow them to understand the (a) strengths and weaknesses of assessing cognitive style using formal measures; (b) need for a second cognitive style measure; (c) use of observations, checklists, and interviews to justify their assessment; and (d) instructional practices for students.

Teacher candidates can evaluate and compare two observation measures such as those developed by Ramírez and Castañeda (1974). They can describe the strengths, needs, and weaknesses of each observation measure as well as which observation measure is a better diagnostic measure. Teacher candidates should be able to justify their responses.

The teacher candidates can try to develop their own measures to identify the students' cognitive styles. Such measures can include tests, interviews, checklists, and observations. The teacher candidates should analyze these measures using the FD and FI characteristics as the criteria.

As a culmination of the assessment component, the teacher candidates should develop a diagnostic project of a student in their classroom.[3] Besides using different measures of cognitive style, they should collect two categories of informal information on this student: diagnostic notes and formal assessment procedures. The diagnostic notes section of this project involves keeping a log of their diagnostic hypotheses, instructional interactions/observations, and their instructional decisions based on the teacher candidates' contact with the student. Teacher candidates will record their thoughts on the following:

1. The students' strengths and needs.
2. Cognitive style characteristics to be addressed in their lessons.
3. After completing the lessons, teacher candidates evaluate the strengths and weaknesses of their lessons and suggest their follow-up plans.
4. At all times, the teacher candidates will justify their decisions.

**Table 11.2**
**Evaluation of a Standardized Cognitive Style Test**

### EVALUATING A COGNITIVE STYLE TEST

*Citation*: author(s), publication date, title of test, and name of publisher.

*Purposes and Uses*: as reported by the author and the cognitive style literature.

*Practical Considerations*: direct costs (e.g., booklets, answer sheets, scoring).

*Format and Layout*: arrangement of items, subsections, and parts.

*Items and Coverage*: basis of item selection.

*Administration*: instructions for individual or group administration; the qualifications of test administrator; time required for administration.

*Scoring*: method of scoring (e.g., hand, machine), required scoring aids (test sheets), directions for scoring.

*Norms*: description of sample that was used for standardization (e.g., nature, size, representative) to obtain the demographic information on sample (e.g., age, sex, education, occupation, region).

*Reliability*: types and procedures of reliability (e.g., test retest, split-half), size and nature of samples used, the scorer reliability.

*Validity*: types and procedures of validation (e.g., content, criterion-related predictive, concurrent, construct), specific procedures used to estimate validity and results acquired; size and nature of samples used.

*Reviewer Comments*: comments from reviewers and users (usually found in *Mental Measurements Yearbook*, *Tests in Print*, and other sources).

*Summary Evaluation*: Summarize your assessment of the cognitive style measure including the test's major strengths and weaknesses.

Adapted from Anastasi (1988).

Teacher candidates can save copies of the student's work on which they based their decisions. They need to learn how to integrate all of the information they collect, such as written work, recorded notes about the interaction, and any observations that are recorded. Teacher candidates will use the students' cognitive styles to develop hypotheses about what students need and adjust their instruction accordingly. They basically will be keeping a running record in informal notes on their hypotheses and actions. The complete diagnostic project will integrate their diagnostic notes with their formal and informal assessments. Table 11.3 outlines this assignment.

### Presenting Information

First, teacher candidates are taught the knowledge of cognitive style and later the necessary background to simplify the understanding of the educational implications of cognitive style.

**Table 11.3**
**Components for the Diagnostic Project**

I. Diagnostic notes

    A. Keep a log of all observations/interactions, diagnostic hypotheses, and instructional decisions based on regular instructional interaction with the identified student.

    B. Include an appendix for running long, sample papers, and other relevant information.

    C. Summarize your comments that you wrote on the student based on the information that the teacher candidates collected.

II. Formal and informal assessments

    A. Administer two cognitive style standardized tests and cognitive style observations. Discuss and compare the results.

    B. Draw conclusions about this student's strengths and weaknesses based on these assessments.

    C. Evaluate the practicality of these assessments.

III. Conclusions

    A. Write comments, hypotheses, and conclusions about this student based on the assessments (formal and informal) and information that was gathered by the teacher candidates.

    B. Describe and justify the follow-up procedures based on the information that was gathered. Provide general principles with specific examples. Identify the diagnosis and instructional strategies that would have made a difference in the student's learning.

IV. Appendices

    A. Diagnostic notes

    B. Running log

    C. Formal and informal assessments used

    D. Samples of the student's work

After the relevant information is taught, the educational implications of cognitive style in various settings should be demonstrated in four special realms: (1) the manner in which students learn, (2) the manner in which teachers instruct, (3) the manner in which teachers and students interact, and (4) the manner in which teachers and students can acquire cognitive flexibility.

## Cognitive Style Content

The presentation of theoretical information should be organized to facilitate learning for the FD teacher candidates. Gillies (1984) found that handouts that

**Table 11.4**

**Strategies to Teach Large and Small According to the Different Cognitive Styles**

| **FD Cognitive Style** | **FI Cognitive Style** |
|---|---|
| 1. Provide pictures of family members to teach big and small people like father and baby brother. | 1. Provide large and small shapes like large circles and dots. |
| 2. Provide pictures of big and small neighborhood houses for them to compare the differences in these two concepts. | 2. Provide large and small blocks for children to build buildings by themselves. |

Adapted from Saracho (1989f).

outlined relevant issues or procedures facilitate the FD students' learning and short-term retention. Recurrent verbal and nonverbal feedback in the actual setting helps to direct and encourage the FD person. This type of interaction between the teacher and student provides a more social, one-to-one relationship for the FD person (Ismeurt, Ismeurt, & Miller, 1992)

**Instructional Content**

Courses contain distinctive suggestions on instructional content and strategies that are effective with FD and FI students. Topics for the content areas and strategies are related for both FD and FI students (Saracho, 1989f).

Toward the end of the course,[4] each teacher candidate could be given a copy of the Educational Testing Service Research Bulletin (Witkin et al., 1977) on the educational implications of cognitive style and a reprint of the article "Role of the Field-dependent and Field-independent Cognitive Styles in Academic Evolution: A Longitudinal Study" by Witkin et al. (1976b). They read, learn, and discuss this material as a final review of the course. Teacher candidates ask questions, raise issues, and plan for future uses of this information (Saracho, 1989f).

When the teacher candidates are enrolled in their methods courses (e.g., reading, language arts, social studies, mathematics, and science), they could enroll in a course on cognitive style that meets periodically to design lesson plans for both FD and FI students. These lesson plans are tested in a school setting. Before developing these lesson plans, teacher candidates reexamine the material they learn in their previous courses and evaluate the lesson plans they have designed and tested in a school setting.

Assignments in the course embody a curriculum guide where concepts are taught first in the students' dominant cognitive styles; while later, when the students feel comfortable in the classroom, concepts are taught in the cognitive style that differs from their own. Table 11.4 provides an example of how to teach the concept large and small for both FD and FI cognitive styles.

The curriculum guide includes content areas, topics, and strategies related to different cognitive styles. The concluding section of the curriculum guide has different instructional strategies for both FD and FI cognitive styles. By this time, students should be flexible in using the different cognitive styles and can shift to and from both FD and FI cognitive styles.

The teacher education program can provide workshops for university supervisors and cooperating teachers to help them become knowledgeable of and understand cognitive style and its educational implications. Before student teaching, a university instructor who is knowledgeable of cognitive style could meet with university supervisors and cooperating teachers to discuss the uses of cognitive style. Each could be given a copy of the Educational Testing Service Research Bulletin (Witkin et al., 1977) and a reprint of the article "Role of the Field-dependent and Field-independent Cognitive Styles in Academic Evolution: A Longitudinal Study" by Witkin et al. (1976b) to inform them about cognitive style and its educational implications.

During student teaching, university instructors or supervisors could hold seminars and follow-up sessions with the teacher candidates and cooperating teachers to make sure that cognitive style information is integrated in their school experiences. No new information would be provided, but discussions can occur or questions can be raised. The last seminar session could be devised to encourage teacher candidates to continue thinking about cognitive style. Educational implications of cognitive style should be reviewed, and teacher candidates allowed to raise questions or issues. Teacher candidates are encouraged to share any successes or complications they experienced with the recommended procedures (Saracho, 1989f).

## CONCLUSION

The FDI dimension of cognitive style influences how teachers teach, students learn, and teachers and students interact (Witkin et al., 1977). Professional preparation curricula must include information about experiences with learning and teaching styles to help teacher candidates identify and accommodate various learning styles (Pettigrew & Buell, 1989). Therefore, knowledge of cognitive style must be included in programs that prepare teachers. Teacher candidates should learn to handle both FD and FI cognitive styles for teaching, learning, and ultimately nourishing cognitive flexibility in themselves and in their students.

Teachers are in the distinct position to manipulate all domains of learning. They should be sensitive to how their students receive and process information and be aware of their students' learning styles in selecting instructional strategies for their lessons (Pettigrew & Buell, 1989).

The practical application of the knowledge gained from the concept of FDI is important for all teacher candidates because information-processing differences of FD and FI persons affect teaching practice. Teachers must be aware of the different student characteristics that inspire the exchange of information to maximize teaching and learning experiences. Knowledge and acceptance of the different personal characteristics in each person promote the development of alternative, affective, and individualized learning strategies for peers, students (Ismeurt, Ismeurt, & Miller, 1992), and teachers.

## NOTES

1. This can be a portion of the human development and learning course.

2. This information can be presented as part of the course on principles and methods of teaching.

3. This section of the assessment can be integrated with the material in the teacher candidates' school service semester where teacher candidates develop conceptual understanding of the teaching-learning process.

4. This course focuses on planning activities, materials, and methods by which educational objectives are attained.

# Chapter 12

# Potential Roles of Cognitive Style in Educational Practice

This book has presented research and theory related to cognitive style as well as suggestions for applying this theory to educational practice at the early childhood level. The field dependence independence (FDI) dimension of cognitive style has been the most extensively studied, and it has had the widest application to educational problems (Witkin et al., 1962/1974; Witkin et al., 1977). This is the dimension of cognitive style that has been dealt with here as it applies to early childhood education. It differentiates between field dependent (FD) and field independent (FI) individuals.[1] Knowing about cognitive style research and theory, teachers can modify their programs to meet the individual differences in cognitive functioning found among the children in their classrooms. This requires them to know the developmental patterns of their children. It is easy to see how children differ in relation to their physical size, height, and weight just by looking at those children who are of the same chronological age. They differ in their cognitive, social, language, and motor competence as well. These differences cannot be seen directly, however, and teachers must use a variety of evaluative instruments and observation techniques to identify differences in these domains.

Teachers typically set different expectations for their children's achievement and learning. Not all children can be expected to learn the same things, at the same time, or in the same ways. Teachers expect some children to learn more than others and expect some children to take more time to learn what is required of them. Children also differ in the styles in which they learn. Stylistic differences in cognitive performance, however, are not necessarily related to intellectual abilities.

Teachers need to provide a variety of learning alternatives for the children in their classes, using many different teaching strategies, curricula, materials, and resources. This is especially important when working with children who differ in their analytic and social abilities.

Education is a social act, and the social dimensions of learning also need to be addressed in the children's educational settings. Interactions with others, both teachers and other children, influence students' learning. Therefore, appropriate learning groups and learning tasks must be established, such as matching learning styles to learning tasks and to learning support systems (Spodek, 1990).

## COGNITIVE STYLE IN CLASSROOM SETTINGS

Information on cognitive style can be used to improve classroom practices in order to optimize learning. One suggestion has been provided by Spodek (1990), who has proposed matching teachers and students and learning tasks in relation to cognitive style and cognitive flexibility.

### Matching

According to Hunt (1970), a "match" provides instruction comparable to the child's ability to profit from it. A match can maximize the teaching and learning process. A mismatch of instruction can lead to frustration and "disconfirmation," possibly a negative learning experience.

*Matching Learning Tasks.* The cognitive style literature suggests matching children's learning tasks to their cognitive styles. FD children, for example, are more successful with socially oriented learning tasks. Teachers could avoid abstract learning tasks and focus on tasks that are set in a social context. FI children are more successful with abstract and less social activities, whereas FD children perform best in personal-social learning activities. To optimize learning, these children can be encouraged to specialize in the activities in which they best succeed. Thus, FI children may focus in mathematics and science activities and FD children may focus in dramatic play and other activities with social content. Or better yet, mathematics and science learning can be put into a social learning context—cooking, for example—for FD children. Similarly, social learning can be approached in a more abstract way for FI children.

This proposal should only be implemented to a limited degree. Children must go beyond their own particular cognitive styles. They should be provided with opportunities that will help them achieve more than what they are presently capable of doing. Children need to be challenged to learn all intellectual skills, including both abstract and concrete. Teachers need to extend rather than restrict the opportunities for success in school for those children who enter school with cognitive styles that mismatch the requirements of school learning tasks.

*Matching Teachers and Students.* Research suggests that both the match and mismatch of teachers' and children's cognitive styles contribute to their learning. The traditional approach to selecting early childhood teachers has been to select those individuals with FD characteristics. It has been believed that these individuals make better teachers of young children. However, findings from several studies demonstrate that this is not necessarily the case. Frequently, the students of FI teachers have been found to have greater educational outcomes, at least in terms of academic achievement. This would suggest that FI individuals might be better teachers for all children, since these teachers also are more supportive of the learning of those children whose cognitive style is different from their own. Apparently, in selecting teachers of young children, individuals should be sought who have FI characteristics. In addition, FI teachers can be trained to acquire FD characteristics. If FD teachers are selected, they also can learn to acquire FI characteristics.

It is important to note that these studies on the match and mismatch of teachers and children have employed academic achievement assessments as outcome measures. Although these assessments may be valid and reliable, they relate only to a narrow range of outcomes of early childhood education. For example, outcomes from tests of social competence have not been used. Limited information has been accumulated on the relationship between the match and mismatch of teachers' and children's cognitive styles and children's social-emotional outcomes or problem-solving outcomes. All of these are important in early childhood education. Perhaps we need to further explore the effects of the teachers' cognitive styles on a broad range of outcomes in early childhood education before applying any cognitive style criteria in selecting teachers or in matching teachers to children.

## Cognitive Flexibility

Teachers need to be responsive to the cognitive styles of their students instead of their own. This requires that they develop cognitive flexibility. That is, individuals can have the ability to use cognitive strategies based on a FD or FI situation.

In achieving cognitive flexibility, a person's cognitive style is identified and then modified to allow her or him to use both FD and FI characteristics. Saracho (1983b) offered support for the value of cognitive flexibility. Both adults and children have demonstrated the ability to function in a cognitive style that differs from their own. This modifies the individual's characteristics but does not wholly change them (Ramírez & Castañeda, 1974; Saracho & Spodek, 1981, 1986).

*Developing Cognitive Flexibility.* Saracho and Spodek (1981, 1986) have recommended that children be educated to have cognitive flexibility. According to Ramírez and Castañeda (1974), Saracho and Spodek (1981, 1986), and Witkin and Goodenough (1981), both FD and FI cognitive styles are equally valuable for cognitive functioning. A variety of learning styles can provide children with the cognitive resources that assist them to achieve a variety of intellectual tasks. Children can be stimulated to cultivate skills that are related to many learning styles. Then children can match the skills from their cognitive repertoires to the requirements of each specific intellectual task. Cognitive flexibility offers overall cognitive growth instead of a narrowly focused intellectual strength in a set of particular skills.

The principle of teaching for cognitive flexibility is complex. Teachers need to first assess their classroom children to determine their dominant cognitive styles. This will help them to identify the various instructional strategies and prioritize them into: (1) FD teaching methods and learning activities, (2) FI teaching methods and learning activities, and (3) neutral teaching methods and learning activities. Teachers can then provide children with activities that match and mismatch their cognitive styles. Teachers need to plan distinctive activities for each individual child based on a judgment as to whether the child needs matched or mismatched activities. Teachers can systematically administer simple and practical measures of cognitive style and systematically use their outcomes as one of the bases for making educational decisions.

In determining the children's cognitive styles for planning instruction, teachers must consider both the cognitive style of each child and that of the child's peers in the classroom to promote learning.

*Flexible Curriculum.* When teachers use information on children's cognitive styles to plan matched and mismatched activities and organize matched and mismatched peer groups, the process may become complex. Rather than develop an unmanageable plan to match children to teachers in relation to cognitive style or children to specific activities based on cognitive style, a flexible curriculum may be needed.

Such a curriculum should be flexible enough to support the children's active learning. Teachers can provide children with opportunities to make choices from learning alternatives. Teachers and children collaboratively make classroom decisions. Such collaboration and mutual decision-making yield a better match of teaching activities to children's learning styles, since the children themselves decide which activities they can best learn.

## FUTURE RESEARCH

The emergence of developmental and individual differences in persons' cognitive styles as well as their interrelationships have been presented in this book. The suggestions for planning for different areas of the curriculum that can be inferred from the research have also been thoroughly discussed. Kogan (1976) summarizes general conclusions or principles that he extracted from the mass of empirical research. Below are his conclusions.

1. *During the preschool years, sex differences in cognitive style and strategies are extensive and consistently favor females.* A developmental timetable exists where females are around six months to one year ahead of males on several cognitive performances. In occasional cases, the female superiority does not appear, but there is the option where usually differences exist, instead of having male superiority. The outcomes on sex differences in early childhood differ

slightly from Maccoby and Jacklin's (1974). Their differences fail to support early systematic sex differences in cognitive styles. The inconsistency in the view between Maccoby and Jacklin (1974) and Kogan (1976) is that Kogan relied on his access to unpublished materials.

2. *Since prominent changes occur within the preschool period, preschoolers should not be considered a homogeneous age group in reference to cognitive styles.* The lack of stability in cognitive styles complicates the identification of groups. This knowledge challenges the importance of individuals' psychological abilities to shift back and forth between cognitive constructs. Identification for children's cognitive styles would differ at ages three and five years. As a matter of fact, this information is unknown. It is imperative to conduct longitudinal research to obtain this information.

3. *The associations between cognitive styles and personality and socioemotional behaviors are magnanimous and multifaceted.* Cognition-personality relationships take on different forms in preschool males and females. A future responsibility should be to justify this diverse sex patterning. Salient age outcomes in the patterning of cognition-personality relationships differ over the course of development. Justification for this change is evasive. For example, an analytic style may relate to a set of highly positive socioemotional behaviors at one stage during the preschool years and lose or reverse this association a year later. Cognitive patterning at one age (e.g., three years) can be studied over a year or more to explore the basis for stability and change.

4. *IQ is moderately related to cognitive style.* The IQ construct considers only a trivial segment of the contention in the cognitive performance of preschoolers. Cognitive style may contribute to young children's performance on IQ tests. Further research needs to be conducted on the influence of cognitive style on IQ.

5. *Capacity for cognitive style modification can be found at an early age.* The evidence to support modifying children's cognitive styles can be found in children as young as two years of age. Young children's cognitive styles can be modified. In addition, young children may find alternative methods of performing a task by simply being asked to do so. Before assessing or modifying children's cognitive styles, it is important to identify the cognitive style strategies that exist in their repertoires. Researchers need to examine if the combination of optimal methods of assessment and exhaustion of the child's repertoire would drastically curtail the degree of individual differences in a specific cognitive style domain.

6. *Assessment of cognitive style since early childhood is influenced by the task content and stimulus materials.* Characteristics of a task and the context can influence the assessment of children's cognitive styles. Their performance may indicate a tribute to young children's sensitivity or susceptibility to environmental contingencies. This is important when preschool children enter school for the first time and children are assessed with unfamiliar materials. Studies on moderator effects are likely to be a high-risk enterprise; however, its success

may represent an enormous increase in understanding the justification for individual differences in young children's cognitive styles.

Research in cognitive style has been conducted for decades, but only in the last two decades has research on cognitive style in early childhood education emerged, and findings from cognitive style research with adults and older children have been related to the field of early childhood education. Although many studies have been conducted applying cognitive style to education, there are some methodological problems in this research, including small sample sizes and samples that are not very representative.

In addition, many times, different researchers have found conflicting results in their studies. This has sometimes resulted from studying different populations, using different instruments, or using different research designs. A more dependable set of outcomes is needed for a solid foundation of knowledge in this area. In addition, researchers need to continue research in cognitive style to increase the available knowledge. The previous studies offer a good beginning of a productive area of educational and psychological studies.

It can be concluded, however, that the knowledge relating to cognitive style in early childhood education is sufficiently valid. The knowledge of teachers' and children's cognitive styles can be used flexibly to improve the quality of education for young children. Flexibility must be used in matching teachers and children in terms of their cognitive styles and in matching and mismatching teaching methods and learning activities to the cognitive styles of children, whether by individual child or by cultural group (Spodek, 1990).

It is important to continue the exploration of the individual differences among teachers and children in school settings and to continue to use the knowledge to upgrade educational opportunities for all children.

### NOTE

1. Chapter 2 describes in detail the difference between FD and FI individuals.

# References

Adejumo, D. (1983). Effect of cognitive style on strategies for comprehension of prose. *Perceptual and Motor Skills, 56*, 859–863.

Anastasi, A. (1988). *Psychological testing.* New York: Macmillan.

Annis, L., & Davis, J. K. (1978). Study techniques comparing their effectiveness. *The American Biology Teacher, 40*, 108–110.

Ash, B. F. (1986). *Identifying learning styles and matching strategies for teaching and learning* (Report No. JC 860 277). Washington, DC: U.S. Department of Education, Office of Educational Research and Improvement. (ERIC Document Reproduction Service 270 142)

Balistreri, E., & Busch-Rossnagel, N. A. (1989). Field independence as a function of sex, sex-roles, and the sex-role appropriateness of the task. *Perceptual and Motor Skills, 68*, 115–121.

Beller, E. K. (1967). *Methods of language training and cognitive styles in lower class children.* Paper presented at the meeting of the American Educational Research Association, New York.

Berry, J. M. (1976). *Human ecology and cognitive style: Comparative studies in cultural and psychological adaptation.* New York: Wiley.

Bertini, M. (1986). Some implications of field dependence for education. In M. Bertini, L. Pizzamiglio, & S. Wapner (Eds.), *Field dependence in psychological theory: Research and application* (pp. 15–25). Hillsdale, NJ: Erlbaum.

Bhasin, M. P. (1987). Learning style. *Indian Psychological Review, 32*(7), 29–34.

Bigelow, G. S. (1971). Field dependence-independence in 5- to 10-year-old children. *Journal of Educational Research, 64*, 397–400.

Black, B. (1992). Negotiating social pretend play: Communication differences related to social status and sex. *Merrill-Palmer Quarterly, 38*(2), 212–232.

Brattesani, K., Weinstein, R., & Marshall, H. (1984). Student perception of teacher expectation effects. *Journal of Educational Psychology, 76*, 236–247.

Brewer, A. (1977). On Indian education. *Integrated Education, 15*(1), 21–23.

Brodzinksy, D. M. (1982). Relationship between cognitive style and cognitive develop-
    ment: A 2-year longitudinal study. *Developmental Psychology, 18,* 617–626.

Brophy, J. E., & Good, T. L. (1972). Teacher expectations: Beyond the Pygmalion con-
    troversy. *Phi Delta Kappan, 54*(4), 276–278.

Brophy, J., & Good, T. L. (1986). Teacher behavior and student achievement. In M. C.
    Wittrock (Ed.), *Handbook of research on teaching* (pp. 328–375). New York:
    Macmillan.

Bruner, J. S. (1972). Nature and use of immaturity. *American Psychologist, 27,* 687–
    708.

Bryson, J. B., & Driver, M. J. (1969). Conceptual complexity and internal arousal. *Psy-
    chonomic Science, 17,* 71–72.

Busch, J. C., Watson, J. A., Brinkley, V., Howard, N., & Nelson, C. (1993). Preschool
    Embedded Figures Test performance of young children: Age and gender differ-
    ences. *Perceptual and Motor Skills, 77,* 491–496.

Bush, D. F., & Coward, R. T. (1974). Sex differences in the solution of achromatic and
    chromatic embedded figures. *Perceptual and Motor Skills, 39,* 1121–1122.

Bush, D. W. (1986). *Relationships among teacher personality, pupil control attitudes
    and pupil control behavior* (Report No. SP 026 564). Paper presented at the
    Annual Meeting of the American Educational Research Association, Chicago, IL.
    (ERIC Document Reproduction Service No. ED 262 002)

Campione, J. C., Brown, A. L., & Bryant, N. R. (1985). Individual differences in learning
    and memory. In R. J. Sternberg (Ed.), *Human abilities: An information-processing
    approach* (pp. 103–126). New York: W. H. Freeman.

Cecchini, M., & Pizzamiglio, L. (1975). Effects of field-dependency on social class and
    sex of children between ages 5 and 10. *Perceptual and Motor Skills, 41,* 155–
    164.

Chadwick, S. S., & Watson, J. A. (1986). Computers and cognitive styles. *Academic
    Therapy, 22*(2), 125–132.

Chan, K. S., Takanishi, R., & Kitano, M. K. (1975). *An inquiry into Asian American
    preschool children and families in Los Angeles* (Report No. UD 015 651). Los
    Angeles: University of California. (ERIC Document Reproduction Service No.
    ED 117 251)

Chapelle, C., & Green, P. (1992). Field independence/dependence in second-language
    acquisition research. *Language Learning, 42*(1), 47–79.

Chapelle, C. A. (1992). Disembedding "Disembedded figures in the landscape . . .": An
    appraisal of Griffiths and Sheen's "appraisal of L2 research on field dependence
    independence." *Applied Linguistics, 13*(4), 375–384.

Charlier, P. S. (1981, Spring). Learn to learn; analysis of learning styles. *Scholar and
    Educator,* 47–53.

Cheney, L. V. (1987). *American memory: A report on the humanities in the nation's
    public schools.* Washington, DC: National Endowment for the Humanities.

Chynn, E. W., Garrod, A., Demick, J., & DeVos, E. (1991). Correlations among field
    dependence-independence, sex, sex-role stereotype, and age of preschoolers. *Per-
    ceptual and Motor Skills, 73,* 747–756.

Clements, D. H., & Gullo, D. F. (1984). Effects of computer programming on young
    children's cognition. *Journal of Educational Psychology, 76*(7), 1051–1058.

Coates, S. (1972). *Preschool Embedded Figures Test.* Palo Alto, CA: Consulting Psy-
    chologists Press.

Coates, S. (1975). Field independence and intellectual functioning in preschool children. *Perceptual and Motor Skills, 41*, 251–254.

Coates, S., Lord, M., and Jakabovics, E. (1975). Field dependence independence, social-nonsocial play, and sex differences. *Perceptual and Motor Skills, 40*, 195–202.

Cohen, J. (1957). The factorial structure of the WAIS between early adulthood and old age. *Journal of Consulting Psychology, 21*, 283–290.

Cohen, R. A., (1969). Conceptual styles, culture conflict, and nonverbal tests of intelligence. *American Anthropologist, 7*, 828–856.

Coop, R. H., & Brown, L. D. (1970). The effects of teaching method and cognitive style on categories of achievement. *Journal of Educational Psychology, 61*, 400–405.

Cooper, R. H., & Sigel, I. E. (1971). Cognitive style: Implications for learning and instruction. *Psychology in the Schools, 8*(2), 152–161.

Copeland, B. D. (1983). The relationship of cognitive style to academic achievement of university art appreciation students. *College Student Journal, 17*(2), 157–162.

Coward, R. T., Davis, J. K., & Wichern, R. O. (1978). Cognitive style and perceptions of the ideal teacher. *Contemporary Educational Psychology, 3*(3), 232–238.

Cox, D. L., & Moore, C. A. (1976). Field independence and the structuring of knowledge in a social studies minicourse. *Journal of Educational Psychology, 68*(5), 550–558.

Cronbach, L. J., & Snow, R. E. (1977). *Aptitudes and instructional methods: A handbook for research on interaction.* New York: Irvington.

Crosson, C. W. (1984). Age and field independence among women. *Experimental Aging Research, 10*(3), 165–170.

Cullanine, D. (1985). *A cognitive style study of Native Indian children.* Unpublished master's thesis, University of British Columbia, Canada.

Damico, S. B. (1985). The two worlds of school: Differences in the photographs of Black and White adolescents. *The Urban Review, 17*(3), 210–222.

Davey, B. (1990). Field dependence-independence and reading comprehension questions: Task and reader interactions. *Contemporary Educational Psychology, 15*, 241–250.

Davey, B., & Menke, D. (1990). The importance of cognitive style in children's acquisition of reading skill. In O. N. Saracho (Ed.), *Cognitive style and early education* (pp. 79–94). New York: Gordon & Breach Science Publishers.

Davey, B., & Miller, D. (1990). Topicalization and the processing of expository prose by children: Mediating effects of cognitive styles and content familiarity. *Educational Psychology, 10*(1), 23–38.

Davies, M. F. (1988). Individual differences in the reading process of field independence and letter detection. *Perceptual and Motor Skills, 66*, 323–326.

Davis, J. K. (1987). The field independent-dependent style and beginning reading. *Early Child Development and Care, 29*, 119–132.

Davis, J. K., & Cochran, K. F. (1982, March). Toward information processing analysis of field independence. In R. E. Schultz (Chair), *Trends in cognitive style research: Directions and dilemmas.* Symposium conducted at the meeting of the American Educational Research Association, New York.

Davis, J. K., & Cochran, K. F. (1990). An information processing view of field dependence-independence. In O. N. Saracho (Ed.), *Cognitive style and early education* (pp. 61–94). New York: Gordon & Breach Science Publishers.

Davis, J. K., & Frank, B. M. (1979). Learning and memory of field independent individuals. *Journal of Research in Personality, 13*, 469–479.

Dawson, J. L., Young, B. M., & Choi, P. P. C. (1974). Developmental influence in pictorial depth perception among Hong Kong Chinese children. *Journal of Cross-Cultural Psychology, 5*(1), 3–22.

De Bello, T. C. (1990). Comparison of eleven major learning styles; variables, appropriate populations, validity of instrumentation and the research behind them. *Journal of Reading, Writing, and Learning Disabilities International, 6*, 203–222.

Deever, S. G. (1968). Ratings of task-oriented expectancy for success as a function of internal control and field independence. *Dissertation Abstracts International, 29*(1). (University Microfilms No. 68–9470)

DeNovellis, R., & Lawrence, G. (1983). Correlations of teacher personality I variables (Myers-Briggs) and classroom observation data. *Research in Psychological Type, 6*, 37–46.

Dinges, N. G., & Hollenbeck, A. R. (1978). Field dependence independence in Navajo children. *International Journal of Psychology, 13*, 215–220.

DiStefano, J. J. (1970). Interpersonal perceptions of field independent and field dependent teachers and students (Doctoral dissertation, Cornell University, 1969). *Dissertation Abstracts International, 31*, 463A–464A.

Dodge, K. A., Pettit, G. S., McClaskey, C. L., & Brown, M. M. (1986). Social competence in children. *Monographs of the Society for Research in Child Development, 51*(2, Serial No. 213).

Doebler, L. K., & Eicke, F. J. (1979). Effects of teacher awareness of the educational implications of field-dependent/field-independent cognitive style on selected classroom variables. *Journal of Educational Psychology, 71*(2), 226–232.

Dor-Shave, Z., & Peleg, R. (1989). Mobile field-independence and rating as a "good teacher." *Educational Psychology, 9*(2), 149–163.

Drane, M. J., Halpin, G. M., Halpin, W. G., vonEschenbach, J. F., & Worden, T. W. (1989). Relationships between reading proficiency and field dependence/independence and sex. *Educational Research Quarterly, 13*(2), 2–10.

Dreyer, A. S., Dreyer, C. A., & Nebelkopf, E. B. (1971). Portable rod-and-frame test as a measure of cognitive style in kindergarten children. *Perceptual and Motor Skills, 33*, 775–781.

Dubois, T. E., & Cohen, W. (1970). Relationship between measures of psychological and intellectual ability. *Perceptual and Motor Skills, 31*, 411–416.

Dunn, R., Dunn, K., & Price, G. E. (1978). *Learning style inventory.* Lawrence, KS: Price Systems.

Dusek, J. B. (1975). Do teachers bias children's learning? *Review of Educational Research, 45*, 661–684.

Dwyer, F. M., & Moore, D. M. (1991). Effect of color coding on visually oriented tests with students of different cognitive styles. *The Journal of Psychology, 125*(6), 677–680.

Edwards, R. V., & Lee, A. M.(1985). The relationship of cognitive style and instructional strategy to learning and transfer of motor skills. *Research for Exercise and Sport, 56*, 286–290.

Ekstrom, R. B. (1976). Teacher aptitudes, knowledge, attitudes and cognitive style as predictors of teacher behavior. *Journal of Teacher Education, 27*(4), 329–331.

Elliott, A. R. (1995). Field independence/dependence, hemispheric specialization, and attitude in relation to pronunciation accuracy in Spanish as a foreign language. *The Modern Language Journal, 79,* 356–371.

Ennis, C. D., Chen, A., & Fernandez-Balboa, J. M. (1991). Cognitive style differences within an analytical curriculum: Examples of success and nonsuccess. *Early Child Development and Care, 74,* 123–134.

Ennis, C. D., & Chepyator-Thompson, J. R. (1991). Learning characteristics of field-dependent children with an analytical concept-based curriculum. *Journal of Teaching in Physical Education, 10,* 170–187.

Ennis, C. D., & Lazarus, J. C. (1990). Cognitive style and gender differences in children's motor task performance. *Early Child Development and Care, 64,* 33–46.

Erdle, S., Murray, H. G., & Rushton, J. P. (1985). Personality, classroom behavior, and student ratings of college teaching effectiveness: A path analysis. *Journal of Educational Psychology, 77*(4), 394–407.

Erikson, E. H. (1950). *Childhood and society.* New York: Norton.

Federico, P. A. (1983). Changes in the cognitive components of achievement as students proceed through computer-managed instruction. *Journal of Computer-based Instruction, 9,* 156–168.

Folman, R. Z. (1973). Therapist-patient perceptual style, interpersonal attraction, initial interview behavior, and premature termination (doctoral dissertation, Boston University). *Dissertation Abstracts International, 34,* 1746B. (University Microfilms No. 73-23, 482)

Forns-Santacana, M., Amador-Campos, J. A., & Roig-López, F. (1993). Differences in field dependence-independence cognitive style as a function of socioeconomic status, sex, and cognitive competence. *Psychology in the Schools, 30,* 176–186.

Frank, B. M. (1983). Flexibility of information processing and the memory of field-independent and field-dependent learners. *Journal of Research and Personality, 21,* 89–96.

Frank, B. M., & Davis, J. K. (1982). Effect of field-independence match or mismatch on a communication task. *Journal of Educational Psychology, 74,* 23–31.

Gardner, R. W., Holzman, P. S., Klein, G. S., Linton, H. B., & Spencer, D. P. (1959). Cognitive control: A study of individual consistencies in cognitive behavior. *Psychological Issues, 1*(4).

Garity, J. 1985). Learning style: Basis for creative teaching and learning. *Nurse Educator, 10*(2), 12–15.

Gelderloos, P., Lockie, R. J., & Chuttoorgoon, S. (1987). Field independence of students at Maharishi school of the age of enlightenment and a Montessori school. *Perceptual and Motor Skills, 65,* 613–614.

Gilbert S. E., II, & Gay, G. (1985, October). Improving the success in school of poor black children. *Phi Delta Kappan, 67*(2), 133–137.

Gillies, D. A. (1984). Effect of advance organizers on learning medical surgical nursing content by baccalaureate nursing students. *Research in Nursing and Health, 7,* 173–180.

Globerson, T. (1985). Mental capacity, mental effort, and cognitive style. *Developmental Review, 3,* 292–302.

Globerson, T., Weinstein, E., & Sharabany, R. (1985). Teasing out cognitive development from cognitive style: A training study. *Developmental Psychology, 21,* 682–691.

Goldberger, L., & Bendich, S. (1972). Field-dependence and social responsiveness as determinants of spontaneously produced words. *Perceptual and Motor Skills, 34*, 883–886.

Good, T. L. (1987). Two decades of research on teacher expectations: Findings and future directions. *Journal of Teacher Education, 38*(4), 32–47.

Good, T. L., & Stipek, D. (1983). Individual differences in the classroom: A psychological perspective. In G. G. Fenstermacher & J. L. Goodlad (Eds.), *Individual differences and the common curriculum: Eighty-second yearbook of the National Society for the Study of Education: Part 1* (pp. 9–43). Chicago: University of Chicago Press.

Goodenough, D. R. (1976). The role of individual differences in field dependence as a factor in learning and memory. *Psychological Bulletin, 83*, 675–794.

Goodenough, D. R. (1986). History of the field dependence construct. In M. Bertini, L. Pizzamiglio, & S. Wapner (Eds.), *Field dependence in psychological theory, research, and application*. Hillsdale, NJ: Erlbaum.

Goodenough, D. R., & Eagle, C. A. (1963). A modification of the embedded figures test for use with young children. *Journal of Genetic Psychology, 103*, 67–74.

Goodenough, D. R., & Karp, S. A. (1961). Field dependence and intellectual functioning. *Journal of Abnormal and Social Psychology, 63*, 241–246.

Gottschaldt, L. (1926). Über den Einfluss der Erfährung auf die Wahrnehmung von Figuren 1: Über den Einfluss Gehäufter Einprägung von Figuren auf Ihre Sichtbarkeit in Umfassenden Konfigurationen. *Psychol. Forsch, 8*, 261–317.

Greene, M. A. (1972). Client perception of the relationship as a function of worker-client cognitive. *Dissertation Abstracts International, 33*, 3030A-3031A. (University Microfilms No. 72–31, 213)

Gregorc, A. F. (1982). *Gregorc style delineator: Developmental, technical, and administrative manual*. Maynard, MA: Gabriel Systems.

Grieve, T. D., & Davis, J. K. (1971). The relationship of cognitive style and method of instruction to performance in ninth grade geography. *Journal of Educational Research, 65*(3), 137–141.

Griffiths, R. T., & Sheen, R. (1992). Disembedded figures in the landscape: A reappraisal of L2 research on field dependence/independence. *Applied Linguistics, 13*(2), 133–148.

Griggs, S. A., & Dunn, R. (1989). The learning styles of multicultural groups and counseling implications. *Journal of Multicultural Counseling and Development, 17*, 146–155.

Gullo, D. F. (1988). An investigation of cognitive tempo and its effects on evaluating kindergarten children's academic and social competencies. *Early Child Development and Care, 34*, 201–215.

Haight, W., & Miller, P. J. (1992). The development of everyday pretend play: A longitudinal study of mothers' participation. *Merrill-Palmer Quarterly, 48*(3), 331–349.

Hale, J. (1983). Black children: Their roots, culture, and learning styles. In O. N. Saracho & B. Spodek (Eds.), *Understanding the multicultural experience in early childhood education* (pp. 17–34). Washington, DC: National Association for the Education of Young Children.

Hall, C. (1988). Field independence and simultaneous processing in preschool children. *Perceptual and Motor Skills, 66*, 891–897.

Halphin, G., & Peterson, H. (1986). Accommodating instruction to learners' field independence/dependence: A study of effects on achievement and attitudes. *Perceptual and Motor Skills, 62*, 967–974.

Halverson, C. F., & Waldrop, M. F. (1976). Relations between preschool activity and aspects of intellectual and social behavior at age 7½. *Developmental Psychology, 12*(2), 107–112.

Hammer, R. E., Hoffer, N., & King, W. L. (1995). Relationships among gender, cognitive style, academic major, and performance on the Piaget water-level task. *Perceptual and Motor Skills, 80*, 771–778.

Hansen, L. (1984, June). Field dependence-independence and testing evidence from six Pacific Island cultures. *TESOL Quarterly, 18*(2), 311–324.

Hardy, R. C., Eliot, J., & Burlingame, K. (1987). Stability over age and sex of children's responses to embedded figures test. *Perceptual and Motor Skills, 64*, 399–406.

Harris, D. B. (1963). *Children's drawings as measures of intellectual maturity.* New York: Harcourt Brace Jovanovich.

Hayes, J., & Allison, C. W. (1992). *Cognitive style and its relevance for management practice* (Industrial Relations/Human Resource Management, Discussion Paper IH92/01). England: School of Business and Economic Studies, University of Leeds.

Hayes, J., & Allison, C. W. (1993). Matching learning style and instructional strategy: An application of the person-environment interaction paradigm. *Perceptual and Motor Skills, 76*, 63–79.

Haynes, M. E. (1992). *The relationship of cognitive styles, cognitive profiles, and the Test of Adult Basic Education among selected adult students in an adult basic education center.* Unpublished master's thesis, University of Wyoming, Laramie.

Haynes, V. F., & Miller, P. H. (1987). The relationship between cognitive style, memory and attention in preschoolers. *Child Study Journal, 17*(1), 21–33.

Hertz-Lazarowitz, R., & Sharan, L. (1979). Self-esteem, locus of control and children's perception of classroom climate: A developmental perspective. *Contemporary Educational Psychology, 4*(2), 154–161.

Hester, F. M., & Tagatz, G. E. (1971). The effects of cognitive style and instructional strategy on concept attainment. *The Journal of Genetic Psychology, 85*, 229–237.

Hiebert, J. (1992). Reflection and communication: Cognitive considerations in school mathematics reform. *International Journal of Educational Research, 17*, 439–456.

Hodges, R. B., & Evans, J. R. (1983). Effect of three instructional strategies with juvenile delinquents of differing learning styles. *Current Trends in Correctional Education, 7*(3&4), 57–656.

Holtzman, W. H., Díaz-Guerrero, R., & Swartz, J. D. (1975). *Personality in two cultures.* Austin: University of Texas Press.

Howard, B. C. (1987). *Learning to persist/persisting to learn.* Washington, DC: The American University.

Howard, D. V., & Goldin, S. E. (1979). Selective processing in encoding and memory: An analysis of resource allocation by kindergarten children. *Journal of Experimental Child Psychology, 27*, 87–95.

Huang, J., & Chao, L. (1995). Chinese and American students' perceptual styles of field independence versus field dependence. *Perceptual and Motor Skills, 80*, 232–234.

Hudak, M. A. (1985). Review of Learning Styles Inventory. In D. J. Keyser & R. C. Sweetland (Eds.), *Test critiques* (Vol. II, pp. 402–410). Kansas City, MO: Test Corporation of America.

Humphries, L., Elam, C. L., & Metzler, E. W. (1988). Use of a tutorial in a psychiatry clerkship: Teaching styles, learning styles. *Journal of Psychiatric Education, 12*(1), 51–55.

Hunt, D. E. (1970). A conceptual level matching model for coordinating learner characteristics with educational approaches. *Interchange, 1*(3), 68–82.

Hunt, D. E. (1971). *Matching models in education: The coordination of teaching methods with student characteristics.* Toronto, Canada: Ontario Institute for Studies in Education.

Hunt, D. E. (1978). Theorists are persons, too: On preaching what you practice. In C. A. Parker (Ed.), *Encouraging development in college students* (pp. 250–266). Minneapolis: University of Minnesota Press.

Hunt, D. E., & Sullivan, E. V. (1974). *Between psychology and education.* Hinsdale, IL: Dryden.

Hunt, J. (1964). How children develop intellectually. *Children, 11*, 83–91.

Hunt, J. (1971). Using intrinsic motivation to teach young children. *Educational Technology, 11*, 78–80.

Hunt, J. McV. (1961). *Intelligence and experience.* New York: Ronald Press.

Huteau, M. (1987). *Style cognitif et personnalité: La dépendance-indépendance a l'egard du champ.* Lille: Presses Universitaires.

Hyde, J. S., Geiringer, E. R., & Yen, W. M. (1975). On the empirical relationship between spatial ability and sex differences in other aspects of cognitive style. *Multivariate Behavioral Research, 10*(3), 289–309.

Ismail, M., & Kong, N. W. (1985). Relationship of locus of control, cognitive style, anxiety, and academic achievement of a group of Malaysian primary school children. *Psychological Reports, 57*, 1127–1134.

Ismeurt, J., Ismeurt, R., & Miller, B. K. (1992). Field-dependence/independence: Considerations for staff development. *The Journal of Continuing Education in Nursing, 23*(1), 38–41.

Jackson, D. N. (1956). A short form of Witkin's embedded figures test. *Journal of Abnormal Psychology, 53*, 254–255.

Jacobs, R. L. (1985–1986). Ratings of social interaction and cognitive style in a PSI course: A multidimensional scaling analysis. *Journal of Educational Technology Systems, 14*(1), 51–59.

Jacobs, R. L., & Gedeon, D. V. (1982). The relationship of cognitive style to the frequency of proctor/student interactions and achievement in a PSI technology course. *Journal of Industrial Teacher Education, 19*(2), 18–26.

James, C. D. R. (1973). *A cognitive approach to teacher-pupil interaction and the academic performance of black children.* Unpublished master's thesis, Rutgers University.

Jamieson, J. (1992). The cognitive styles of reflection/impulsivity and field independence/ dependence and ESL success. *The Modern Language, 76*, 491–499.

Jennings, K. D. (1975). People versus object orientation, social behavior, and intellectual abilities in preschool children. *Developmental Psychology, 11*, 511–519.

Jolly, P. E., & Strawitz, B. M. (1984). Teacher-student cognitive style and achievement in biology. *Science Education, 68*(4), 485–490.

Kagan, J. (1971). *Change and continuity in infancy.* New York: Wiley.

Kagan, J., Moss, H. A., & Sigel, I. E. (1963). Psychological significance of styles of conceptualization. In G. C. Wright & J. Kagan (Eds.), Basic cognitive process in children. *Monograph of the Society for Research in Child Development, 28*(2, Serial No. 86).

Kagan, S., & Buriel, R. (1977). Field dependence-independence and Mexican American culture and education. In J. L. Martínez (Ed.), *Chicano Psychology* (pp. 279–328). New York: Academic Press.

Kalyan-Masih, V., & Curry, W. (1987). Cognitive performance and cognitive style of young children. *Perceptual and Motor Skills, 65,* 571–579.

Karp, S. A., Kissin, B., & Hustmyer, F. E. (1970). Field dependence as a predictor of alcoholic therapy dropouts. *Journal of Nervous and Mental Disease, 150,* 77–83.

Karp, S. A., & Konstadt, N. L. (1963). *Manual for the Children Embedded Figures Test.* Brooklyn, NY: Cognitive Tests.

Karp, S. A., & Konstadt, N. L. (1971). Children's Embedded Figures Test. In H. A. Witkin, P. K. Oltman, E. Raskin, & S. A. Karp (Eds.), *A manual for the Embedded Figures Tests* (pp. 21–26). Palo Alto, CA: Consulting Psychologists Press.

Kaulback, B. (1984). Styles of learning among native children: A review of the research. *Canadian Journal of Native Education, 11,* 27–37.

Keefe, J. W. (1986). *The NASSP Learning Style Profile.* Reston, VA: National Association of Secondary School Principals.

Keefe, J. W., & Farrell, B. G. (1990). Developing a defensible learning style paradigm. *Educational Leadership, 57,* 61–62.

Kiewra, K. A., & Frank, B. M. (1988). Encoding and external storage effects of personal lecture notes, skeletal notes, and detailed notes for field-independent and field-dependent learners. *Journal of Educational Research, 81*(3), 143–148.

Kitano, M. K. (1983). Early education for Asian-American children. In O. N. Saracho & B. Spodek (Eds.), *Understanding the multicultural experience in early childhood education* (pp. 45–66). Washington, DC: National Association for the Education of Young Children.

Kloner, A., & Britain, S. (1984). The relation between sex-role adoption and field independence in preschool children. *Journal of Genetic Psychology, 145,* 109–116.

Kogan, N. (1971). Educational implications of cognitive styles. In G. S. Lesser (Ed.), *Psychology and educational practice* (pp. 242–292). Glenview, IL: Scott Foresman.

Kogan, N. (1976). *Cognitive styles in infancy and early childhood.* Hillsdale, NJ: Erlbaum.

Kogan, N. (1983). Stylistic variation in childhood and adolescence: Creativity, metaphor, and cognitive styles. In P. H. Mussen (Ed.), *Handbook of child development* (Vol. III, pp. 630–706). New York: Wiley.

Kogan, N. (1987). Some behavioral implications of cognitive styles in early childhood. *Early Child Development and Care, 29,* 595–598.

Kogan, N., & Block, J. (1991). Field dependence-independence from early childhood through adolescence: Personality and socialization aspects. In S. Wapner & J. Demick (Eds.), *Field dependence-independence: Cognitive style across the life span* (pp. 177–207). Hillsdale, NJ: Lawrence Erlbaum.

Kolb, D. A. (1984). *Experimental learning.* Englewood Cliffs, NJ: Prentice-Hall.

Konstadt, N., & Forman, E. (1965). Field dependence and external directedness. *Journal of Personality and Social Psychology, 1,* 490–493.

Kornbluth, J. A., & Sabban, Y. P. (1982). The effect of cognitive style and study method on mathematical achievement of disadvantaged students. *School Science and Mathematics, 82*(2), 132–140.

Lee, L. C., Kagan, J., & Rabson, A. (1963). The influence of a preference for analytic categorization upon concept acquisition. *Child Development, 34*, 433–442.

Linn, M. C. (1978). Influence of cognitive style and training on tasks requiring the separation of variables schema. *Child Development, 49*, 874–877.

Linn, M. C., & Kyllonen, P. (1981). The field dependence-independence construct. *Journal of Educational Psychology, 73*, 261–273.

Linn, M. C., & Swiney, J. F. (1981). Individual differences in formal thought: Role expectations and aptitudes. *Journal of Educational Psychology, 73*, 274–286.

Lyons, C. A. (1985). The relationship between prospective teachers' learning preference/ style and teaching preference/style. *Educational and Psychological Research, 5*(4), 275–297.

Lytton, H., Watts, D., & Dunn, B. E. (1986). Stability and predictability of cognitive and social characteristics from age 2 to age 9. *Genetic Social and General Psychology Monographs, 112*, 361–398.

MacArthur, R. (1968). Ecology, culture and cognitive development: Canadian Native youth. In L. Drieger (Ed.), *The Canadian ethnic mosaic* (pp. 133–146). Toronto: McClelland & Stewart.

Maccoby, E. E., & Jacklin, C. N. (1974). *The psychology of sex differences.* Stanford, CA: Stanford University Press.

Mahlios, M. C. (1981). Instructional design and cognitive styles of teachers in elementary schools. *Perceptual and Motor Skills, 52*, 335–338.

Mahlios, M. C. (1990). The influence of cognitive style on the teaching practices of elementary teachers. In O. N. Saracho (Ed.), *Cognitive style and early education* (pp. 129–147). New York: Gordon & Breach Science Publishers.

Marshall, E. A. (1985). Relationship between client-learning style and preference for counselor approach. *Counselor Education and Supervision, 24*(4), 353–399.

Martinetti, R. F. (1994). Relationship between cognitive processing style and academic achievement. *Perceptual and Motor Skills, 78*, 813–814.

Massari, D. (1975). The relation of reflection-impulsivity to field dependence-independence and internal external control in children. *Journal of Genetic Psychology, 126*, 61–67.

McCarthy, B. (1980). *The 4MAT system: Teaching to learning style with right/left mode techniques.* Barrington, IL: Excel.

McCleod, B. (1987). An examination of development trends in field dependence among age groups of 13 to 21 years of age. *Perceptual and Motor Skills, 64*, 117–118.

McCutcheon, J. W., Schmidt, C. P., & Bolden, S. H. (1991). Relationships among selected personality variables, academic achievement and student teaching behavior. *Journal of Research and Development in Education, 24*(3), 38–43.

McDonald, E. R. (1984). The relationship of student and faculty field dependence-independence congruence to student academic achievement. *Educational and Psychological Measurement, 44*, 725–731.

McGillian, R. P., & Barclay, A. G. (1974). Sex differences and spatial ability factors in Witkin's differentiation construct. *Journal of Clinical Psychology, 30*(4), 528–532.

Meng, K., & Patty, D. (1991). Field dependence and contextual organizers. *Journal of Educational Research, 84*(3), 183–189.

Meredith, G. M. (1985). Transmitter-facilitator teaching style and focus-scan learning style in higher education. *Perceptual & Motor Skills, 61*(2), 545–546.

Messick, S. (1976). Personality consistencies in cognition and creativity. In S. Messick & Associates (Eds.), *Individuality in learning* (pp. 4–22). San Francisco, CA: Jossey-Bass.

Messick, S. (1984). The nature of cognitive styles: Problems and promise in educational practice. *Educational Psychologist, 19*(2), 59–74.

Messick, S., & Damarin, F. (1964). Cognitive styles and memory for faces. *Journal of Abnormal and Social Psychology, 69*, 313–318.

Messick, S. K. (1982). *Cognitive styles in educational practice* (Research Bulletin No. RR-8). Princeton, NJ: Educational Testing Service.

Mirandé, A. (1985). *The Chicano experience.* South Bend, IN: University of Notre Dame Press.

Moore, C. A. (1973). Styles of teacher behavior under simulated teaching conditions. *Dissertation Abstracts International, 34*, 3149A-3150A. (University Microfilms No. 73-30, 449)

Moore, D. M., & Bedient, D. (1986). Effects of presentation mode and individual characteristics of cognitive style. *Journal of Instructional Psychology, 13*, 19–24.

Moran, A. (1991). What can learning styles research learn from cognitive psychology? *Educational Psychology, 11*(3 & 4), 239–245.

More, A. (1984). *Okanagan/Nicola Indian quality of education study.* Penticton, British Columbia: Okanagan Indian Learning Institute.

More, A. J. (1987a). Native Indian learning styles: A review for researchers and teachers. *Journal of American Indian Education, 27*(1) 17–29.

More, A. J. (1987b). Native Indian students and their learning styles: Research results and classroom applications. *British Columbia Journal of Special Education, 11*, 23–37.

Mrosla, H., Black, W. L., & Hardy, C. A. (1987). Cognitive learning style and achievement in mathematics. *Journal of Instructional Psychology, 14*, 26–28.

Nagata, H. (1989). Grammatical judgment of sentences and field-dependence of subjects. *Perceptual and Motor Skills, 69*, 739–747.

Nakamura, C. Y., & Finck, D. N. (1980). Relative effectiveness of socially oriented and task oriented children and predictability of their behaviors. *Monographs of the Society for Research in Child Development, 45*(3-4, Serial No. 185).

Niaz, M. (1989a). Relation between Pascual-Leone's structural and functional M-space and its effect on problem solving in chemistry. *International Journal of Science Education, 11*(1), 93–99.

Niaz, M. (1989b). The role of cognitive style and its influence on proportional reasoning. *Journal of Research in Science Teaching, 26*(3), 221–235.

Nummedal, S. G., & Collea, F. P. (1981). Field independence, task ambiguity and performance on a proportional task. *Journal of Research in Science Teaching, 18*(3), 255–260.

OFSTED (1993). *Curriculum Organization and Classroom Practice in Primary School.* London: HMSO.

Ohnmacht, F. M. (1966). Effects of field independence and dogmatism on reversal and nonreversal shifts in concept formation. *Perceptual and Motor Skills, 22*, 491-497.

Ohnmacht, F. W. (1967a, February). *Relationships among field independence, dogma-*

*tism, teacher characteristics and teaching behavior of pre-service teachers* (Report No. SP 001 071). Paper presented at the meeting of the American Educational Research Association, New York. (ERIC Document Reproduction Service No. ED 011 525)

Ohnmacht, F. W. (1967b). Teacher characteristics and their relationship to some cognitive styles. *Journal of Educational Research, 60*, 201–204.

Ohnmacht, F. W. (1968). Factorial invariance of the teacher characteristics schedule and measures of two cognitive styles. *Journal of Psychology, 69*, 193–199.

Olstad, R. G., Juarez, J. R., Davenport, L. J., & Maury, D. A. (1981). *Inhibitors to achievement in science and mathematics by ethnic minorities.* Seattle: University of Washington Press.

Oltman, E. (1968). A portable rod-and-frame apparatus. *Perceptual and Motor Skills, 26*, 503–506.

Oltman, P. K., Goodenough, D. R., Witkin, H. A., Freedman, N., & Friedman, F. (1975). Psychological differentiation as a factor in conflict resolution. *Journal of Personality and Social Psychology, 32*, 730–36.

Oltman, P. K., Raskin, E., & Witkin, H. A. (1971). *Group Embedded Figures Test.* In H. A. Witkin, P. K. Oltman, E. Raskin, & S. A. Karp (Eds.), *A manual for the Embedded Figures Tests* (pp. 15–20). Palo Alto, CA: Consulting Psychologists Press.

Packer, J., & Bain, J. D. (1978). Cognitive style and teacher-student compatibility. *Journal of Educational Psychology, 70*(5), 864–871.

Papert, S. (1980). *Mindstorms: Children, computers, and powerful ideas.* New York: Basic Books.

Páramo, M. F., & Tinajero, C. (1990). Field dependence/independence and performance in school: An argument against neutrality of cognitive style. *Perceptual and Motor Skills, 70*, 1079–1087.

Park, K. A., Lay, P., & Ramsay, L. (1993). Individual differences and developmental changes in preschoolers' friendships. *Developmental Psychology, 29*(2), 264–270.

Partridge, R. (1983). Learning styles: A review of selected models. *Journal of Nursing Education, 22*, 243–248.

Pascual-Leone, J., Ammon, P., Goodman, D., & Subleman, I. (1978). Piagetian theory and neo-Piagetian analysis as psychological guides in education. In J. M. Gallagher & J. Easeley (Eds.), *Knowledge and development, Vol 2: Piaget and education* (pp. 116–138). New York: Plenum.

Pawelkiewics, W. M., & McIntire, W. G. (1975). Field dependence-independence and self-esteem in pre-adolescent children. *Perceptual and Motor Skills, 41*, 41–42.

Pellegrini, A. D. (In press). Play and assessment of young children. In O. N. Saracho & B. Spodek (Eds.), *Play in early childhood education* (pp. 216–234). Albany: State University of New York Press.

Pennell, L. (1985). Academic intervention program: Applying brain and learning styles concepts. *Theory into Practice, 24*(2), 131–134.

Peplin, C. M., & Larsen, J. D. (1989). Field dependence: Experimenters' expectancy, sex difference or no difference? *Perceptual and Motor Skills, 68*, 355–358.

Pepper, F. C., & Henry, S. (1986). Social and cultural effects on Indian learning style: Classroom implications. *Canadian Journal of Native Education, 13*, 54–61.

Perney, V. H. (1976). Effects of race and sex on field dependence independence in children. *Perceptual and Motor Skills, 42*, 974–980.

Pettigrew, F., & Buell, C. (1989, January-February). Preservice and experienced teachers' ability to diagnose learning styles. *Journal of Educational Research, 82*(3), 187-189.

Pettigrew, F., & Heikkinen, M. (1985). Increased psychomotor skill through eclectic teaching. *The Physical Educator, 43*(3), 140-146.

Pettigrew, F. E., Bayless, M. A., Zakrajeck, D. B., & Goc-Karp, G. (1985). Compatibility of students' learning and teaching styles on their ratings of college teaching. *Perceptual and Motor Skills, 61*, 1215-1220.

Piaget, J. (1962). *Play, dreams, and imitation in childhood.* New York: International Press.

Pitblado, C. (1977). Orientation bias in the Rod-and-Frame Test. *Perceptual and Motor Skills, 44*, 891-900.

Pohl, R. L., & Pervin, L. A. (1968). Academic performance as a function of task requirements and cognitive style. *Psychological Reports, 22*, 1017-1020.

Quinlan, D. M., & Blatt, S. J. (1972). Field articulation and performance under stress: Differential predictions in surgical and psychiatric nursing training. *Journal of Consulting and Clinical Psychology, 39*, 517.

Ramírez, M. (1990). A bicognitive-multicultural model for a pluralistic education. In O. N. Saracho (Ed.), *Cognitive style and early education* (pp. 151-158). New York: Gordon & Breach Science Publishers.

Ramírez, M., & Castañeda, A. (1974). *Cultural democracy, bicognitive development, and education.* New York: Academic Press.

Ramírez, M., & Price-Williams, D. R. (1974). Cognitive styles of children of three ethnic groups in the United States. *Journal of Cross-Cultural Psychology, 5*, 212-219.

Ramírez, M., III (1982, March). *Cognitive styles and cultural diversity.* Paper presented at the Annual Conference of the American Educational Research Association, New York.

Ramírez, M., III (1989). A bicognitive-multicultural model for a pluralistic education. *Early Child Development and Care, 51*, 129-136.

Reiff, J. (1982, April). *Identifying learning preferences of young children.* Paper presented at the meeting of the Association for Childhood Education International Conference, Atlanta, Georgia.

Renninger, K. A., & Sigel, I. E. (1987). The development of cognitive organisation in young children: An exploratory study. *Early Child Development and Care, 29*, 133-161.

Renninger, K. A., & Snyder, S. S. (1983). Effects of cognitive style on perceived satisfaction and performance among students and teachers. *Journal of Educational Psychology, 75*, 668-676.

Rhodes, R. W. (1988, January). Holistic teaching/learning for Native American students. *Journal of American Indian Education, 27*(2), 21-29.

Riding, R., Burton, D., Rees, G., & Sharratt, M. (1995). Cognitive style and personality in 12-year-old children. *British Journal of Educational Psychology, 65*, 113-124.

Riding, R., & Douglas, G. (1993). The effect of cognitive style and mode of presentation on learning performance. *British Journal of Educational Psychology, 63*, 297-307.

Riding, R., & Mathias, D. (1991). Cognitive styles and preferred learning mode, reading attainment and cognitive ability in 11-year-old children. *Educational Psychology, 11*(3 & 4), 383-393.

Riding, R., & Read, G. (1996). Cognitive style and pupil learning preferences. *Educational Psychology, 1*, 81–106.

Rink, J. E. (1985). *Teaching physical education for learning.* St. Louis, MO: Times Mirror/Mosby Publishing Company.

Roach, D. (1985). Effects of cognitive style, intelligence, and sex on reading achievement. *Perceptual and Motor Skills, 61*, 1139–1142.

Roberge, J. J., & Flexer, B. K. (1983). Cognitive style, operativity, and mathematics achievement. *Journal for Research in Mathematics Education, 14*(5), 344–353.

Rollock, D. (1993). Field dependence/independence and learning condition: An exploratory study of style vs. ability. *Perceptual and Motor Skills, 74*, 807–818.

Rosenthal, R., & Jacobson, L. (1968). *Pygmalion in the classroom: Teacher expectations and pupils' intellectual development.* New York: Holt, Rinehart and Winston.

Ross, H. G. (1980). Matching achievement styles and instructional environments. *Contemporary Educational Psychology, 5*(3), 216–226.

Ross, J. A. (1990). Learning to control variables: Main effects and aptitude treatment interactions of two rule-governed approaches to instruction. *Journal of Research in Science Teaching, 27*(6), 523–539.

Rubin, K. H. (1976). Relation between social participation and role-taking skill in preschool children. *Psychological Reports, 39*, 823–826.

Rubin, K. H. (1980). Fantasy play: Its role in the development of social skills and social cognition. *New Directions for Child Development, 9*, 69–84.

Rubin, K. H., Watson, K. S., and Jambor, T. W. (1978). Free play behaviors in preschool and kindergarten children. *Child Development, 49*, 534–536.

Ruble, D. N., & Nakamura, C. Y. (1972). Task orientation versus social orientation in young children and their attention to relevant social cues. *Child Development, 43*, 471–480.

Sanders, M., Scholz, J. P., & Kagan, S. (1976). Three social motives and field independence-dependence in Anglo-American and Mexican American children. *Journal of Cross-Cultural Psychology, 7*(4), 451–462.

Saracho, O. N. (1980). The relationship between teachers' cognitive styles and their perceptions of their students' academic competence. *Educational Research Quarterly, 5*, 40–49.

Saracho, O. N. (1982a, March). *The cognitive style of teachers and their perceptions of their matched and mismatched children's academic competence.* Paper presented at the annual meeting of the American Educational Research Association, New York.

Saracho, O. N. (1982b). The effects of a computer assisted instruction program in basic skills achievement and attitudes toward instruction of Spanish-speaking migrant children. *American Educational Research Journal, 19*(2), 201–219.

Saracho, O. N. (1983a). Assessing cognitive style in young children. *Studies in Educational Evaluation, 8*, 229–236.

Saracho, O. N. (1983b). Cognitive style and Mexican American children's perceptions of reading. In T. H. Escobedo (Ed.), *Early childhood bilingual education: A Hispanic perspective* (pp. 201–221). New York: Teachers College Press, Columbia University.

Saracho, O. N. (1983c). Cultural differences in the cognitive style of Mexican American students. *Journal of the Association for the Study of Perception, International, 18*(1), 3–10.

Saracho, O. N. (1983d). Relationship between cognitive style and teachers' perceptions of young children's academic competence. *Journal of Experimental Education, 51*, 184–189.

Saracho, O. N. (1983e). The relationship of teachers' cognitive styles and their ethnicity to predictions of academic success and achievement of Mexican-American and Anglo-American students. In E. Garcia & S. Vargas (Eds.), *The Mexican-American child: Language, cognition and social development* (pp. 107–122). South Bend, IN: University of Notre Dame Press.

Saracho, O. N. (1984a). Construction and validation of the play rating scale. *Early Child Care and Education, 17*, 199–230.

Saracho, O. N. (1984b, April). *Educational implications of the matched and mismatched of students' and teachers' cognitive styles.* Paper presented at the annual conference of the American Educational Research Association, New Orleans, Louisiana.

Saracho, O. N. (1984c). The Goodenough-Harris Drawing Test as a measure of field-dependence/independence. *Perceptual and Motor Skills, 59*, 887–892.

Saracho, O. N. (1984d). Young children's academic achievement as a function of their cognitive styles. *Journal of Research and Development in Education, 18*, 44–50.

Saracho, O. N. (1985a). A modification in scoring the ABC Scale. *Journal of Personality Assessment, 49*, 154–155.

Saracho, O. N. (1985b). Young children's play behaviors and cognitive styles. *Early Child Development and Care, 21*(4), 1–18.

Saracho, O. N. (1986a). Play and young children's learning. In B. Spodek (Ed.), *Today's kindergarten: Exploring the knowledge base, expanding the curriculum* (pp. 91–109). New York: Teachers College Press, Columbia University.

Saracho, O. N. (1986b). Validation of two cognitive measures to assess field-dependence/independence. *Perceptual and Motor Skills, 63*, 255–263.

Saracho, O. N. (1987a). Cognitive style characteristics as related to young children's play behaviors. *Early Child Develpment and Care, 28*, 163–179.

Saracho, O. N. (1987b). Cognitive styles: Characteristic modes of individuality and diversity. *Early Child Development and Care, 29*, 81–93.

Saracho, O. N. (1987c). The match and mismatch of students' and teachers' cognitive styles: A case study of two kindergarten classrooms. *Early Child Development and Care, 29*, 209–238.

Saracho, O. N. (1988a). Cognitive style and early childhood practice. In B. Spodek, O. N. Saracho, & D. L. Peters (Eds.), *Professionalism and the early childhood practitioner.* New York: Teachers College Press, Columbia University.

Saracho, O. N. (1988b). Cognitive style and young children's learning. *Early Child Development and Care, 30*, 213–220.

Saracho, O. N. (1988c). Cognitive styles: Implications for the preparation of early childhood teachers. *Early Child Development and Care, 30*, 1–11.

Saracho, O. N. (1988d). Cognitive styles in early childhood education. *Journal of Research in Childhood Education, 3*(1), 24–35.

Saracho, O. N. (1988e). The early childhood teachers' cognitive styles. In B. Spodek, O. N. Saracho, & D. L. Peters (Eds.), *Professionalism and the early childhood practitioner.* New York: Teachers College Press, Columbia University.

Saracho, O. N. (1988f, April). *Matching students' and teachers' cognitive styles.* Paper presented at the annual conference of the American Educational Research Association, New Orleans, Louisiana.

Saracho, O. N. (1989a). Cognitive style and the evaluation of young children's educational programs. *Early Child Development and Care, 51*, 13–28.

Saracho, O. N. (1989b). Cognitive style: Individual differences. *Early Childhood Development and Care, 53*, 75–81.

Saracho, O. N. (1989c). Cognitive style in the play of young children. *Early Child Development and Care, 51*, 65–76.

Saracho, O. N. (1989d). Cognitive styles and classroom factors. *Early Child Development and Care, 47*, 149–157.

Saracho, O. N. (1989e). Cultural differences in the cognitive style of Mexican American students. In B. J. R. Shade (Ed.), *Culture, style and the educative process* (pp. 129–136). Springfield, IL: Charles C. Thomas Publisher.

Saracho, O. N. (1989f). Early childhood teachers' instructional styles and their instructional behaviors. *Early Child Development and Care, 49*, 94–109.

Saracho, O. N. (1989g). The factorial structure of three- to five-year-old children's social behavior: Cognitive style and play. *Journal of Research and Development in Education, 22*(4), 21–28.

Saracho, O. N. (1990a). Cognitive style and the evaluation of young children's educational programs. In O. N. Saracho (Ed.), *Cognitive style and early education* (pp. 43–58). New York: Gordon & Breach.

Saracho, O. N. (1990b). The match and mismatch of teachers' and students' cognitive styles. *Early Child Development and Care, 54*, 99–109.

Saracho, O. N. (1990c). Preschool children's cognitive style and their social orientation. *Perceptual and Motor Skills, 70*(3), 915–921.

Saracho, O. N. (1991a). Cognitive style and social behavior in young Mexican American children. *International Journal of Early Childhood, 23*(2), 21–38.

Saracho, O. N. (1991b). Social correlates of cognitive style in young children. *Early Child Development and Care, 76*, 117–134.

Saracho, O. N. (1991c). Students' preference for field-dependence-independence teacher characteristics. *Educational Psychology, 11*(3 & 4), 323–332.

Saracho, O. N. (1991d). Teacher expectations and cognitive style: Implications for students' academic achievement. *Early Child Development and Care, 77*, 97–108.

Saracho, O. N. (1991e). Teacher expectations of students' performance: A review of the research. *Early Child Development and Care, 76*, 27–41.

Saracho, O. N. (1992). The relationship between preschool children's cognitive style and play: Implications for creativity. *The Creativity Research Journal, 5*(1), 35–47.

Saracho, O. N. (1993). The effects of the teachers' cognitive styles on their students' academic achievement. *International Journal of Early Childhood, 25*(2), 37–40.

Saracho, O. N. (1994). Relationship of preschool children's cognitive style to their play preferences. *Early Child Development and Care, 97*, 21–33.

Saracho, O. N. (1995a). Preschool children's cognitive style and their selection of academic areas in their play. *Early Child Development and Care, 112*, 27–42.

Saracho, O. N. (1995b). Relationship between the cognitive styles and play behaviors of preschool children. *Educational Psychology, 15*(4), 405–415.  `

Saracho, O. N. (1995c). Relationship between young children's cognitive style and their play. *Early Child Development and Care, 113*, 77–84.

Saracho, O. N. (1996a). Preschool children's cognitive style and their play behaviors. *Child Study Journal, 26*(2), 125–148.

Saracho, O. N. (1996b). The relationship between the cognitive style and play behaviors of three- to five-year-old children. *Personality and Individual Differences, 21*(6), 863–876.

Saracho, O. N., & Dayton, C. M. (1980). Relationship of teachers' cognitive styles to pupils' academic achievement gains. *Journal of Educational Psychology, 72*, 544–547.

Saracho, O. N., & Gerstl, C. K. (1992). Learning differences among at-risk minority students. In H. C. Waxman, J. W. Felix, J. E. Anderson, & H. P. Baptiste (Eds.), *Improving the education of at-risk students* (pp. 105–135). Newbury Park, CA: Corwin Press, Inc.

Saracho, O. N., & Hancock, F. M. (1983). Mexican-American culture. In O. N. Saracho & B. Spodek (Eds.), *Understanding the multicultural experience in early childhood education* (pp. 3–15). Washington, DC: National Association for the Education of Young Children.

Saracho, O. N., & Spodek, B. (1981, January). Teachers' cognitive styles and their educational implications. *Educational Forum, 45*(2), 153–159.

Saracho, O. N., & Spodek, B. (1986). Cognitive style and children's learning: Individual variations in cognitive processes. In L. G. Katz (Ed.), *Current topics in early childhood education* (Vol. VI, pp. 177–194). Norwood, NJ: Ablex.

Saracho, O. N., & Spodek, B. (1994). Matching preschool children's and teachers' cognitive styles. *Perceptual and Motor Skills, 78*, 683–689.

Schimek, J. G. (1968). Cognitive style and defenses: A longitudinal study of intellectualization and field independence. *Journal of Abnormal Psychology, 73*, 575–580.

Schmidt, C. P., & Lewis, B. E. (1987). Field-dependence/independence, movement-based instruction and fourth graders' achievement in selected musical tasks. *Psychology of Music, 15*, 117–127.

Shade, B. J. (1981). Racial variation in perceptual differentiation. *Perceptual and Motor Skills, 52*, 243–248.

Shade, B. J. (1982). Afro-American cognitive style: A variable in school success? *Review of Educational Research, 52*(2), 219–244.

Shade, B. J. (1983). Cognitive strategies as determinants of school achievement. *Psychology in the Schools, 20*, 488–493.

Shade, B. J. (1984, August). *The perceptual process in teaching and learning: Cross-ethnic comparisons.* Paper presented at the annual meeting of the American Psychological Association, Toronto, Canada.

Shade, B. J. (1990). The influence of perceptual development on cognitive style: Cross-ethnic comparisons. In O. N. Saracho (Ed.), *Cognitive style and early education* (pp. 177–195). New York: Gordon & Breach Science Publishers.

Shade, B. J., & Edwards, P. A. (1987). Ecological correlates of the educative style of Afro-American children. *Journal of Negro Education, 56*(1), 88–99.

Sheen, R. (1993). A rebuttal to Chapelle's response to Griffiths and Sheen. *Applied Linguistics, 14*(1), 98–100.

Sherman, J. A. (1967). Problems of sex differences in space perception and aspects of intellectual functioning. *Psychological Review, 74*, 290–299.

Sigel, I. E. (1963). How intelligence test units help understand intelligence. *Merrill-Palmer Quarterly, 9*, 39–56.

Sigel, I. E., Jarman, P., & Hanesian, H. (1967). Styles of categorization and their intellectual and personality correlates in young children. *Human Development, 10*, 1–17.

Solas, J. (1992). Investigating teacher and student thinking about the process of teaching and learning using autobiography and repertory grid. *Review of Educational Research, 61*(2), 205–225.

Spodek, B. (1990). Responding to individual differences. In O. N. Saracho (Ed.), *Cognitive style and early education* (pp. 217–221). New York: Gordon & Breach.

Spodek, B., & Saracho, O. N. (1987). The challenge of educational play. In D. Bergen (Ed.), *Play as a learning medium for learning and development: A handbook of theory and practice* (pp. 9–22). Portsmouth, NH: Heinemann.

Spodek, B., & Saracho, O. N. (1990). Early childhood curriculum construction and classroom practice. *Early Child Development and Care, 61*, 1–9.

Stasz, C., Shavelson, R. J., Cox., D. L., & Moore, C. A. (1976). Field independence and the structuring of knowledge in a social studies minicourse. *Journal of Educational Psychology, 68*(2), 550–558.

Steele, C. (1981). Play variables as related to cognitive constructs in three- to six-year-olds. *Journal of Research and Development in Education, 14*(3), 58–72.

Stevenson, H. W. (1954). Latent learning in children. *Journal of Experimental Child Psychology, 47*, 17–21.

Stodolsky, S. S., & Lesser, G. S. (1967). Learning patterns in the disadvantaged. *Harvard Educational Review, 37*(4), 546–593.

Stone, M. K. (1976). The role of cognitive style in teaching and learning. *Journal of Teacher Education, 27*(4), 332–334.

Swisher, K., & Deyhle, D. (1987). Styles of learning and learning of styles: Educational conflicts for American Indian/Alaskan native youth. *Journal of Multilingual and Multicultural Development, 8*(4), 345–360.

Swisher, K., & Deyhle, D. (1989, August). The styles of learning are different, but the teaching is just the same: Suggestions for teachers of American Indian youth. *Journal of American Indian Education 16*, 1–14.

Tafoya, T. (1989, August). Coyotes eyes: Native cognition styles. *Journal of American Indian Education, 21*(2), 21–33.

Tamir, P. (1975). The relationship among cognitive preference, school environment, teachers' curricular bias, curriculum, and subject matter. *American Educational Research Journal, 12*(3), 235–264.

Tarantino, S. J., & Loricchio, D. F. (1989). Field dependence, language ability, and self-concept as a function of fathers' absence. *Perceptual and Motor Skills, 69*, 431–434.

Thornell, J. G. (1977). Individual differences in cognitive styles and guidance variables in instruction. *Journal of Experimental Education, 45*(4), 9–12.

Tong, B. (1978). Warriors and victims: Chinese-American sensibility and learning styles. In L. Morris, G. Sather, & S. Scull (Eds.), *Learning styles from social/cultural diversity. A study of five American minorities* (pp. 153–167). Washington, DC: Southwest Teacher Corps Network, U.S. Department of Health, Education and Welfare.

Trout, J. S., & Crawley, F. E. (1985). The effects of matching instructional strategy and selected student characteristics on ninth grade physical science students' attitudes and achievement. *Journal of Research in Science Teaching, 22*, 407–419.

Turner, N. D. (1993). Learning styles and metacognition. *Reading Improvement, 30*(2), 82–85.

Tyler, L. E. (1974). *Individual differences: Abilities and motivational directions.* Englewood Cliffs, NJ: Prentice-Hall.

Vaidya, S., & Chansky, N. (1980). Cognitive development and cognitive style as factors
in mathematics achievement. *Journal of Educational Psychology, 72,* 326–330.

Van Blerkom, M. I. (1987). Haptic lateralization, field dependence, and sex. *Perceptual
and Motor Skills, 64,* 907–914.

Vaught, G. M., Pittman, M. D., & Roodin, R. A. (1975). Developmental curves for the
portable rod-and-frame test. *Bulletin of the Psychonomics Society, 5,* 151–152.

Vernon, P. E. (1972). The distinctiveness of field-independence. *Journal of Personality,
40,* 366–391.

Victor, J. B. (1976). Peer judgments of teaching competence as a function of field independence and dogmatism. *Journal of Experimental Education, 44*(3), 10–13.

Wapner, S., & Demick, J. (1991). Some open research problems on field dependence-
independence: Theory and methodology. In S. Wapner & J. Demick (Eds.), *Field
dependence-independence: Cognitive style across the life span* (pp. 401–429).
Hillsdale, NJ: Lawrence Erlbaum.

Weinstein, R. (1983). Student perceptions of schooling. *Elementary School Journal, 83,*
287–312.

Weinstein, R. (1985). Student mediation of classroom expectancy effects. In J. B. Dusek
(Ed.), *Teacher expectancies* (pp. 222–237). Hillsdale, NJ: Erlbaum.

Weinstein, R., Marshall, H., Brattesani, K., & Middlestadt, S. (1982). Student perceptions
of differential teacher treatment in open and traditional classrooms. *Journal of
Educational Psychology, 74,* 678–692.

Weitz, J. (1971). *Cultural change and field dependence in two native Canadian linguistic
families.* Unpublished doctoral dissertation, University of Ottawa, Canada.

Wheeler, R. H., & Perkins, F. T. (1932). *Principles of mental development: A textbook
in educational psychology.* New York: Crowell.

Winnie, P. H., & Marx, R. W. (1980). Matching students' cognitive styles to teaching
skills. *Journal of Educational Psychology, 72*(2), 257–264.

Witkin, H. A. (1949). Perception of body position and of the position of the visual field.
*Psychological Monographs, 63* (Whole No. 302).

Witkin, H. A. (1950). Individual differences in ease of perception of embedded figures.
*Journal of Personality, 19,* 1–15.

Witkin, H. A. (1952). Further studies of perception of the upright when the direction of
the force acting on the body is changed. *Journal of Experimental Psychology, 43,*
9–20.

Witkin, H. A. (1965). Some implications of research on cognitive style for problems of
education. *Archivio Di Psicologia Neurologia E Psichiatria, 26,* 27–54.

Witkin, H. A. (1976). Cognitive styles in academic performance in teacher-student relations. In S. Messick & Associates (Eds.), *Individuality in learning* (pp. 38–72).
San Francisco, CA: Jossey-Bass.

Witkin, H. A. (1978). *Cognitive styles in personal and cultural adaptation.* Worcester,
MA: Clark University Press.

Witkin, H. A., & Asch, S. E. (1948). Studies in space orientation IV. Further experiments
on perception of the upright with displaced visual fields. *Journal of Experimental
Psychology, 38,* 762–782.

Witkin, H. A., & Berry, J. W. (1975). Psychological differentiation in cross-cultural
perspective. *Journal of Cross-Cultural Psychology, 6,* 4–87.

Witkin, H. A., Dyk, R. B., Faterson, H. F., Goodenough, D. R., & Karp, S. A. (1974). *Psychological differentiation: Studies of development*. Potomac, MD: Erlbaum (originally published, New York: Wiley, 1962).

Witkin, H. A., Faterson, H. F., Goodenough, D. R., & Birnbaum, J. (1966). Cognitive patterning in mildly retarded boys. *Child Development, 37*, 301–316.

Witkin, H. A., & Goodenough, D. R. (1977). *Field dependence revisited* (Research Bulletin No. RB 77–16). Princeton, NJ: Educational Testing Service.

Witkin, H. A., & Goodenough, D. R. (1981). Cognitive control: Essence and origins field dependence and field independence. *Psychological Issues, Monograph 51*(Serial No. 51).

Witkin, H. A., Goodenough, D. R., & Karp, S. A. (1967). Stability of cognitive style from childhood to young adulthood. *Journal of Personality and Social Psychology, 7*(3), 219–300.

Witkin, H. A., Lewis, H. B., Hertzman, M., Machover, K., Meissner, P. B., & Wapner, S. (1972). *Personality through perception*. Westport, CT: Greenwood Press (originally published, New York: Harper & Row, 1954).

Witkin, H. A., Lewis, H. B., & Weil, E. (1968). Affective reactions and patient-therapist interactions among more differentiated and less differentiated patients early in therapy. *Journal of Nervous and Mental Disease, 146*, 193–208.

Witkin, H. A., & Moore, C. A. (1974, April). *Cognitive style and the teaching learning process*. Paper presented at the annual meeting of the American Educational Research Association, Chicago, IL.

Witkin, H. A., Moore, C. A., Friedman, F., & Owen, D. R. (1976a). *A longitudinal study of the role of cognitive styles in academic evolution during the college years* (Graduate Record Examinations Board Research Report No. 76–10R). Princeton, NJ: Educational Testing Service.

Witkin, H. A., Moore, C. A., Goodenough, D. R., & Cox, P. W. (1977). Field-dependent and field-independent cognitive styles and their educational implications. *Review of Educational Research, 47*(1), 1–64.

Witkin, H. A., Moore, C. A., Oltman, P. K., Goodenough, D. R., Friedman, F., Owen, D. R., & Raskin, E. (1976b). Role of the field-dependent and field-independent cognitive styles in academic evolution: A longitudinal study. *Journal of Educational Psychology, 69*(3), 197–211.

Witkin, H. A., Oltman, P. K., Raskin, E., & Karp, S. A. (1971). *A manual for the Embedded Figures Tests*. Palo Alto, CA: Consulting Psychologists Press.

Wittrock, M. C. (1987). Teaching and student thinking. *Journal of Teacher Education, 38*(6), 30–33.

Wollman, W. T. (1986). The effects of lesson structure and cognitive style on the science achievement of elementary school children. *Science Education, 70*(4), 461–471.

Wu, J. J. (1968). Cognitive style and task performance—A study of student teachers. *Dissertation Abstracts International, 29*, 176A. (University Microfilms No. 68-7408)

Yore, L. D. (1986). The effects of lesson structure and cognitive style on the science achievement of elementary school children. *School Children, 70*, 461–471.

Young, H. (1959). A test of Witkin's field dependence hypothesis. *Journal of Abnormal Social Psychology, 59*, 188–192.

Yuill, N. (1992). Children's conception of personality traits. *Human Development, 35*, 265–279.

# Author Index

# Subject Index

**About the Author**

OLIVIA NATIVIDAD SARACHO is Professor of Education in the Department of Curriculum and Instruction at the University of Maryland at College Park. For several decades, Dr. Saracho has conducted research related to cognitive style, including young children. She is coauthor of *Right from the Start* (1994), *Dealing with Individual Differences in the Early Childhood Classroom* (1994), and *Foundations of Early Childhood Education* (1991).

ISBN 0-89789-486-3

HARDCOVER BAR CODE